A CANOE QUEST IN THE WAKE OF CANADA'S "PRINCE OF EXPLORERS"

Welcome
to the
Prince of Wales
...hern Heritage Centre
Enjoy your visit

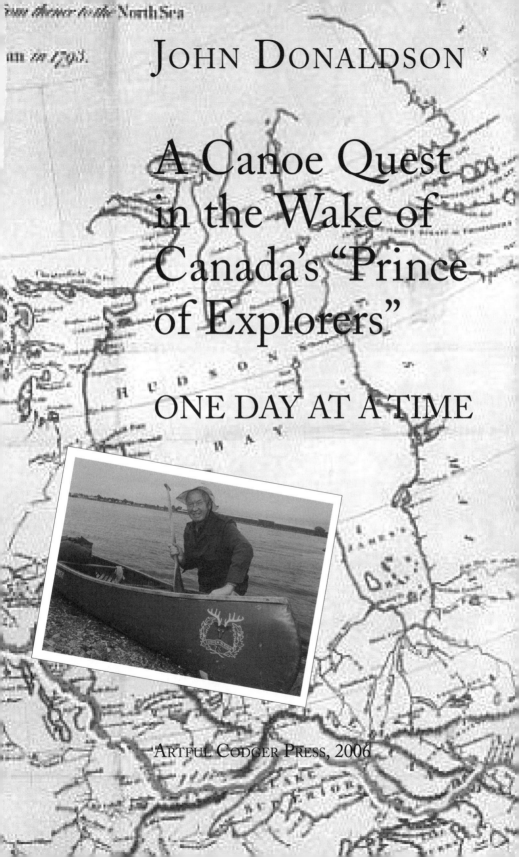

JOHN DONALDSON

A Canoe Quest
in the Wake of
Canada's "Prince
of Explorers"

ONE DAY AT A TIME

ARTFUL CODGER PRESS, 2006

© John Donaldson, 2006
Printed in Canada

ISBN 0-9736161-8-0

LIBRARY AND ARCHIVES CANADA CATALOGUING IN PUBLICATION

Donaldson, John, 1930-
A canoe quest : In the wake of Canada's prince of explorers / John Donaldson.
ISBN 0-9736161-8-0

1. Donaldson, John, 1930- – Journeys – Canada. 2. Mackenzie, Alexander, Sir, 1764-1820. 3. Alexander Mackenzie Voyageur Route. 4. Northwest, Canadian – Discovery and exploration. 5. Canada – Description and travel. 6. Canoes and canoeing – Canada.
I. Title.
FC3212.1.M46D65 2006   917.104   C2006-904375-2

ARTFUL CODGER PRESS
10 Gordon Street, Kingston Ontario K7M 3R9

Contents

"Old men should be explorers."
T.S. ELIOT

Modern day explorers follow the path of Alexander Mackenzie

Lone canoeist shares experiences with the explorer Mackenzie

By Rob Cotton
The News

Frying on top and freezing on the bottom.

That's how canoeist John Donaldson, his face burnt and peeling, described life in a canoe on Lake Superior as he follows the route fur trader and explorer Alexander Mackenzie took to the Pacific Ocean.

Donaldson, 59, a retired university professor now living in Sharbot Lake near Perth, Ont. arrived on the Pumphouse Beach at Terrace Bay on Sunday, June 23, two and a half weeks after leaving Sault. Ste. Marie.

"This beach is a luxury," he said.

He has not always had the luxury of a sand beach or calm water when he is landing his cedar strip canvas covered canoe.

More often he has to land on rocky beaches and that means getting his feet wet.

"I have suffered from hypothermia twice because of this," he said.

In order to warm himself up in these situations Donaldson runs around on the beach.

"Sometimes I light my small Primus stove and lean over it holding my towel over my head," he said.

As evidence he held up an old towel that was more than a little charred at the edges.

"You have to take Lake Superior one day at a time," he said.

"You can start out with a flat calm, a beautiful day, but soon a little frown will come on the water and then it becomes a ripple and then you're right into it."

Lake Superior fog is one thing that Donaldson has never experienced

John Donaldson on the Pumphouse Beach in Terrace Bay.

before.

Although he uses a compass to maintain his course, he said he still had difficulty.

Continued on page 12

Student voyageurs bring Canadian history to life along Mackenzie's routes

By Rob Cotton
The News

Fur trading voyageurs, appearing out of the mists of history if not out of the mists of Lake Superior, will arrive in Terrace Bay on July 13, to remind us reflect on things that make us Canadian.

These voyageurs are actually students from Lakehead University following the route explorer Alexander Mackenzie took across Canada.

This is the second stage of The Sir Alexander Mackenzie *Canada Sea-to-Sea Bicentennial Expeditions*, a project to commemorate the 200th anniversary of Mackenzie's achievement, the first recorded crossing of Canada from the Atlantic to the Pacific Ocean.

The first stage of the *Canada Sea-to-Sea* expedition was completed in the summer of 1989 when a group of voyageurs/students paddled from Ft. McMurray, Alberta, to the the mouth of the Mackenzie River on the Arctic Ocean - a distance of more than 3,400 km.

This year 36 voyageurs/university students will follow the voyageur routes of commerce, paddling from Lachine, Quebec to Winnipeg, Manitoba.

Canada Sea-to-Sea stopping at communities along the route, informs Canadians about a significant part of Canadian history. When the modern-day voyageurs arrive in Terrace Bay they will present a historical pageant, including skits, dances and songs, to commemorate Mackenzie's search for the Northwest Passage.

This event will take place Saturday July 13, at 7:30 in the park area in front of Simcoe Plaza.

Between 1789 and 1793 Alexander Mackenzie made two remarkable journeys in search of the Northwest Passage. The first voyage was unsuccessful

Continued on Page 12

Local adventurer to be honoured in Scotland

Lynn Rees Lambert
KINGSTON THIS WEEK

An intrepid Kingstonian, who retraced the arduous, 14,000 kilometre voyage of explorer Alexander Mackenzie, will be the guest of honour at a ceremony in Scotland June 13.

John Donaldson, a retired neuroscientist, followed the Scottish explorer's watery route from Montreal to Bella Coola on the Pacific coast and then to the Beaufort Sea alone in a 16-foot wood and canvas Cree-built canoe over four summers.

Donaldson landed his canoe July 22, 1993 on the same spot where Mackenzie had first scrawled "Alexander Mackenzie from Canada by Land" 200 years earlier — the first white man to make the claim.

The adventurous Donaldson had many "near misses" with disaster, including 25-foot waves on Lake Superior, confrontations with black bears, getting lost in the

John Donaldson retraced the canoe route of Scots-Canadian explorer Alexander Mackenzie

Mackenzie delta and a "canoe-jacking" by an escaped prisoner near Buffalo Narrows.

He was spared certain death several times, he says, through a combination of divine intervention and the kindness of strangers.

His exploits were both a personal challenge and an effort to raise the profile of a "great Scots-Canadian explorer" who has been relegated to dusty history books.

Donaldson will be the guest of honour at a special ceremony in Avoch in the Scottish Highlands, the burial place of Mackenzie .

Last fall, Canadian Airlines flew Donald's canoe — *Spirit of Mackenzie* —

to Scotland, where it will form part of a museum collection dedicated to Alexander Mackenzie.

Attending the ceremony will be the Canadian High Commissioner for the United Kingdom and special guests — including actor Sean Connery, who, Donaldson says, is a strong supporter of historic figures and fervent Scottish nationalist.

A book in the works

After the museum opening, Donaldson will continue to work on a book about his adventure. He has also set up the Mackenzie Heritage Trust to raise funds to be used to foster an exchange between First Nations and students from Scotland.

Donaldson would also like to see canoe construction and bushcraft workshops in the Northwest Territories, to curb the decline in traditional heritage skills among First Nations youth.

About John Donaldson

John Donaldson is a neurological biochemist with a primary interest in the role of trace metals in the brain. In the industrial milieu, he was formerly a vice-president of scientific affairs and head of molecular biology in the pharmaceutical industry. In the academic area, he served as Associate Professor of Pharmacology at the University of Manitoba and as Professeur Agrere at the Université de Montréal. He holds a BSc in chemistry, an MSc in microbiology and a doctorate in experimental medicine, all gained at McGill University, Montreal. He is a former Garfield Weston Scholar in medical research, as well as the recipient of several awards from the American Parkinson's foundation.

John grew up in Scotland and came to Canada in 1955. Following an active academic and industrial career, he now lives in Kingston with his wife, Ishbel. They are proud parents and grandparents, love the great outdoors, and have travelled extensively. John has great interest in Scottish and Canadian history, the fur trade in Canada, aviation, and World War II. On the spiritual side, he is a lay oblate of the Benedictine Order and follows Christian meditation.

At aged 60, armed with a little recreational canoeing experience and a grand sense of adventure, John retraced the voyages of the great Scottish-Canadian explorer, Sir Alexander Mackenzie, his boyhood hero. John's travels spanned five years and took him more than 12,000 kilometres from Montreal (Mackenzie's starting point) to the Pacific and Arctic oceans.

About
Sir Alexander Mackenzie

Alexander Mackenzie was born in 1764 in
Stornoway on the Isle of Lewis off the west
coast of Scotland. He travelled to New York with his father and went to
school in Montreal. In 1779 he entered a company that eventually joined
with other Montreal firms involved in the fur trade, forming the North
West Company. Mackenzie became a determined young fur trader who
eventually found routes overland across the continent to the Arctic and
Pacific oceans.

In June 1789 he embarked on his first remarkable journey by canoe
from Fort Chipewyan on the shores of Lake Athabasca. He was
accompanied on the expedition by French-Canadian voyageurs and
native hunters and interpreters. They dicovered the De-Cho River, now
known as the Mackenzie, and travelled by it to the Arctic Ocean before
returning to Fort Chipewyan in September that same year.

In October 1792 Mackenzie again left Lake Athabasca in search of
the elusive North West Passage. Travelling along the Peace River, he
arrived at winter quarters in Fort Fork. In spring he set out again, together
with Alexander McKay and natives and voyageurs. Following the Parsnip,
McGregor and Fraser rivers through the Rocky Mountains, they then
headed west on foot along 2,000 year old trails of the Carrier people.
After a gruelling journey they reached the Pacific Ocean. There, on a
prominent rock near Bella Coola, Mackenzie wrote:

ALEXANDER MACKENZIE
FROM CANADA BY LAND,
THE TWENTY-SECOND OF JULY,
ONE THOUSAND, SEVEN HUNDRED
AND NINETY-THREE

Preface

Two hundred years after the Scottish-born explorer Alexander Mackenzie completed the first crossings of Canada to the Arctic and Pacific oceans by canoe, I fulfilled a personal dream by making the same voyages. One of my reasons for doing so was to heighten awareness in this country of Canada's extraordinarily rich history.

When I first came to Canada from Scotland as a young man in the mid-1950s, I used to hurry home from work to listen to *The Land Is Bright* on CBC Radio, a marvellous documentary of Canada's rich history, highlighting the lives of many of the country's greats. I enjoyed all the dramatizations of the deeds of Canada's gifted explorers, military men, and inventors. Coming from a country where history as taught was a tedious exercise in recalling dates of an unending compendium of royal personages, I found Canada's history, in contrast, refreshingly vibrant and exciting. I particularly thrilled to the accounts of explorers like Radisson, La Verendrye, de Groseilliers, Brule, Fraser, Mackenzie, Thompson, and Henry. They cemented my love for a country that had fostered such intrepid individuals. Other names like Banting and Best, brilliant medical scientists and the creators of insulin, evoked my admiration and awe. Then there were the immortal flying aces like Billy Bishop and those others whose courage, skills and endurance opened up the North, like "Wop" May, and Grant MacConnachie, who rose from flying string-bag biplanes to founding Canadian Pacific Airlines, thus pioneering commercial aviation in this country. The British might revel in the glamour of their Great Train Robbers, but what Canadian could fail to be enthralled at the exploits of the flying bandit Ken Leishman, even if he steered to the wrong side of the law?

Despite their relatively smaller numbers in both world wars, Canadians were renowned as gifted aerial warriors, their superior flying skills enabling them to down high numbers of enemy aircraft. The vastness of Canada provided ideal training grounds to develop not only advanced flying skills but also intrepid individuals with stamina and panache. Under the enormously successful British Empire Training Scheme in World War II, thousands of pilots, navigators, and bomb aimers received their training in Canada, producing desperately needed aircrew.

In more recent times, another major first in aviation was Canada's development of the fastest fighter aircraft in the world, the Avro Arrow. This brilliant achievement in aircraft design and engineering put even the U.K. and U.S.A. in the shade, even if it did end up being sacrificed to political expediency.

Today I am puzzled and disappointed that many Canadians are unaware of the hardship, ingenuity, and perseverance of the brave pioneers who opened up this wonderful country. By remembering our past, we regain our spirit and enthusiasm for the future. Sadly, Canadians show little interest in this country's history. The banal celebration of our annual "heritage day" is designed to offend no one, and consequently fails to reflect what or whose heritage we celebrate!

The inability to step forward with pride for what we truly represent as Canadians is our major problem. It is an ominous legacy for the future when our younger generation hasn't the faintest idea what Canada stands for. Our governments and school systems are largely to blame for graduating young citizens with no idea of the events that shaped our country.

As historian Jack Granatstein observes in an article on the Dominion Institute website, "There is scarcely a school system in Canada that obliges its students to learn anything of world history or European history. The key to understanding of our civic institutions, British history, has been eliminated because the British are seen as just another ethnic group deserving no special attention. Four provinces have no compulsory Canadian history in their high schools, others bury the past in a mishmash of civics, pop sociology and English as a second language, eliminating anything that might offend students, parents, and school trustees in an attempt to produce an unbiased past free of warts (except for the officially approved historical sins) that can be used for present day social engineering."

Granatstein continues his indictment: "Schools put process over learning. History is hard, and to master the Canadian past is difficult. But this is its great virtue. History requires thought, demands wide study and almost forces those who study it to write … History happened, and must not be twisted out of shape for present day purposes … not for indoctrination, but presented warts and all."

He concludes, "History matters. The way it is taught – or not taught

– has shaped a tuned-out generation that can use a computer and surf the Net, but that knows almost nothing about anything of importance, except that anything important must be inexpressibly boring. Kosovo? Immaterial. Social Union? Incomprehensible. The future? Unknowable, but surely bleak."

With the traditional bias towards the English version of history in Canadian schools, the considerable part played in Canada's development by Scottish men and women has been little understood. Historian W. Stanford Reid of the University of Toronto points out that the Scottish role in Canada "predates that of the French, Portuguese and English," going back as far as 1010! Scots were among the crew of Thorfinn Karlsevnis's voyage to North America and sent by him to explore Vineland (Newfoundland and Nova Scotia).

Scottish seamen were also among the crew of Jacques Cartier's ships, because of the "Auld Alliance," the concord between Scotland and France drawn up in 1295. Based on the two countries' shared need to curtail English expansionism, it lasted some 400 years. It gave the Scots dual citizenship with France. Even more appealing to many, Scotland received first choice of the finest French wines of Bordeaux. Although whisky is considered the drink of the Scots, it was only the commoners that drank it. Scottish intellectuals and other elite drank claret!

The two leading centres of the Enlightenment were in fact Edinburgh and Paris. Voltaire acknowledged the debt that French intellectuals owed to Scotland, since many of the new trends and theories of the day emanated from Edinburgh. Scottish scholars studied in France at the Scots College in the Sorbonne.

Many Scots emigrated to France, particularly Brittanny. Scottish soldiers fought in the great European campaigns and aided Joan of Arc in her famous relief of Orleans, then went on to form the Garde Ecossais, the loyal bodyguard of the French kings. A battalion of exiled Scots fresh from the killing fields of Culloden swelled Montcalm's ranks on the Plains of Abraham, staring across at fellow clansmen in Wolfe's army. Their Sorbonne-educated officers were fluent in French. Remarkably, Montcalm's Scottish aide de camp, Chevalier Johnstone, by his single-handed action in moving horse-drawn cannon directly in front of Wolfe's crack division, the Fraser Highanders, almost turned the tables and came within a hair's breadth of bringing about a last-minute victory for the French. Even after the conquest, the harsh directives from London to subjugate French Canadians were never implemented thanks to the loyal Jacobite, General Murray, first British governor of Quebec.

Canadian history is enormously influenced by the Scots who came to Canada in huge numbers following the tragic battle of Culloden. In the *Scottish Tradition in Canada*, Stanford Reid describes the destruction of highland culture following this defeat: "The immediate British reaction to the Jacobite rising of 1745-6 was an effort to break the spirit of the men who had served the Jacobite cause. Rapine, slaughter and torture, all were used with relentless vindictiveness by the king's son who commanded the British government forces (Prince William, Duke of Cumberland) ... Through the glens and over the hills, ["Bloody Butcher" Cumberland's] patrols laid waste the land, plundered the houses, burned the crofts, killed suspected Jacobites, raped the women and drove the Highanders cattle to the military posts." Terrible as these reprisals were, the Duke considered them inadequate. Three months after Culloden he wrote, "I am sorry to leave this country in the condition it is in; for all the good that we have done is a little blood letting, which has only weakened the madness, but not at all cured it, and I tremble for fear that this vile spot may still be the ruin of this island and of our family."

The "clearances" of the clans began. The only choices left to the highlanders were to starve, emigrate, or fight England's wars. Allowing Scots to join newly formed regiments of the British army was a clever ploy, a two-bladed sword for the "final solution" of the troublesome highlanders. On one hand it gave England an excellent force of great fighting men with which to build her empire. At the same time, it removed the major thorn in England's side. As British Prime Minister Pitt observed to General Wolfe, "Tis no great matter should they fall."

Expendable they were and fall they did, in far-off places around the world as they enlarged the British Empire over the following two hundred years. But they also left their mark in many of those places, none more than in Canada. From the exploration of its vast wilderness to the establishment of its universities, they left a legacy. As a first-generation Canadian Scot, it is one I have been proud to commemorate.

PART 1

THE FIRST YEAR: 1990

FROM MONTREAL TO SAULT STE MARIE

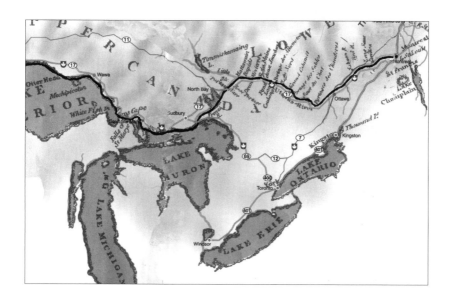

A tea break offers a welcome respite from the fierce current and plunging logs on the Ottawa River.

Portaging along the rocky footpaths of the Ottawa River is an exhausting task.

1

The Spirit of Mackenzie

As a young man in Glasgow, I used to pass the Canadian Pacific posters in Central Station every day on my way to and from work. "Canadian Pacific: Password for excellence," the message ran. Gazing enthralled at the magnificent lakes and canoes crossing emerald-green waters, I dreamed about paddling on lakes like these in the pristine wilderness. In 1955 I emigrated to Canada with my wife, Ishbel, and our three-month-old daughter, Anne. But though I never forgot my dream, for many years it lay dormant.

Some 35 years later, I made preparations to launch my five-metre (16 foot) Cree-built wood-canvas canoe, *Spirit of Mackenzie*, on a transcontinental adventure. My hope was to emulate the voyages of the great Scottish-Canadian explorer, Sir Alexander Mackenzie, when he made the first crossing of the continent in 1793 – twelve years before the expedition of America's renowned Lewis and Clark. It would be a voyage of some 12,000 kilometres through North America's toughest waters.

My qualifications for this daunting venture were unimpressive. Taking the kids canoeing on my vacation in the Thousand Islands or on Lake St Francis for two or three weeks every year constituted the bulk of my paddler's resume. I remember the first time I brought home a canoe. The newly purchased craft atop my car, I sped down the road towards Lake St Louis, intending to try it out even before I went home. Not even the owner's warning, "Watch it, she's tippy," curbed my euphoria.

Fresh from work, I was dressed in jacket, collar and tie. I figured on paddling only a short way, then heading home to show off my acquisition. Hauling the canoe from the car roof, I launched it, quickly paddling out 50 metres or so. It handled beautifully. As the canoe glided silently over the tranquil water, the sun shone through the trees lining the lake. The cry of a loon echoed along the lakeshore, and I felt decidedly at one with nature. That's when I shifted in the seat to a more comfortable position. My new acquisition turned over, throwing me into the water.

The canoe in which I was now setting out into the wilderness was of a very different order. Resting on the grass, its thwarts and ribs gleaming, it was sturdily built by the Cree First Nations people of James Bay, a culture that considers a canoe as not only transport but an ancient and treasured heritage. This is reflected especially in the final act of construction, when in sacred ceremony the breath of the Great Spirit is imbued into the very innards of the canoe. Only when the craft has been fully endowed with the qualities of strength, endurance, and perseverance and is protected from numerous and treacherous manitous can it be called a "Cree-built canoe." It now gleamed with a new coat of green paint highlighting the white and red Clan Mackenzie crest of the famed Seaforth Highlanders – a stag with the Gaelic "*Cuidich n'righ*"– "Save the King."

The site I had chosen as my point of departure for the *pays d'en haut*, as the voyageurs used to call it, was appropriate. It was directly behind the reconstructed Fur Trade Museum at Lachine, once a warehouse of the Hudson's Bay Company. All around the museum were artefacts and memorabilia of those giants of Canada's past who had launched their *canots de maître* at the same spot: Brûlé, Radisson, Le Verendrye, Mackenzie, Fraser, Thompson. The very names create a historical resonance of the Canada of our ancestors as they carved out a civilization across the North American continent. It was fitting also that across the river lay the reservation of Kahnewake, and nearby ran the treacherous Lachine Rapids, where many a voyageur or *coureur du bois* had met a tragic end.

In the halcyon days of the voyageurs, great armadas of canoes as many as a hundred strong were provisioned and made ready on the spot where I prepared to launch the *Spirit of Mackenzie*. In his book *Rivers of Canada*, Hugh McLennan writes: "They had the pride of champions. They sprang from European peasants who had never been allowed to leave their villages or their lords' estates ... but in the West of Canada they were their own masters and lived with the freedom of kings."

They would leave in the early spring as soon as the Ottawa River was free of ice and head out for the northlands. Quebecois mothers in those days prayed to deliver a son with broad shoulders to handle the paddle along the wild waters and savage forests stretching from Lachine to Superior and beyond in the fierce *terre sauvage* of the Athabasca region. Youths eagerly signed on for a voyage that would take them out of sight of the vigilant church spires of Montreal, with the promise, boasted of by old canoemen, of amorous delights with the aboriginal inhabitants.

Such fantasies were dispelled after a few days of rigorous paddling. But the pay was good and food not too bad even if the Hudson's Bay Company, implacable foes of the Norwesters, derisively called them "pork eaters."

No one was there to see me set off into Lake St Louis on that afternoon in early June. I was only taking up this venture on a one-day-at-a-time basis. I wasn't even carrying provisions – there were plenty of grocery stores along the way. I paused for a moment to reflect once again on why in God's name I was undertaking this piece of romantic folly. There were a lot of reasons.

I hoped my transcontinental odyssey would help bring to prominence the role played by Mackenzie in shaping our country. My own interest in the great explorer had begun early. My father was born on the Black Isle on the Moray Firth in the Scottish highlands, the country to which Mackenzie retired after being knighted for his discoveries. He is buried in the village of Avoch near Inverness, and his tomb is becoming a major site for tourists from Canada visiting Scotland. It was one of Mackenzie's relatives, Kenneth Mackenzie, the Earl of Seaforth, who formed the famed Seaforth Highlanders in which my dad and several uncles served in the First World War. The crest of the Seaforths adorned the bow of my canoe.

In my young life Mackenzie, Canada, and the Seaforth Highlanders somehow became synonymous. My dad never talked about his war experiences, but my aunts told me that at the age of fifteen in the Battle of the Somme, Dad was befriended by an officer in the Canadian Seaforth Highlanders who, aghast at his young age, was instrumental in getting him a safe job behind the lines.

A more compelling reason for taking on my Mackenzie odyssey was that I had been downsized into early retirement from my job as a research scientist. Ostensibly, a lack of funding from research-granting bodies was the reason. In reality I was a casualty of intensive turf wars between department heads. In the highly competitive area of academic research, items that can enable a laboratory to seize a lead over its competitors are sought with the avidity of a starving hound seizing a bone. Thus a job – which if I had been a millionaire, I would have paid to have – was lost to the cupidity of grant procurement. Medical and biological research was for me not employment but a vocation in which I immersed myself not only intellectually but with body, heart, and soul. When it disappeared, it left me bereft and spiritually bankrupt. I had lots of time, the children were no longer at home, and my wife was working. I had Ishbel's support and encouragement. She figured that the enormity of such a challenge would bring me out of my doldrums.

Another reason: The continuing erosion of our heritage gnaws at my innards. Ask a student today who Mackenzie was and you'll get a blank stare. Our pioneering bush plane heritage is also fading into obscurity. Names like Wop May, Punch Dickens, or Billy Bishop, or even Banting and Best are unknown.

It's important that people know their roots. But in today's Canada, this knowledge is rapidly being lost. I am deeply concerned that we are losing our Canadian identity. In attempting to repeat the voyages of Mackenzie, I fervently hoped to remind Canadians that we possess a priceless cultural heritage which is being eroded. Pierre Trudeau expressed these sentiments well: "I know a man whose school could never teach him patriotism, but who acquired that virtue when he felt in his bones the vastness of his land and the greatness of those who founded it."

Maybe my trip could do something to spark an interest in today's younger generation. Some of them might think that if an old guy like me could finish the Mackenzie marathon, they might try it too!

I canoed past the many architectural gems that line Lake St Louis. I felt nostalgia for many of these beautiful edifices of English-Canadian life, sadly now suffering the ravages of architectural vandals. The red-tiled roofs of MacDonald College came into view. The college, once renowned internationally as a centre of excellence in agricultural research, is now a CEGEP, a community college.

Swinging alongside the dock at the picturesque village of Ste Anne de Bellevue, I tied up and crossed the road towards a little stone church near the busy locks. Ste Anne's was a major stop for voyageurs, heralding their entry into the Lake of Two Mountains. At the church they would leave an offering with the priest to gain the protection of good Ste Anne along the wild rivers leading to the savage interior. At the first camp down the lake, they broke out a keg of rum.

Ste Anne's is also the junction of the Ottawa and the St Lawrence rivers – my first portage. I swung the canoe above my head for a trifling 100-metre carry past the locks that have tamed once-formidable rapids that guarded entry to the broad expanse of the Lake of Two Mountains. Next to the locks is Simon Fraser House. This delightful stone house is often mistaken as having belonged to the famous explorer who travelled the mighty Fraser River in British Columbia but in fact is named for a kinsman. Now a tea-room supporting the work of the Victorian Order of Nurses, it is maintained much as it was 200 years ago. In his book *Ottawa Waterway*, historian Robert Legget quotes a young Irish traveller, Thomas Moore, who stayed in the house in 1804. He was so enchanted with the idyllic scene that he captured it in verse with his classic "Canadian Boat Song." It begins:

> Faintly as tolls the evening our voices
> Keep tune and our oars keep time.
> Soon as the woods on shore look dim,
> We'll sing at St Anne's our parting hymn,
> Row, brothers, row, the stream runs fast,
> The rapids are near and the daylight's past

I paddled under the span of the great bridge that links Montreal with eastern Ontario, an endless stream of cars and trucks passing overhead. Underneath the central span lies the small island of Ile aux Tourtes, which gained international distinction for the virulence of its mosquitoes. During the American War of Independence it was a POW camp for some 250 American soldiers. Eventually they were transported to another camp across the lake at Vaudreuil, but two prisoners left behind were later rescued by Benedict Arnold's troops. Their condition was so poor that the Continental Congress made a formal protest to the British government over their "cruel treatment." Legget records wryly, "It was probably the only occasion in history when exposure to the famed mosquitoes of the Ottawa Valley resulted in diplomatic action!"

On the Quebec shore towards the small village of Oka, the Trappist monastery looks serenely down from on top of the mountain. Known for its excellent Oka cheese, it made a pretty picture from my canoe. As I paddled across the mirror-like surface of the lake that summer of 1990, however, things were not so tranquil. In the brasserie at Ste Anne's I had watched television reports of a violent encounter between the Quebec police and local First Nations protesters. Approaching the shoreline, I was thrust into history in the making. Barricades bristled with barbed wire, while heavily armed military personnel clustered around armoured vehicles. An ugly situation was unfolding in a tense confrontation between First Nations People and Canada. The fracas created a deep rift that will take a generation to heal.

It was a relief to pass through the ferry crossing and continue out into the lake. Over 100 years ago, the tiny village of Como on the south shore had one of the largest glass factories in the country. A few kilometres upstream lies the delightful town of Hudson. Near the yacht club I found a likely camping spot under a clump of trees close by the water. Lifting my canoe onto the grass, I spread my ground sheet and set up my tent for my first camp along the trail. Too bushed to make a proper meal, I broke out my regular standby of Harvest Crunch.

My first day as a voyageur had gone well: I hadn't dumped my canoe. From my sleeping bag I watched the sun sinking across the lake. As sleep took over, I resolved to take it one day at a time. For the voyageurs, anyone past forty was over the hill. I was on the wrong side of sixty. If circumstances arose that meant heading for home, I would face that when it came.

I awoke next morning full of energy. After a breakfast of cereal and coffee brewed on my new backpack stove, it was time to head out. Exquisitely painted white churches lined the Ottawa River on the Quebec side. Fish were jumping everywhere around my canoe. I couldn't help smiling as several fishermen in high-powered boats were vainly trying to get a bite. One of the great advantages of the canoe is that it blends so easily with the natural environment. At least this is usually the case – but as I glided along the shoreline, an Arctic tern came fluttering up and beat her wings in my face. Obviously she had young in the nest nearby.

As I headed out into mid-channel, dark clouds appeared. In no time a wild east wind was whipping up the river. Through the mist and rain ahead rose the magnificent spire of the Catholic church at Hawkesbury. The fine rain was penetrating my clothing, but my spirits were undampened. I was looking forward to a change into dry clothes and footwear. Shangri La for a canoeist is a pair of dry socks!

Following a visit to the local laundromat and an excellent meal at a restaurant called Le Caveau, it was time for a walkabout of downtown Hawkesbury. At the local bank I fell into conversation with a young lady who introduced herself as Sharon Russell. We were engrossed in talking about canoes and white water when her mother, Eleanor, met us outside the bank. She suggested that her husband would also like to meet with me, and extended an invitation to visit them at their house further along the river.

Gliding along the shore I searched for the Russell house. As I turned into a bay, peeping out between several trees was a pretty little house exactly as Eleanor had described it. The family had been keeping a lookout for me.

Herb Russell, an Air Canada pilot, flies gliders out of the airfield at Pendleton during his off-duty times. Since flying is a major interest of mine, we spent some time swapping stories. Herb warned me that squalls could arise very fast along this part of the river, churning the water into high choppy waves.

In their kitchen I helped myself to freshly made delicious pancakes with the Russells' personal brand of maple syrup. After a couple of hours of conversation I reluctantly took my leave. And sure enough, as Herb predicted, the wind whipped up the waves. Soon *Spirit of Mackenzie* was being battered by a miniature squall. Despite my frantic efforts to turn the bow into wind, I was driven across the river to the Ontario shore.

A large pier loomed through the driving rain. I clung to it grimly in the howling wind to prevent capsize. Slipping into the leeside, I heard a muffled shout. An elderly lady was gesturing at me. "C'mon in for coffee!" she hollered. After securing the canoe, I bolted through the rain to the house.

As I dripped on the hallway carpet, she introduced herself as Mrs. Holmes. She led me into the large living room where others of the family were gathered. While rain battered the windows we exchanged pleasantries over steaming mugs of coffee. As the conversation deepened, we discovered that one of them had been a student of mine at the University of Manitoba some years earlier. There was much laughter at the remarkable coincidence of a rain-soaked stranger blown ashore turning out to be an old acquaintance.

The storm blew itself out and I made my farewell. Further down the river, when it was getting dark with no sign of a camping spot, I suddenly saw ahead a large sign for "Claude's Cabins." As I pulled up to the dock, a diminutive figure strolled out to greet me. Even from a distance it was plain he had been imbibing freely.

Grabbing the rope, he helped me secure the canoe and introduced himself as Claude. He seemed pleased to see me. "Just make yourself at home," he said, pointing out a good spot for my tent. "There's no other campers, so pick any spot you like. Anyway, I'm going off for a nap, so you run the place!"

Next morning Claude called me over to his cabin. He was preparing bacon and eggs for my breakfast, all the while profusely apologizing for leaving me alone. His regular clients were becoming fewer each year, he said, confessing that this was likely due to his drinking binges. He refused to accept any payment, pleading with me to stick around for a day or two. I was grateful for his hospitality, but I was reeling from the heightened emotion that seemed to accompany our conversation. I was anxious to be moving on.

The voyageurs delighted in the beauty of the Ottawa, which they called the Grande Rivière. As I headed towards Montebello, I admired the attractive homes set amidst rolling meadows, the Gatineau hills rising behind them. No wonder voyageur hearts leaped on their return from the *terre sauvage*. Their vermilion paddles would beat a fast cadence on reaching Grande Rivière, and they burst into song, grateful to good Ste

Anne for sparing them from the perils of a vast unforgiving wilderness.

Mackenzie made several trips through the Ottawa waterway. His description of the Ottawa route from Montreal to Fort Chipewyan is considered a classic. After his epic second journey in 1793 to the Pacific Ocean, he returned by way of the Great Lakes and called on Governor Simcoe at Niagara, presenting him with a sea-otter skin to prove that he had reached the ocean. That journey marked him as among the great travellers of all time. The American writer Bernard de Voto considers Mackenzie's exploits unsurpassed: "In courage, in the faculty to command, in ability to meet the unforeseen with resources of craft and skill, in the will that cannot be overborne, he has no superior in the history of American exploration."

The scenery was idyllic and I belted out a few choruses from my own repertoire of Scottish and Irish ditties. A seagull arose abruptly, screeching at this vulgar intrusion. Meanwhile, since I had said goodbye to Claude, the sky was darkening, with a blustering wind rising from the north. The waves were beginning to look nasty, with a fine rain to boot. Under such conditions, it's easy to lose sight of even prominent landmarks. This helps explain why my navigation skills fell apart, resulting in an extra six kilometres as I guided the canoe down a blind alley. I had wandered into a wildlife refuge brimming with diverse populations of ducks and other waterfowl.

After I backtracked to the main channel, the enormous edifice of Chateau Montebello appeared suddenly over the bow. A north wind was now sweeping across the river. It seemed like a good time for break, and what better place to stop than the impeccable grounds surrounding the flagship of the Canadian Pacific Hotels, the Chateau Montebello. Once the former residence of the prestigious Seigneury Club, today Montebello still has a select clientele who enjoy its superb accommodation and gourmet cuisine. Amazingly, the magnificent chateau is really Canada's biggest log cabin! An incredible 10,000 red cedar logs were used in its construction. The huge hexagonal fireplace in the main hall provides a stunning spectacle, especially in winter with a roaring fire burning. In the early 1970s my wife and I used to find excuses to take a weekend break at the hotel. I fondly recalled relaxing in one of the comfortable chairs at the long mahogany bar, sipping a Drambuie. Unfortunately, my present travels did not allow for a stay at the hotel, never mind a stopover.

Guiding my canoe into the yacht club, I tied up alongside the expensive yachts at the long dock. I strolled around the chateau's lovely gardens, stretching my cramped legs. Later, amidst all this affluence, I relaxed on the lawn over a modest repast – coffee and a mouthful of Harvest Crunch – hoping the staff would not take me for a squatter and kick me out.

So far I had yet to see another canoe. Near Thurso that changed. Lulled into a reverie by the monotony of paddling, I was suddenly aroused by the sound of splashing. Rapidly overtaking me was a yellow fibreglass canoe with a lone occupant. Swinging alongside, a young man in his mid-twenties thrust out his hand.

"Jerome Orange, from France," he said, in halting English. A teacher from Normandy, he spoke only a little English, but together with my fractured French we made out.

I was delighted and incredulous to learn that he too was following the trail of Mackenzie! Remarkably, we were even using the same journals and diaries of prominent fur trade historians and explorers, although his were in French. Like me, he had been entranced with Eric Morse's *Fur Trade Routes of Canada Then and Now*, a little gem describing Canada's voyageur era. But the book that had pride of place among his journals was the Bible.

Jerome was a remarkable young man. He had walked all the way from Paris to Jerusalem covering the medieval pilgrimage trails through France and Spain. As a canoeist, he was, like me, a rank amateur. He told me his experience had consisted solely of a few trips down the Seine from Paris in an old canoe. Now on a one-year sabbatical from his school, he was living the wilderness experience. He was also an avid reader of Jack London, whose tales of the Canadian North had fired his imagination. Despite a forty-year difference in our ages, there was no sense of a generation gap. We were just two travellers meeting on the trail. One thing we did not agree on was food, however. While my canoe was heavily laden with provisions, Jerome's had only a large bag of rice, which was his breakfast, lunch and dinner.

Meeting this young Frenchman was a highlight of my trip thus far. We were evidently driven by the same love and romantic ideals of Canada's past history. It did not escape either of us that a strong rapport between the Scottish explorers and the French-Canadian voyageurs had resulted in an entrepreneurial alliance that forged our Canadian roots. Jerome, however, was following the route of Mackenzie to the Beaufort Sea and hoped to be North of Sixty by summer's end, well down the Mackenzie River.

It was a very ambitious venture, but he was young, eager, and brimming with enthusiasm and likely would make it. He was anxious to get on his way and reach Athabasca before winter. I insisted he forge ahead without having to mark time with a laid-back paddler.

Although the sun was below the horizon, there was still plenty of light. A few kilometres down the river I pulled up onto a sandbank, secured my canoe, and with my gathering experience soon had my tent up and tea brewing.

Next day was hot and humid, and paddling was an effort. Eventually, to my delight, I glimpsed the water tower at Masson in the distance. The huge tower is a great landmark for recreational flyers around this part of the country, and usually I viewed it from several thousand feet overhead. When I flew my old Aeronca Superchief, from Montreal to Ottawa, it was a terrific aid in lining up for final approach to the Gatineau airport.

A coffee break seemed like a great idea when I got to Rockland, the classy suburb of Ottawa. I headed towards a grassy verge at the riverside, pulling the canoe well out of the water. Sitting in a local restaurant, it dawned on me that a few curves on in the river lay Canada's capital. Despite the short distance, it turned out to be a strenuous paddle, particularly the last few kilometres. The current was very strong due to the confluence of the Gatineau and Rideau rivers mingling with the Ottawa.

Near the Ottawa Canoe Club where I was headed, a tour boat packed with tourists suddenly swung towards me. A guide was giving the passengers lining the decks a talk on the history of Canada. Observing the decals on my canoe, his voice boomed out, "Now here's a voyageur in a replica canoe." This evoked a great cheer. I raised my paddle in acknowledgment. It was heartening to receive such a welcome to Ottawa.

Altogether, it had taken six days to paddle the 170-kilometre stretch from Montreal. While it was only a short distance, completing it gave my morale a great boost. I was well aware of the many formidable obstacles still ahead. But my resolve to continue on to the *pays d'en haut* was strengthened.

I tied up at a vacant slip at the Ottawa Canoe Club. The atmosphere felt decidedly melancholy, and the property had an atmosphere of neglect. I was incredulous to see the remains of a heritage Montreal canoe sticking out of a dumpster. Neatly sawn in half in order to fit, the canoe had obviously been in excellent condition. There seemed no valid reason why such a historical treasure should be disposed of so ignominiously. When I enquired, several people told me with some embarrassment that the club had run out of room to store the canoe. However, nobody could provide a more coherent explanation. Many museums around the country would have killed for such a valuable artefact.

Heading out to the middle of the river, I pointed the bow towards the Museum of Civilization on the Quebec side. This route goes right through the meeting place of the Gatineau, Rideau, and Ottawa rivers.

While the current was strong, it was manageable. I had a marvellous view of the Parliament Buildings like a great castle atop the huge limestone cliffs rearing up from the river. Of course I had no idea then that two years later I would be a guest in the chambers of the Speaker of the House.

My daughter Anne lives in nearby Aylmer across the river from Ottawa. When I called, she told me she would come to pick me up. Within the hour a van pulled off the road, and Anne and two of my grandchildren strolled across the roadway towards me.

"Hi, Dad! So you made it okay," she called out and gave me a hug. Despite my protests, since she was six months pregnant, Anne helped me load the canoe on the cartop carrier.

Later, while my son-in-law Bob and I were chatting in the living room, surrounded by my other three grandchildren, Anne dropped a bombshell. She had just been to the Ottawa General for an ultrasound. She was expecting triplets!

After a pleasant night in a real bed, still somewhat dazed by news of the forthcoming additions to my family, I took my leave and headed out towards the river. Becoming a grandfather three more times – and all at once – was going to take a little getting used to!

A short paddle up the river from Aylmer lies Quoyn, a pleasant little town on the Pontiac and my first stop after the Deschenes Rapids. I picked up some supplies at the general store. Frequently along the trail my presence was met by quizzical glances. However, the young girl behind the counter was not fazed in the least by a lobster-faced old guy with an Aussie hat, several days' beard, and eyes like a raccoon's. I decided to splurge on a meal at the local restaurant. There conversation ceased immediately and a hush fell over the dining salon: no doubt that I was the subject of bemused scrutiny by the middle-aged patrons. It's curious that younger people are more accepting of the eccentric than the senior generation.

The Ontario provincial park at Fitzroy Harbour lies directly across the river from Quoyn. This location turned out to be a great camping spot with a broad expanse of sandy beach. The ready availability of excellent camping spots is one of the marvellous spin-offs in canoeing the Ottawa. The downside to the grandeur of the river, however, is the presence of so many dams, which pose a real environmental problem. Despite repeated pledges by politicians when the dams were being proposed that access to the river would be unhindered, small boat traffic is completely blocked from moving upstream. Because of continued pressure by the sports fishing industry and small boat operators, steps are finally being taken to install boat lifts in several locations.

I spent the next morning searching for a suitable detour around the dam at Fitzroy Harbour. It became clear there was no simple way to get around the monstrous granite structure. When I returned to the village and enquired at the general store for advice, an 82-year-old retired employee of Ontario Hydro kindly volunteered to provide portage services. Calling a friend with a pickup truck, he helped me load my canoe and gear in the back. We took off along a private hydro road that led past the dam. Although entrance to the other side of the dam was guarded by a fenced door, my new friends had a key.

About half a kilometre on, the pickup screeched to a halt. The banks of the river were lined with enormous rocks, so getting my canoe and gear down to the water was fraught with difficulties. It was struggle to keep my footing on the rocks; even a goat would have had problems. Ultimately, with some nifty footwork, this precarious operation was accomplished. Thanking my helpers profusely, I pressed ten dollars on them, which they reluctantly accepted. Relieved that the canoe and all my gear was in one piece, I plunged my paddle into the lake. Waving my thanks to my helpers high up on the road, I gratefully headed upstream.

The current became progressively swifter, and I was hard pressed to make headway, especially when I tried to pass under a bridge that spans the river at Lac des Chats. A man and boy fishing from the bridge watched my progress. Despite deep, savage thrusts of the paddle, my repeated tries ended in failure. Fatigued, I would drift helplessly back downstream as I regained strength for another assault. Finally, on my fifth attempt, intensive paddling and sheer physical stamina paid off. Accompanied by cheers from the two fishermen on the bridge, I gained the broad expanse of the lake.

I had no time to rest. Westerly winds were picking up and cresting the bow. By hugging the shoreline I was able to avoid most of the turbulence, but with a stiffening wind in my face, it was a relief to pull into the municipal park at Arnprior. A friendly young attendant bent the rules and allowed me to camp overnight. Her friend volunteered to drive me into town. On the banks of the Madawaska River, once the epicentre of the logging industry in the last century, Arnprior is now a dormitory community for Ottawa commuters. I enjoyed my walk past tidy homes along tree-lined streets and watched the sunset turn the river to gold.

Sunday threatened rain, and a strong east wind was making cat's-paws across the water. I decided I would launch anyway and try to hug the shoreline. Suddenly the wind shifted so that it was dead on the stern. It's a rare event to catch a following wind heading northwest, as prevailing winds are generally westerly. Hastily rigging a spinnaker by lashing a paddle to the mid-thwart and using cords to attach the tent fly to the paddle, I was soon bowling across the water. It was marvellous to get a break from paddling, even if only for a short while.

The wind pushed me steadily along at about three knots. At Sand Point a huge log boom forced me to lower the sail. Stepping out onto the logs and trying to manoeuvre a heavily laden canoe to clear this formidable obstacle was difficult. The logs were slippery and constantly rolled around. The task gave me great respect for the log-rolling skills of the Ottawa rivermen.

About ten kilometres further upstream, the river narrowed. I had to negotiate four rapids in swift succession. Three of them were so tricky that several times, despite my prodigious efforts, the bow slewed around and I headed downstream again. Then a second log boom appeared. Nearby, two "alligators" – strange little craft like mini-tugboats, with high bows – were threshing around the water, corralling logs like sheep dogs. The Ottawa River shore used to reverberate to the roar of dozens of these busy craft as they marshalled the logs into rafts for the journey downriver.

Later versions had flat bottoms and were known as "winch boats." Equipped with a large winch in the bow, their hauling power was such that they could actually pull themselves out of the water and portage between lakes. As I steered past, I realized that these were probably the last two winch boats on the river. The imminent demise of the logging industry on Canada's Grande Rivière was sounding their death knell.

2

Highway to the West

The Chenaux Rapids lie at the top end of Lac des Chats, where the course of the river is bridged by a small archipelago. The current is fast, and several times I had to jump out and haul the canoe upstream using a line tied to both sides of the mid-thwart. Over and over, my canoe was turned in the turbulent current and carried downstream. I could only make progress by grabbing branches and shrubs along the shoreline while I slid and stumbled on the rocky bottom. Although it was only a short distance to the Portage Dufort dam, I found myself in several dangerous skirmishes with logs hurtling downriver. Later I learned that a log drive was in progress.

Immediately before the dam, the current was extremely fast, and the raging river was filled with enormous logs shooting by at incredible speed. Any one of these would have smashed my canoe to pieces. The only way I could make headway was by placing a halter around my shoulders, securing it to a mid-thwart, and wading chest deep in the swirling current. Then I was stopped by a logjam. The only solution was to wade around the logs in near mid-stream in neck-high, fast water, trying to keep my balance on the slippery bottom. Logs shot past like torpedoes. These exhausting encounters took up most of the afternoon.

Fortunately, just before sundown, further upstream but on the other side of the river, a little bay appeared. The thick brush along the shore could make it difficult to pitch a tent, but from my position in the river with a bucking canoe and a halter around my neck, it looked great.

I climbed into the canoe and paddled furiously, steering a diagonal course to avoid the full force of the current. In this fashion it was possible to cross the fast-moving water into the sheltered bay. Just ahead I could see a tiny clearing between two trees in a thickly wooded area. Not ideal, but I was unlikely to find anything better further upstream. I was beat and looking forward to a meal.

I tied the canoe to an enormous log on the shore. As I set up the tent in the thicket, pine branches lashed my face, but it felt great to be out of the constant jarring of the fast water. Eventually I managed to flatten the brush and remove most of the nettles, compressing the tent floor into the tiny space.

Setting up camp and preparing supper were welcome events any day, but especially so this evening. That huge log made a great table. Leaving the dishwashing and other chores until morning, I tumbled into my sleeping bag, barely able to keep one eye open to watch an exquisite sunset. Though the ground was definitely stubbly, I had no trouble sleeping.

Next morning, groggily unzipping the tent, I was jarred into instant wakefulness. All the cooking gear, dishes and supplies I'd left on top of the huge log had vanished. So had the log – and my canoe! I gazed wildly around. There, out in the centre of the bay, was the log, complete with my stove, pots, pans and cutlery, plus my canoe, still tethered, spiralling around carousel-like in a giant whirlpool!

Any minute everything would be swept out of the bay into the mainstream and dashed to pieces in the rapids. I plunged into the water, swimming frantically to the log. Levering myself into the canoe, I swept the cooking utensils in as well. Then, undoing the rope, I made a mad dash to shore. Incredibly, the river level had increased by some four metres during the night!

I packed up my gear and made my way upriver once more, thankful to leave the formidable Chenaux rapids behind. Along with the massive logs coming down the fast water, the haphazard way in which water levels were controlled created an extremely dangerous situation.

That summer of 1990 was the last year of the log drives on the Ottawa. After nearly 300 years a remarkable era in Canada's history was rolling to an end. The demise of the logging industry was already creating a great downturn in the Ottawa Valley economy. Entire communities like Portage Dufort were scrambling desperately for revenue sources. It's sad that so many villages and small towns were left in grim economic straits. Some communities even competed aggressively for the "golden" opportunity of hosting Canada's largest garbage dump. Today, formerly tidy communities show neglect as hard times continue to tighten their grip. However, Valley folk are a hardy breed and have overcome hardships in the past. They will do so again.

A short distance upriver from the Chenaux lies the dam at Portage Dufort, once the major portage route around five awesome cataracts. Many of the giants of Canada's history trod the portage, the oldest footpath in North America. In 1613 Champlain battled his way along it before spending the winter in Ile aux Allumettes. Prior to this, a party of Algonquins, accompanied by the first white scout, Nicholas Vignau, passed through en route to a powwow at Calumet Island. For centuries the portage path rang with the curses of explorers and traders heading to the Upper Great Lakes, the Mackenzie basin, and way down south via the Mississippi to the Gulf of Mexico. I was following in their footsteps.

A few kilometres further, just below the Bryson Dam, I encountered more fast water. The frequent detouring around logjams and menacing log build-ups was tricky. However, I found it less stressful than my earlier battles with the current.

The portage path at Bryson is just off a small lake. I could see at once that it was going to be a challenging haul. Dense bush, tree stumps, roots, and fallen trees blocked the only route past the dam. The high ground and cliff face were going to make it nearly impossible to haul up the canoe. Most portages meant one haul for the canoe and two for the packs. A portage involving a total of five packs over the trail, for a total of 12 kilometres, is quite a trek. I swore that in future I would make do with one pack.

Sprawled on the beach, my head cushioned by sand, I considered my options. Getting the canoe up the steep bluff would be very tricky. Manoeuvring it through the bush would be even more so. It was clearly impossible to carry it through the hanging branches along the trail.

The longer I contemplated this predicament, the more hopeless it seemed. My anxiety intensified. Negotiating this portage seemed insoluble. The sensible thing to do was to pack up and head home.

Sheer stubbornness drove me on. The only way to get the canoe up the cliff was to haul it up. Fastening a rope to the mid-thwart of the canoe, I climbed the steep rock and tied the other end around a tree. Slipping and slithering on the muddy track, I managed to get the canoe to the top of the ridge.

Elated, I now faced the problem of carrying it through dense bush. The low branches meant I couldn't carry it on my shoulders. Would it be possible to drag it? No, the thin-skinned canvas covering would be ripped apart by the roots, stumps and rocks along the track. To protect the skin was vital. I wrapped rope so tightly around the canoe from bow to stern it appeared to be encased in a cocoon. My hope was that the rope would keep the canvas from being torn apart.

I made slow progress through the dense thicket, dragging the canoe behind me. When sharp rocks appeared, I laid down a layer of leaves or small branches. In this way I negotiated my way through all the snags until I reached the other side of the dam. Humping the packs through the bush was much easier.

Back on the river, my confidence went up a notch. Facing obstacles at this early stage taught me valuable lessons, enabling me to overcome some life-threatening hazards later in my journey. But isn't that what life is all about? Adversity squarely faced is ultimately shaped into that precious commodity we term experience. The gruelling Bryson portage was memorable physically, but I learned important psychological and spiritual lessons too. Whoever said "pain is the touchstone of all spiritual progress" had it right.

Paddling upriver past the dam into the tiny community of Bryson, I pulled in and tied my canoe to a tree. Above me on a high embankment overlooking the river was a large building and a sign indicating it was the local watering hole. I toiled my way up the grade. In the welcoming cool of the tavern, the few patrons looked up in surprise at the weather-beaten apparition. There were no strange cars in the parking lot, so how did this stranger get into town?

Curiosity eventually overcame the natural Valley reticence. "Where do you hail from?" someone asked. When I told them my personal watercraft was parked just below the hotel, their expressions turned to incredulity. One fellow observed scornfully, "There's no way anyone can come upriver now they're sending logs down!"

Finally someone went outside, returning shortly to report that indeed a canoe was tied up. With reluctance they considered that I might not be lying. They were astounded that not only had I overcome the rapids but I'd navigated through all the logs hurtling downriver. As they plied me with congratulations, the tables soon groaned with a variety of brews. In this sleepy Valley hamlet, any excuse for a pint was seized on. My adventures made their day.

Next morning I glided through the pass towards Ile du Grand Calumet, an exquisite panorama of pristine forest and placid lake. The journey was enhanced by knowing that for thousands of years this was an ancient meeting place for First Nations Peoples across North America. Further along the lake a small island came into view. I could see the wreck of a shallow-draft wood canoe abandoned on the rocky shore. Who knew what tales it could tell?

After a heavy pull against the current, the village of Grand Calumet was dead ahead. I tied up outside the Auberge Albert and went in for a leisurely breakfast of bacon and eggs with fresh croissants. Over excellent coffee, Albert Bedard, cordial owner and raconteur, entertained me with fascinating accounts of local folklore. He told me there used to be a large pipe outside his restaurant to commemorate the ancient meeting place of the tribes who held their powwows there. It had long since rotted away with the weather.

I asked about the impressive obelisk visible from the river just outside the village and set in a pretty knoll among a grove of trees. After refilling our cups, Albert leaned across the table with the anticipation of a veteran storyteller. "The monument is dedicated to the brave exploits of a coureur de bois named Jean Cadieux," he began. "He was taking his wife and family by canoe down to Trois Rivières when he was ambushed by a hunting party of Iroquois. Realizing he could not elude them, he jumped from the canoe and told his family to paddle on. He then created a diversion by running through the forest and firing occasional shots at the Iroquois over his shoulder.

"His pursuers wounded him with an arrow, but not before he had killed two of them with his hatchet. Leaving him to die, they went in search of the canoe. But they called off the chase when they saw that the heavily laden craft was swiftly being carried towards the dreaded seven chutes at Ile du Grand Calumet. These rapids had never been run, even by the most experienced paddlers. They had taken the lives of all those foolish enough to try to pass through them.

"The terrified women and children gave themselves up for lost, praying loudly to Ste Anne, great intercessionary of those in peril on the water. Legend has it that Ste Anne entered the canoe and guided it through the dreaded waters. Cadieux's wife, a very pious woman, said later, 'I saw nothing in the Seven Falls but a noble lady in white who hovered over us and showed us the way.' The canoe miraculously made it through all seven rapids. On arrival at Trois Rivière, the family attributed their survival to Ste Anne who answered their plea by lifting them above the waters.

"Meanwhile," Albert concluded, "Cadieux, a voyageur, poet and warrior, dying from his wounds, had dug himself a grave. On a piece of birch bark he wrote his death chant in his own blood."

Part of Cadieux's famous lament, recounted in full in Edith Fowkes' *Folklore of Canada*, reads:

Nightingale, go tell my wife.
Tell my children, that I take my leave of them,
That I have kept my love and my faith.
And henceforth they must give me up.

The legend of Cadieux was the first song composed in Canada about a Canadian incident. He is thought to have died in 1709; by 1800 his story was known to every voyageur. Albert said a lady from Trois Rivières, believed to be a descendant of Cadieux, appeared once a year at his monument to offer prayers and pay homage to his memory. The Ottawa Valley abounds with legends and river lore, but among tales authentic or suitably embellished, it is unlikely that the legend of Jean Cadieux could be surpassed. Unquestionably for Albert, Cadieux's story rang true.

After numerous cups of excellent coffee it was time to leave. In the austere conditions of the *pays d'en haut*, I would look back with nostalgia on all the wonderful rest stops along the Ottawa.

That night I had trouble finding a decent campsite. Just outside Campbell's Bay, I saw from a distance what looked like an acceptable spot. Unfortunately, it turned out to be a swamp. All night long the frogs croaked something awful. The place was plagued with snails and leeches, and in the morning my legs were covered with them. It was a relief to rise, throw my gear into the canoe, and head out.

Although an early morning fog lay heavily over the river, it was easy to navigate by the shoreline. At the small riverside community of Campbell's Bay, I left my canoe on a sandy beach while I had a quick breakfast, then headed upriver towards Fort Coulonge.

Fort Coulonge is the oldest community on the Ottawa. At its dock, a local fisherman, Rick Romaine, introduced himself. After we chatted a while, he extended an invitation for lunch. Rick lived in a habitant-style home overlooking the river. Recently laid off from the local mill, he had time to explain the local economy to me. The end of the logging era was a crippling blow for the town.

Back in the canoe, a few kilometres on I came to the Marchand Bridge connecting Fort Coulonge with the logging sites in the interior. At 129 metres, it is said to be the third-largest covered bridge in Quebec, a popular drawing card for tourists. Along the main street is an exquisite little stone Presbyterian church. Fort Coulonge was once home to lumber baron George Bryson, a man whose ego was so prodigious he opened his own bank and issued money with his face on it. Since the lumber company also owned the stores along the river, there was no problem about anyone refusing the "Bryson buck."

Bryson had Napoleon to thank for his wealth. Back in the 1840s when the French navy blockaded and cut off Britain's supply of timber from the Baltic, Bryson bought up huge tracts along the Ottawa River. To circumvent the waterfalls at Fort Coulonge, he created a 3,000-foot bypass that carried the 60-foot timbers past the bottlenecks. It took six men all day to square one log. The massive timbers were then shipped out in huge rafts of 2,000 and more.

Some indication of the intense logging activity that took place in the area is recorded by Joan Finnigan in her *Guide to the Ottawa Valley*. Local inhabitant Emile Bertrand records that one memorable logjam was over sixteen metres high. It took 150 men with bulldozers nearly a month to break it. When it finally was pried loose, the cascade swept the shores like a giant tidal wave, ripping great trees off by their roots. One local recalled that the noise was so frightful that "cows quit milking and sheep died of fright!"

The Paquette Rapids run for about six kilometres and are particularly fast on the Ontario side. Nonetheless I had no real difficulty as I attached a rope to the bow and pulled the canoe through the shallows. This process, termed "lining," was often used by the voyageurs.

At the little general store in Westmeade, an elderly French-Canadian lady and her daughter were interested to hear of my exploits as a voyageur, even pleading for me to entertain them by singing a voyageur song. I politely declined, but they appeared satisfied at my recounting of the legend of Jean Cadieux.

That night I camped on a soft sandy beach among some pines. The view of the sun going down over the Gatineau hills was spellbinding. Next morning the sky was cloudless and the lake was like a mirror. In the distance was the bridge across the river near Pembroke. But to my consternation I could see a stretch of formidable rapids about ten kilometres away. My anxiety grew as the distance to this enormous area of turbulent white water shortened.

Then, suddenly, the fearsome vision of raging white water disappeared. The lake was perfectly calm. There were no wind or waves to disturb the surface, nothing except my paddle. The only explanation was the atmospheric conditions. As I faced into a strong sun, the mirror-like water conditions likely played a role in creating this mirage. In flying floatplanes, one of the great hazards is making landings when glassy-water conditions prevail. A very calm surface with no wind creates a false perception of depth. The illusion is so convincing that inexperienced pilots are astounded when they come a-cropper. A similar explanation probably accounted for my delusion.

Rain started in the afternoon. It continued through the night I spent just west of Pembroke. The weatherproofing on my tent was totally inadequate to withstand it. Surrounded by wet clothes and down to my last dry sweater, I hunched in my dripping tent, thoroughly depressed. I knew I had to have something more weather-worthy. Hitching a ride back into town, I bought new camping gear – an expensive process.

Pembroke reflects its Valley history in baronial-like homes like the massive Booth Mansion on Main Street, built by egocentric timber tycoons who went to great lengths to build bigger than their rivals. It was late in the day, and as I was still waiting for my clothes to dry in the laundromat, I checked into a motel. At sunset I watched flocks of swallows circle over the water in an incredible display of aerobatics. According to locals, they compare in numbers as well as aerial virtuosity to those of San Juan Capistrano in California.

Next morning I packed my new gear into the canoe and pointed the bow towards Chalk River, home to Canada's atomic research centre.

Upriver lies Deep River, a pleasant bedroom community for the research centre's staff. It also marks the spot considered by the voyageurs as the beginning of their incursion into the wilderness. The Canadian Shield directly across the river from the town rises over 200 metres out of the water. The pine-clad rock face marked the beginning of serious paddling.

Point Bapteme, a short distance from Chalk River, is a historic portage where baptism of new recruits took place. The name derived from initiation ceremonies, consisting mainly of endurance tests, that all novice voyageurs had to undergo before proceeding further. After the new recruits were admitted to the exalted ranks of the voyageurs, it was mandatory for them to provide a "*regale*," or drinks all round.

A nearby beach looked like a good stopping-off place for the night. But several kilometres away a powerboat started dashing around, creating huge waves. This was a show-off performance by tanked-up youths flourishing bottles of beer. The high-speed boat, a skier in tow, started to make ever-decreasing circles around my heavily laden craft. Each circuit set up fountains of water that almost swamped the canoe. My frantic efforts to paddle away only caused the powerful boat to tighten the circle. There was no escape from the turbulence and roar of the engine. The water was churned into choppy waves, and despite my efforts to maintain course, the canoe reared and rocked as if in serious white water. My shouts only seemed to increase the merriment. Since we were in the middle of a deep-water channel, capsize would result in my losing all my gear.

Finally my tormentors tired of the sport and roared away. Badly shaken, I paddled to shore. Several people on the beach had witnessed the incident. "You ought to call the RCMP," one man said angrily.

I struggled to control my feelings. I wanted to get my paddle and go after the yobos who had endangered my life, but I decided it was best to put the experience behind me.

Next morning after several hours of paddling I pulled into a quiet beach about six kilometres west of Deep River for a coffee break. I left my canoe on the shore, close to a vintage floatplane. The beach turned out to be part of Ryans' Campsite, a recreational fishing and camping spot run by Bob and Jean Lucier. Bob owns a Piper Supercub in which he takes customers on sightseeing flights. We chewed the fat over aircraft types and flying characteristics of different airplanes – always a hot topic when fellow pilots meet. It's not surprising that aviation buffs are usually canoe enthusiasts as well. Until the advent of the airplane, the open canoe was the vehicle for exploring much of Canada.

Bob treated me to coffee and muffins in his combination gift shop and restaurant and let me use his phone to report to Ishbel that all was well. He checked my map, offering helpful suggestions for lining white water further upriver near Rapide des Joachims.

Like several other Valley communities, Des Joachims was an Ottawa River ghost town, melancholy and run down. But Bradley's Air Service, which transports canoeists up the Dumoine River, was busy. Staff were loading passengers and strapping canoes onto float planes. Ron Forbes, the pilot of the Beaver on floats, was quite taken with my proposed continental voyage. Learning that I had never flown a Beaver, he offered to take me out sometime in the fall when tourist trade was quiet. The De Havilland Beaver is not just a plane but a part of our Canadian heritage. To fly one of them had long been a dream of mine. I hoped one day to take up Ron's generous offer.

Arriving in Mattawa was a trip highlight, marking the end of my journey along the Ottawa River. The current became stronger as the confluence with the diminutive Mattawa River drew near. I was thrilled to see a few kilometres ahead the railway bridge spanning the junction. Noting a large restaurant sign high on the riverbank, I decided to celebrate by treating myself to ham and eggs.

The town's location has an Ojibwa heritage extending back some 6,000 years. It is regarded almost as a place of pilgrimage by modern-day long distance canoeists. The name is derived from the Ojibwa, meaning "meeting of the waters." The historic significance of the junction is indicated by the Explorers Park. Set on the banks of both rivers, the park marks the site of a Hudson's Bay post chosen by Governor George Simpson, "the Little Emperor," in 1837. It also has plaques commemorating the great cross-waterway of Canada, citing the names of intrepid pioneers like Champlain, Radisson, Brûlé, Brebeuf, Mackenzie, Thompson, and Fraser. These men pushed back wild frontiers, sharing knowledge of their explorations of the savage interior. But long before them, the Huron and Ojibwa had used this route to trade with the French, travelling down as far as Trois Rivière and Lachine with their furs.

Running some 65 kilometres to North Bay, the Mattawa River winds through a 600-million-year-old fracture in the earth's crust. The name will always evoke fond memories for me of a summer week canoeing through this region - despite the number of exhausting portages I had to endure. Or the countless beaver ponds whose prickly branches left me cursing in neck-high water – they seemed never-ending as I struggled to manhandle my canoe over dams constructed with thorny masses that tore at my hands and arms. But much later in my journey, paddling through a muddy wasteland of prairie lakes and rivers, my memories of this gem in the Ontario heartland made me nostalgic for the mellow southern landscapes.

The names given to the many portages along the 57-kilometre length of the Mattawa between the Ottawa and Trout Lake provide a commentary on the character of the voyageurs. Portage des Rochers reflects the boulder-strewn pathway past the rapids. There's Portage Pin de Musique, "the singing pines," and Portage de la Mauvaise Musique, "the evil music." But the one that causes a wry smile even several hundred years on is that of Portage des Paresseux, "portage of the lazy-bones." It traces its name to Etienne Brûlé, who in 1610 wrecked his canoe at this point. Leaving two of his crew to portage the goods along the trail, he made the tedious journey by foot back to Montreal for another canoe to continue their journey. Returning weeks later, he found his crew had not moved a muscle, and the trading goods and supplies were just where he had left them!

The Mattawa River was once one of the most dangerous stretches for the voyageurs. As they travelled the 2,000-kilometre stretch to Grande Portage on Lake Superior, danger lurked along its many portages: fierce rapids, dangerous wildlife. The Voyageur Heritage Centre in Samuel de Champlain Provincial Park, about 12 kilometres along the river from Mattawa, contains several exhibits that recreate the rugged voyageur life. These include a 12-metre (40-foot) Montreal canoe and the 40-kilogram packs carried by the hardy travellers.

When a rapid was too fast or tricky to run, voyageurs would cut saplings and shape them into "setting poles" about four metres long, sometimes shod with metal. Standing in the canoe, usually one man in the bow and the other in the stern, they would pole their way along the waterway. This technique required the skill of a ballerina in timing and balance. If the riverbed was gravel, good progress could be made.

Poling the river was preferred to humping the 40-kilo *pieces*," as they were termed, along the portage trail. Usually, a voyageur would carry two *pieces* attached to a tumpline around his forehead – sometimes more, if he was showing off. When the waters ahead were straightforward, the poles, or "*perches*," could be chucked away; hence the name Decharge des Perches referred to an area where they were able to dispense for a while at least with their setting poles.

Next day as I cruised down the river, the forest echoed to the panting and gasping of dozens of sweat-soaked individuals hauling their burdens along the portages. Canoes with two pairs of legs beneath them brushed past me, blundering against trees, heading at breakneck speed to the next launching point. It was a hot day, and after running several rapids and some stiff portages, I was pooped. Litres of sweat poured down my face, blinding me, and my shirt was saturated.

At one rocky ridge near Talon chute, while I was pondering how to get my canoe up the high ridges of rock, two kindly Samaritans came to my aid. College students Stephen Standen and Robert Spina explained that one of the near-North highlights of the year, the North Bay to Mattawa canoe race, was underway. They were overseeing the race as part of the water safety group. Quickly shouldering my canoe, they carried it to the top. Their assistance was especially appreciated. I decided to make an early camp at Boivin Lake and found a reasonable site near the high cliffs overlooking the lake.

Turtle Portage, a narrow stretch of water between two large cliff faces, was my next port of call in the morning. It is the last portage on the Mattawa. It's a misnomer to call it a portage since, thanks to a local dam, it has long since been flooded. Derisively, Eric Morse in *Fur Trade Routes of Canada, Then and Now* considers it merely "a tight rocky gut." Paddling rapidly through the narrow passage to avoid conflict with boat traffic, I was taken by surprise as a large motor launch roared out from the shore. It was crammed with teenagers clutching bottles of beer. The youngsters had laid in wait until my canoe was halfway through the narrow gap, then ambushed me. Gunning their motor to a frightening crescendo, magnified by the constricted space, they reared the boat like a spooked stallion, causing a tidal wave of wash. Despite my frantic efforts, my canoe was driven onto the rocks. I barely avoided capsize. As it was, the crash landing inflicted several large gashes along the bow.

Jumping onto shore, I screamed angry curses and vowed dire retribution as the louts tore away. How I longed to have a small cannon mounted on my bow!

Trout Lake at the head of the Mattawa is predominantly an area of affluent cottagers with large toys matching their egos. Despite the over-saturation of the lake by powerboats, little police presence is evident to curtail the lethal actions of nautical drunks.

A heavy morning fog lay across the lake next morning as I proceeded down the lake on the last leg of my journey towards North Bay. Visibility was hampered by the mist that rose from the water to a height of about one metre. The canoe and most of my body were shrouded in its clammy embrace, but with my head floating above, it was still possible to navigate. As I hugged the shoreline, a man in front of his cottage dropped the pail he was carrying, at the sight of my disembodied head floating swiftly across the water.

After a heavy pull across the lake, I found myself battling a norwesterly wind kicking up a brisk chop. The weather was changing dramatically. Blinding rain swept the lake, stinging my cheeks and lowering visibility to nothing. Suddenly, through the cascading rain, an odd craft appeared beside me. Curiously, the canoeist was paddling in a standing position. Above the wind I heard a muffled shout of "Follow me." Needing no second invitation, and astonished at the canoeist's ability in an erect position, I swung my canoe after my guide through the deluge. An hour later we arrived at the Trout Lake Canoe Club in North Bay. Only then did I realize that my benefactor was an attractive young woman.

Barb Olmstead was an avid racing canoeist, working for the summer at the club. I accepted the invitation to get out of my wet clothes and have a hot shower. Barb explained that while standing in a canoe is generally considered taboo, for paddling the very narrow-beamed racing canoes, this was the usual position. After coffee in the clubhouse, the weather had cleared. Barb gave me directions to North Bay's sights and restaurants and offered to store my canoe and gear at the club while I was gone.

Trout Lake is connected to Lake Nipissing by many granite ridges and innumerable bogs that comprise the divide. To continue on the trail I would have to cross the lake to the French River, which leads into Lake Huron, Sault Ste Marie, and points west of Lake Superior to Thunder Bay.

The next phase of my journey was the portage of La Vase, between Trout Lake and Lake Nipissing. The trail crosses Highway 17, where it is marked by a historical plaque. Unfortunately, access through from Trout Lake was blocked by a wire fence, thanks to the operation of a large chemical company. This unexpected intrusion on a national historic trail meant I had to rethink my plans. To get to Lake Nipissing. I was going to have to portage around the other side of North Bay to Callander, the closest community to the lake.

Fortunately, an old buddy of mine lived outside the city close to Turtle Lake. I called him, and after I explained my predicament, a major transportation problem was solved. Jim Watson turned up with his pickup truck in half an hour, loaded my canoe and gear on board, and whisked me over to Callander, where he dropped me off.

It was pouring rain again but I passed a pleasant afternoon at the local Legion hall, planning my strategy for crossing Lake Nipissing. I was welcomed by the members, one of whom signed me in. Sitting around a table groaning with drafts, I recounted my nautical adventures.

The beer flowed steadily while my new friends' tales of the fierce dragons inhabiting mighty Lake Nipissing became taller. Since I planned to head out across the lake the following morning, their stories were unsettling. There was no doubt in their minds that this naive stranger had little idea of the formidable character of their lake. But the *piece de resistance* came when a man in his fifties with reddish complexion joined us. The other members deferentially made room for him. From their behaviour I could see that his presence represented my final put-down.

Settling into his chair, Bill told us he had worked for several years in search and rescue on the lake. He had finally quit the job. "I got stressed out from fishing bodies from the lake – particularly canoeists!" the big man guffawed. Lifting his tankard, he regaled the table with macabre details. Later, as I left, the company around the table nudged each other, noting my forlorn countenance. They had succeeded in convincing me their lake was the most formidable impasse in Canada.

I camped on the grass by the Legion parking lot, rising before dawn the next day to get a really early start. The wind soon picked up and the waves became choppy. Lake Nipissing is not a large lake, but it is given to unpredictable winds of considerable velocity. Its fairly shallow depth results in waves with a steep but short crest. In a canoe this means a bumpy ride, making it difficult to maintain direction. Fortunately, the spray covers customized for my craft cut down on wind resistance and kept my gear and supplies dry and my lower body warm. A few hours later I pulled into the shelter of a small island.

Later I headed back out on the lake, making for a small island near Cross Point, just a speck on the horizon. The wind gradually increased. Driving rain stung my face and obscured visibility, signalling the end of paddling for the day. As I searched in vain for a camping spot, through the misty rain a pale apparition materialized just a few metres away. Astonished, I saw it was a large houseboat. From the gathering dark a cry rang out across the water,

"How about a cup of coffee?"

To me, soaked even through my rainwear, my pants cold and sodden against my legs, a cup of coffee sounded fantastic. In no time my canoe was tied up alongside the houseboat of Ruth and Howard Bruce from Callander. It felt marvellous to be warm and out of the deluge, dripping on the carpet in their comfortable floating living room. As I sipped my coffee, Ruth asked, "How does a steak sound, John?"

Bucketing rain outside with a miserable fog, and here I was tucked up in a warm floating hotel with a steak dinner underway. How lucky can you get! Although I am a staunch canoeing enthusiast, at times like these I confess to a twinge of envy for those boat owners with all the comforts of home.

After a marvellous supper, and despite an invitation to stay the night, with the rain now off, it was time to take my leave. Howard insisted on steering close to an island where he said there was a cabin that would make a great camping spot for the night. Paddling the few metres to the island and securing my canoe, I found the cabin and spent a comfortable night out of the rain.

In the fall Ruth would write to say that her friends had heard me being interviewed on CBC Radio North. I had mentioned on the air having spent a pleasant evening aboard the Houseboat Hilton and raved about the Bruces' excellent cuisine and great hospitality. I was delighted that their friends had heard about their kindness and gracious hospitality to a stranger on the water.

3

30,000 Islands

While the rain stopped the next day, the weather was still uncertain. The clouds were low and the wind was freshening. I decided to chance it anyway. Unfortunately, two hours after I launched, the wind increased dramatically, and soon waves were crashing against the bow. I was thankful once again that I had a decent spray cover, giving me a kayak-like ability to deflect the odd waves that flicked across the bow.

As conditions rapidly worsened, the time had come to hightail it off the water. But where could I make a landing? Fortuitously, dead ahead through the spray I saw the outline of a tiny rocky island. It wasn't the best camping spot, but it was better than continuing on in the hope of finding something better. Making a landing wasn't easy as the rock surface was slippy. Eventually, though, I unloaded my gear and hauled the canoe out of the water.

The "island" turned out to be simply an oversized rock. I managed to tether the tent by tying it with long ropes to the branches of several stumpy trees. From the comfort of my newfound sanctuary, I watched the lowering clouds and mounting seas. Waves festooned with greyish streaks rather than whitecaps crashed angrily onto the shore. In a couple of hours there wasn't a boat to be seen on the lake. I vividly recalled the prophetic warnings in the Legion hall about this unpredictable body of water. Rock-strewn, cold, and uninviting as this sparse island might be, I was lucky to have stumbled on it.

Because of a deep recess in the rocky ground my tent was sheltered from the ferocious wind. I didn't even need to crawl into my sleeping bag for warmth. It's interesting how my humble abode felt more "homely" the longer I was on the trail. While I had a lot to learn, it was comforting to know that I had done everything I could think of to protect me against the elements.

All day the waves continued to pound the rocky shoreline, sending spray high into the air and occasionally drenching the tent. The wind shrieked through the stunted trees. The din continued unabated through the night, making sleep almost impossible. To my dismay, morning showed little improvement. In fact the grey rollers seemed to have gained strength, while the cacophony of crashing and pounding continued through the day. The wind raced across the water at 70 to 80 kilometres. There was no way of making safe passage to the French River.

At first after the rigours of paddling the enforced idleness was welcome. I had a good stack of literature on hand, so sitting out the day in a tent was okay. My tastes were eclectic, ranging from John Main's Christian meditation journals through Bloom's *Closing of the American Mind* to a motley selection of Word War II adventure stories.

Because of the wind, I did my cooking on my Coleman backpack stove in the tent. I was aware that this could be a dangerous procedure, but the circumstances left me no alternative. As long as I was scrupulously careful, particularly in lighting the stove as well as extinguishing it outside, over time I had found it safe.

The following day the wind dropped. It was possible that I could make some headway, but the large open stretch of Simpson Bay was only a few kilometres away. Crossing it was going to be difficult with the lake still so agitated.

On the morning of my third day of exile, it looked like there might be a weather window for a quick run hugging the shoreline. Bored to tears by now, I was chafing to get out on the water. I was strongly tempted to launch but sober second thought forced me to accept that the angry seas made it too dicey. As the storm continued to rage, I knew I'd made the right choice.

The day passed into late afternoon then evening. I couldn't bear the thought of another excruciating day in rock-bound exile. After supper, I determined to risk it. Most evenings there is some decrease in the prevailing norwesterlies. In any event, it should be possible to make it to a safe haven near Cross Point. I made preparations to launch into an unsettled but somewhat mollified lake

Dismantling the tent, I packed it and threw my gear into the canoe. Poised with the canoe at the waterline, I scanned the lake once again. Incredibly, the wind, which had been moderating, was now starting to freshen and the wave tops had risen. I had no choice but to continue to wait out the weather. Maybe I could head out for a night crossing – the voyageurs used this method when weather conditions were difficult.

I continued my weather watch with as much patience as I could muster. The night turned chilly and to endure my vigil more comfortably, I set the tent up again. Around 2 a.m. the wind was calm and the wave heights seemed manageable. The moon appeared, a good omen. It would aid navigation considerably. Once again I dismantled my tent and launched the canoe.

I crept along as close to shore as I dared, screwing up my eyes to identify landmarks. Though I was elated to be on the water again, I was apprehensive about this night venture. The moonlight cast shadows everywhere. It was nerve-wracking and eerie creeping through the half-light, but anything that got me moving was an improvement. At least the wind was slight and the waves relatively calm. Occasionally I crossed broad stretches from headland to headland.

I felt chilled and pulled on an extra sweater. After several hours of hard paddling, I could see light on the horizon. A spreading grey mist made progress along the shore tricky, but after a couple of hours, the fog disappeared. After my three days of forced inactivity it felt good to be again working up a sweat with vigorous paddling. Before I realized it, I was off the large expanse of Lake Nipissing and turning into the quiet waters of the French River heading to the Dokis Reserve. It was a great relief.

Once known as the "gateway to the continent," the French River was an important connecting link to the rest of the country and played an important part in our history. In the mid-nineteenth century it was even proposed as the key route to open up the Great Lakes to international shipping. The route's surveyor was the distinguished explorer David Thompson. At sixty-six, after a lifetime career of arduous wilderness adventures, he probably considered his new assignment a mellow retirement project.

Although Ottawa dragged its heels through that decade and beyond, the results of several other surveys and commissions concluded in 1836 that the most desirable route from the Ottawa River to Georgian Bay was the Ottawa Waterway. The distance from Montreal to Thunder Bay via the Ottawa is only 934 miles compared to 1,216 miles by way of the St Lawrence

This route would include the Ottawa, Mattawa, Lake Nipissing, and then the French River to Lakes Huron and Superior. Interestingly, the preliminary government survey had started out as a military project, no doubt fuelled by phobias of American expansionism. Should war break out once more along the troubled frontier, the St Lawrence River route would certainly make it easy for the United States to set up maritime blockades.

From a lacklustre start, the project became an economically viable proposition overnight when it dawned on politicians that the Ottawa

River route would mean a tremendous saving in distance as well as shipping costs. However, the undertaking was eventually ditched by Sir Robert Borden because of financial difficulties accruing from the vast sums spent on the country's transcontinental railway.

During his travels in 1786, Mackenzie recorded in his journal: "There is hardly a foot of soil to be seen from one end of the French River to the other, its banks consisting entirely of rock." It is a beautiful river, and it was delightful canoeing down its moss-covered banks, passing the numerous islands on which Mackenzie commented.

The French River is also home to the only poisonous snake in Ontario. The Massasauga rattlesnake is prolific along the mouth and offshore islands. Fortunately it is quite timid and hard to find among the rocky areas where it hunts mice. But in the 1960s a fisherman who was bitten by a rattler later died, unable to locate a source of anti-snake venom. Although my chances of encountering a rattler were small, I kept a wary eye on the ground when I set up camp.

The rapids along this stretch of river are easily runnable, provided they have been scouted and thoroughly appraised. In fact, once the heavy spring runoff is over, the rapids in all of the French River's 80-kilometre length are fairly straightforward. Those that may present a problem can easily be lined from the bank or portaged. An interesting series is Five Finger Rapids, where the river is broken into channels.

Further downriver, Big Pine Rapids proved exciting as the standing waves were quite steep. Running these rapids without much difficulty was greatly reassuring to my morale, indicating that my canoe was up to the challenge of serious white water. Although I bashed into rocks several times, the canvas proved durable enough to withstand the impact.

While I was reconnoitring one particularly easy rapid, little more than a fast, shallow stream, I was surprised to come across a canoeist portaging this tranquil stretch. He was wearing the latest in expensive flotation devices and loaded down with all kinds of gear, binoculars strung round his neck, compass dangling from his shirt. All the gadgetry considered de rigueur for the "professional" canoeist protruded from his Kevlar canoe.

Glancing derisively at my craft, he enquired in a thick southern accent, "What's yer canoe all made of?" An expression of disbelief crossed his face when I told him my "wooden canoe" had travelled from Montreal. I found this sort of scepticism about the merits of a wood-canvas canoe frequent throughout my travels. The wisdom of the marketplace on "acceptable" gear for the wilderness canoeist is merely a glib sales pitch designed to unload high-priced gear on the inexperienced. Later on in British Columbia when I was completing my trip down the Fraser River, one of these "experts" gave me his card, which actually described him as a "professional canoe consultant." He adamantly refused to believe I had travelled across Canada in a wood-canvas craft. "A trip like that would necessitate having at least three custom-designed canoes for the different waterway conditions!" he insisted.

It delights me to pick up Bill Mason's classic, *Path of the Paddle*, and view his recommended wilderness gear. His lean-to tent would induce apoplexy in the ranks of "wilderness experts." Bill notes his favourite choice of book on long expeditions is the Bible – a very unpolitically correct piece of literature these days and a fact rarely mentioned by Mason's yuppie devotees. It's as if this somehow detracts from his abilities as master canoeist and adventurer.

But great spiritual masters like Meister Eckhart taught that there is nothing in the world that resembles God as much as silence. Silence is one of the great blessings of the wilderness, a place where, through meditation, we can follow our own spiritual navigational beacons towards conscious contact with the Great Spirit. Despite the bleatings from the canoeing establishment that solo wilderness canoeing is sheer folly, it is a vital way to discover who and what we really are. This is put aptly in the I Ching:

> When three people journey together
> Their number decreases by one.
> When one man journeys alone,
> He finds a companion.

After the frenetic pace of the rapids, it was pleasant to meander downriver in quiet water for a while. With the approach of evening, mosquitoes formed clouds around me. They followed in my wake, despite my vigorous paddling to shake them off. When I pulled alongside a flat, moss-covered rock that looked just large enough to hold my tent, they redoubled their attack. I hurried to get the tent up and take refuge inside.

The cries of loons echoed in the still air as night fell. At one point I counted fourteen calling in unison. This delightful lullaby soon sent me off to sleep.

At dawn I was once more on my way. The sun darted in and out of the trees, creating misty swirls above the water. The Five-Mile Rapids did not present much of a problem. Nonetheless, I was happy to pull into a nice cove for lunch. Absent-mindedly, I threw a few pieces of my sandwich to the gulls (a practice I am always criticizing others for) when a heron suddenly came swooping down, plaintively squawking, and alighted close by. With a stilt-like gait it crossed to where I was sitting and begged for crumbs!

Heading down the main channel I passed close to an island with a cottage perched on it like an eyrie atop a craggy bluff. The morning stillness was broken by a shout. I looked up to see a figure leaning over the deck. Carl Sutherland from Columbus, Ohio, reached out a hand to introduce himself, then helped me tie up. Carl told me he had fallen in love with Canada decades ago and kept coming back year after year. Sitting on the deck above the idyllic river scene below, I passed a pleasant hour with this delightful American. He explained that he and his wife were ardent canoeists. Noting my questioning look at the small motor on his 17-foot Grumman canoe, he grinned wryly. "A little extra boost for my retirement years."

The Recollet Falls on the river traces its name to the early missionary fathers from France, to whose incredible zeal and resourcefulness we owe a great deal for opening up much of our wilderness. Sometimes their incursions into Iroquois territory led to their cruel deaths. The falls are particularly treacherous. At one time devout voyageurs would doff their caps to kneel and pray for the many who had drowned in the falls.

Despite my frantic search, there seemed no way to locate the elusive voyageur channel that, so my map indicated, would take me into Georgian Bay. All of the many bays on the river eventually proved to be dead ends. Each of the countless channels appeared to offer a tempting opportunity for passage. The problem was my flawed navigation – my map had a chunk missing from it representing some eight kilometres at precisely the spot to identify the right channel.

The rain suddenly came down in torrents. Pulling under a clump of bushes and holding my tent fly over my head to protect my map, I agonized over my position. As I huddled there, I heard the sound of a small motor. Soon a curious kayak-like craft – indeed, it looked more like a mini-sub – appeared, with two men in it. When I hailed them from shore, they pulled into my shelter, relieved to be out of the worst of the weather. One of the men, an engineer at the University of Toronto, told me he had designed the motorized canoe for cruising Lake Huron. He assured me it was seaworthy, despite its odd appearance.

To my relief, they had a map. They indicated some prominent landmarks. I could find a way out of the labyrinthine-like channel by cutting around Petite Faucille, or "Little Sickle" Rapids, which Mackenzie noted in 1786 required only a 25-metre carryover.

I headed off, greatly relieved to be heading down a known channel. But I was disconcerted as the riverbank began to narrow considerably. Eventually my arms were almost touching the rocky banks with their jack pine on either side! Rounding a bend, I was astonished at the sight of the enormous expanse of Lake Huron.

After my confined river journey through Shield country, I was taken aback by the dramatic change of scenery. The sun shone on crystal-clear water, the myriad of rocky islets seemingly stretching to the horizon. It made me think of the jewel-studded islands along the Amalfi coast near Capri. Although I would later view some stunning scenery in my travels across the country, that experience has remained with me.

My ears picked up the crashing of surf at a position my chart indicated as Point Grondine. The name again reminded me of how apt the descriptions were that the voyageurs had chosen for prominent geographical features. Le Grondine – "The Groaning" – evoked the sound of the waves as they cascaded over the rocks. The powerful surf indicated that while this lake appeared benign, appearances were deceptive, as ample testimony from historical records shows.

Observing large cumulus build-ups on the horizon, I made evening camp on a nearby island. Next morning's run was a magnificent trip across Georgian Bay cruising among hundreds of islands of all shapes and sizes. The voyageurs used them as breaks from the winds that spring up readily. Each tiny island made a magnificent camping spot as well as a great place to tie up for morning coffee or lunch. Later when I cursed the mud and mosquitoes along the Saskatchewan River or other blighted areas in the Northland where my camp was often a hastily erected tent on a slippery mud bank, I looked back nostalgically to this pristine canoeing paradise on the shores of Lake Huron.

However, there were embarrassingly frequent occasions when my craft would grind to a halt with a bone-crunching screech, and throw me cursing into the scuppers. I would pray there were no witnesses to my folly. These mishaps were caused by long shelves of rock prominent along the shore. Heading west, I was frequently dazzled by the sun on the water. Such occasions made me grateful to be in a craft that only draws a few inches of water.

As I approached Killarney, a quaint village in the heart of the provincial park, an enormous cabin cruiser took station at my stern, actually keeping pace behind me for a little while. Looking up to the fly bridge I saw a figure intently regarding me. Finally it pulled out and left me behind.

Once I'd secured my canoe in the Killarney marina and located a camping spot, I had time before sunset for a stroll in the cool of the evening. After being in the canoe all day, it always felt great to stretch my legs. At home I put in about ten kilometres a day summer and winter. Tonight, as I strolled past the marina dock, a voice hailed me from a large cabin cruiser, inviting me to come aboard for a drink. Pete, from Chicago, told me he had been watching my paddle strokes as he was entering harbour. He was curious why, despite the unequal thrust produced by strong strokes on one side, the bow of the canoe maintained a straight course.

I explained the Indian stroke, which puts a slight deflection on the blade before it is withdrawn from the water. Pete, a highly experienced sailor, was most impressed with the canoe's versatility. I found it delightful to be passing the time on a millionaire's yacht discussing the finer points of paddling. Later, in my sleeping bag, thinking over our conversation, I was grateful to be a free spirit roaming the waterways in a humble canoe. While I had enjoyed the evening and my visit, I wouldn't have swapped places.

After checking my chart next morning, I decided to make the trip from Killarney to Little Current on Manitoulin Island using an unusual detour that involved portaging directly into Fraser Bay. While it seems ludicrous to make a portage on the vast expanse of Lake Huron, it would allow me to avoid the legions of boats using the navigation channel between Badgeley Point and Badgeley Island. Two carryovers through the middle of Badgeley Point took me through. Later, on the busy sea-lane near Manitoulin Island, powered craft ran frenetically around me, nearly swamping my canoe. Portaging had definitely been a good move.

The lake started out like a millpond, but as the sun rose higher, the wind increased. White-crested waves rose to about two metres. When a lighthouse appeared dead ahead, I gratefully pulled into shore, unloading and dragging the canoe high up the beach. The lighthouse was clearly uninhabited, though the living quarters were in excellent condition. Regrettably, deserted lighthouses have become a common sight along the Great Lakes as government cuts or privatizes critical services that mariners have come to depend on.

Close by the lighthouse was a shed containing four canoes. While several had no canvas covering, they were heritage canoes and quite valuable. The forlorn appearance of these dilapidated old warriors indicated they had been abandoned by their owner. Despite its melancholy appearance, the lighthouse made an excellent camping spot. The next day's crossing to Little Current on Manitoulin Island was uneventful. But one thing that struck me was all the traps lying in wait for unwary keelboats. Shoals of flat rock lay everywhere just inches below the surface – pity the poor sailors who strayed from the flagged channel markers!

Rather than head into the busy harbour, I decided to tie up about two kilometres from the town. There was an ideal spot on a sandy beach a few metres from a large and beautifully constructed log house. The owners, Gary Trimmer and his partner, Julie, suggested I might be better camping on their lawn than using the town park.

Gary, who is also a pilot, told me he had just bought the second-hand float plane anchored close by my canoe. We exchanged the usual hangar flying anecdotes of aviation buffs. A raconteur and delightful companion, Gary wore several hats as pilot, fireman, electrical contractor, and general all-round great guy. After he helped me pull the canoe up onto the lawn, he gave me a present of a huge roll of duct tape. This became a treasured possession, serving me faithfully for a multitude of repair tasks.

Next morning Gary and Julie served me a colossal breakfast. As the exquisite aroma of brewing coffee drifted across the kitchen, Julie readily agreed with me that their home was "the most beautiful log house in the North." She explained that it had been built to exacting standards by Manitoulin Indians. It was a great visit, albeit too short, and the Trimmers made me so welcome that when they wished me bon voyage it was like bidding farewell to old friends.

My destination was Clapperton Island. The morning was crisp and clear, the sun over the hills sparkling on the water between the numerous tiny little islands. The weather was perfect, and I decided to push on for Blind River. With a soft easterly breeze filling my sail, I easily reached my goal. There weren't many camping sites around the lakeside in town. I rationalized that a night at the local hotel in a soft cushy bed could be a welcome change from my pup tent. What a bad idea that turned out to be!

Things were relatively peaceful as I headed for my room on the second floor. I was asleep by 10 o'clock. Some time later, an incredible cacophony bounced around my room, shaking the mirror and rattling the dishes in the kitchenette. It sounded like Mardi Gras in full swing as feet thumped up and down the corridor, accompanied by raucous shouts and screams. To think I had exchanged a warm bedroll along the shores of a pleasant island for this madhouse!

Next morning a contrite management sheepishly refunded my bill. Like most hotels along the towns and villages of the Great Lakes, they are trying to eke out a precarious living. As most of their revenue comes from the bar and entertainment, overnight guests are largely an inconvenience they could do without. However, their liquor licence depends on providing beds for travellers

As I headed out, a gentle breeze induced me to raise my sail, and soon I was bowling along nicely. But while Lake Huron can present an idyllic side, it is distinctly temperamental. When I rounded Thessalon Point, the wind suddenly freshened, and the wave heights increased to about two metres. The wind rose as I tore along at breakneck speed. Waves scudded over the gunwales. The bow dipped and rose alarmingly, and stability, always a number-one priority in a canoe, became precarious. My efforts to dismantle the sail only resulted in increased pitching. I gave up and put all my energy into trying to control a canoe turned bucking bronco.

We reared and plunged towards the shore, which I was aghast to see was strewn with rocks. It would be near impossible to avoid the needles of volcanic rock waiting to tear my thin-skinned craft to pieces. I had to keep the driving wind straight on my stern – even a slight change of course could result in foundering. Through the spray and rain I made out a small patch of sand among the sharp rocks. Desperately plunging my paddle into the water at an angle to break my headlong course, I prayed not to capsize. There was a thud, and the heavily laden canoe came to a dead stop.

Great stuff! I had run aground on a sandbank a few metres from shore. I took down the runaway sail and dragged the canoe towards the beach. After unloading the heavy packs, I tied up to a tree and threw myself exhausted on the sand. As I lay there listening to the pounding seas and watched the clouds scud across the sky, my gratitude to be safely ashore knew no bounds.

Later, with my tent up, I enjoyed a hearty supper of beef stew and walked along the rocky shoreline. I stubbed my toes, but it felt good to stretch my legs. The pounding of the surf later lulled me to sleep, warm and secure in my sleeping bag.

A couple of days later, the broad outline of St Joseph's Island spread its bulk across the horizon. This huge island signals the entrance to St Mary's River, the final waterway leading to Sault Ste Marie. The dawning realization thrilled me: I was now within reach of this northern city, gateway to the mighty Lake Superior and the wild lands beyond. At this monumental milestone in my cross-Canada odyssey, I was about 1,200 kilometres from Lachine where I had started my journey almost three months ago.

Cruising the narrow stretch of water separating Michigan from Ontario, I could make out the American shore through the bulrushes. Unexpectedly, an east wind arose, quickly changing to a northeasterly and increasing to a formidable 20 knots. It became difficult to keep to the Canadian side of the channel. The canoe was engulfed in high grass as I was blown steadily across the river. The vegetation served one useful purpose – it cut down the large waves now whipping up whitecaps across the channel. However, it interfered with my paddle stroke, slowing my progress to a crawl.

Forcing a passage through the weed took up most of the afternoon. It was hard work. There was no way I could make it back to the Canadian side before sunset. At times I stood up in the canoe like a Venetian boatman and thrust the paddle deep into ooze and weeds. At other times I pulled myself along by grabbing handfuls of bulrushes – a wearying process.

It was now almost sundown. I needed to pick a spot, any spot, that would get me off the water. I dreaded darkness falling before I found a campsite. Most of the shore was occupied by farmland with stout fences or homes with fairly large acreage. Suddenly, I realized I was being observed. Two men in hunting clothes were watching me intently through the grass clumps, one of them through binoculars. I hailed them, and one man returned my greeting, regarding me warily. The other was holding a shotgun, the barrel directed at the ground. It was clear he knew how to use it.

As I pulled into shore, we exchanged pleasantries, civil but guarded. It was obvious they were suspicious. As we stood exchanging small talk, the older man, who looked to be about my age, revealed he had been in the U.S. army and had been based in Hanover, Germany, after the war. There in the 1950s he'd got to know several officers of the Canadian Seaforth Highlanders from Vancouver. He had met on social occasions with officers from the regiment, developing a great respect for the Canadians. I told him I had actually stayed at the base at that time as a guest of the regiment while hitchhiking through Germany.

Apparently that convinced them my presence didn't represent a security threat for the good old U.S. of A. The chilly atmosphere melted. Whatever had aroused their suspicions in the first place appeared now to be dispelled. "I'm heading off home and I'll notify the sheriff," the older man said. "Strictly speaking, you're an illegal alien."

The other man, Bob Selke, owned the beautiful waterfront property where my canoe was now beached. He readily gave me permission to camp on the lawn. After I organized my camp and settled down for the night, a lady appeared outside my tent and introduced herself. "I'm Tedi Selke. Thought you could use this." She handed me a steaming mug of coffee. Settling herself on the grass, she said she was an artist and would like to take my picture for a magazine. She appeared enthralled at my quest to repeat the voyages of Alexander Mackenzie and quizzed me regarding my experiences en route. Most Americans are unaware that Mackenzie crossed the continent twelve years before the famous American explorers Lewis and Clark. Given the opportunity, I was never shy in letting them know that, regardless of what Hollywood said, Mackenzie was the first across the continent. It gave me a kick to put in a plug for our own Canadian hero!

Tedi invited me up to the house. As we crossed the enormous lawn rolling down to the St Mary's River, she explained that they were located about 30 kilometres from Sault Ste Marie, Michigan.

Bob Selke handed me another mug of coffee. A clean-cut, early retired U.S. Air Force general, he was a veteran of Vietnam, writing a book on his wartime experiences there. As former commanding officer at the U.S. air base in Troy, New York, his last assignment had been to plan and coordinate the air strike on Iraq during the Gulf War. He was intrigued to learn that I had in fact flown into the base, home of the B52 bombers of Strategic Air Command, during Air Force Day when it was open to the public.

We talked into the small hours. The Selkes urged me to stay in their house overnight, but I turned down their generous offer. My tent was all set up, and I was delighted to have their manicured lawn for a camping spot

In the morning I was awakened with a shout of "Here's your breakfast!" Sleepy-eyed, I peered through the tent fly to see Tedi balancing a plate of bacon and eggs in one hand and a coffee pot and cup in the other. Holed up in many remote and bleak wilderness spots across the country, I would think with nostalgia of that particular moment when I had room service in my tent!

After breakfast it was time to continue my journey, and Bob helped launch my canoe. Although regulations are strict about reporting landing in the U.S. and clearing customs on returning to Canada, he assured me that there would be no problem. In isolated northern communities along the border, however, there is some concern in regard to strangers, much of it related to drug trafficking.

My windblown cross-border encounter had turned into an enjoyable experience, but Jerome Orange, the young French canoeist I had encountered on the Ottawa River, was not so fortunate. He later told me that he too had been blown across the river to the American side in an identical weather scenario just the week before. As a foreigner and not speaking much English, he had promptly been arrested by the sheriff and spent a couple of days in the local jail while his papers were checked! It was then clear why my unexpected appearance had caused concern among the residents.

As the St Mary's River narrowed near Sault Ste Marie, the current grew progressively stronger, in some places as much as four knots. I passed a navigation marker clearly showing the number 242. No matter how hard I paddled, the same number kept reappearing. Finally I figured out why. After I passed the marker, fatigue would set in. My paddle strokes became weaker until gradually I lost the battle with the current and drifted downstream – to the same marker! God knows how long this water treadmill had been going on. By the time it dawned on me that something was wrong, exhaustion and heat stroke had taken their toll.

A great roaring noise behind me shook me out of my stupor. I turned to see a large freighter rapidly coming up behind me. The deep reverberation from its huge engine bounced off the riverbanks. I struggled desperately to get out of the way. The bulk of the ship was magnified by the constricted space of the riverbank, while the wash from the massive propellers almost capsized me. Only by paddling furiously and running the canoe up the sloping sandy bank did I avert calamity.

As I continued the struggle upriver, my head throbbed and my eyes ached. My arms were also aching unbearably. It was a great relief to find a shady spot on the riverbank. Stretched on the sand, I flaked out for a couple of hours. When I awoke, my whole body was sore. I forced myself up and pushed the canoe into the river to once again continue upstream against the stiff current and torturous effects of the sun.

I knew I was going to have to do something about my hypersensitivity to the sun before travelling further. The sun blocker I was using was obviously useless. My hat also wasn't doing much. Thankfully, I saw in the distance a large building signalling the outskirts of Sault Ste Marie. Eventually I pulled up to the grounds of what conveniently turned out to be the city hospital. Dazed and somewhat disoriented as I was, it felt wonderful to sit in the shade along the riverbank.

After crossing the parking lot to the hospital, my first stop was the washroom. I could hardly believe the slits staring back from the mirror were my eyes. I looked like a raccoon! A nurse treated me with some soothing lotion. Later, following an infusion of caffeine and a chicken sandwich in the cafeteria, my spirits rose considerably. However, the stares from around the room indicated my appearance was attracting attention, even in a hospital!

A woman at the next table introduced herself as Bonnie Baranski and struck up a conversation. We were soon discussing the hazards of Lake Superior. It was a subject in which she was experienced, having worked on the lake boats plying the waters between Thunder Bay and the Gulf of St Lawrence. Despite my painful and puffy eyes I listened fascinated to her accounts of fierce Lake Superior storms. On one occasion she recounted, waves broke over the bow and flooded the ship. "It looked like a submarine, with only the radio antenna showing above water." Carrying meals to the bridge from the galley was a hazardous operation!

When Bonnie told me that during storms the waves had sometimes reached the bridge 60 feet above the waterline, I felt a chill in the pit of my stomach. Paddling a canoe across this enormous inland sea was going to be no picnic!

Bonnie lived across the road from the hospital and offered to store my canoe in her garage over the weekend. Although it was a most generous offer, I declined since I was planning to continue further downriver to the town centre. Fate, however, had other plans for me. On my way back across the parking lot to the beach, I was horrified to see that my canoe, packs, and gear had vanished! A panicky search along the waterfront yielded nothing. My belongings had disappeared. Not even my dirty old socks, which had been drying on the thwarts, were left. I frantically questioned a young girl nearby but she knew nothing.

The main street in front of the hospital finally yielded a clue. Away in the distance, I could see sticking out of the back end of a moving pickup truck the bow of a canoe. It was clearly *Spirit of Mackenzie*!

Flagging a passing motorist, I explained the situation. We gave chase. This pursuit rapidly changed to a crawl as it became apparent the vehicle we were chasing was a police truck! As my driver pulled alongside, I signalled desperately to the policemen in the truck. Finally, they pulled over. The excitement of the chase had all the elements of a Keystone Cops episode, with a citizen chasing the constabulary down Main Street!

As I explained that I was the canoe's owner, the officer said that they assumed it was likely stolen or that the owner had had a mishap. Convinced at last that I was the rightful owner, they asked where they should deliver everything. Embarrassed at their haste in "arresting" my canoe, they pleaded with me not to inform the press. It was an understandable miscall on their part since there were problems at the time with petty theft along the waterfront. Possible drug-smuggling across the border was also cause for concern. Nonetheless, from my point of view it was wonderful to have the boys in blue portage my canoe and gear around the Soo!

I suddenly remembered Bonnie Baranski's kind offer and gave them her address. I hoped I could catch her and explain the circumstances before the police truck and cruisers descended on her unsuspecting household. This hope was dashed as an entourage of a large police truck and three cruisers swept to a halt in front of Bonnie's house. Police carrying bits and pieces of my equipment filed into the yard, heading for the garage.

Bonnie's husband was home alone looking after their baby, completely unaware of what had transpired between Bonnie and me. Open-mouthed, he stared at the police vehicles around his property. Neighbours peered through their drapes at the flashing strobe lights. Had their friendly neighbours suddenly developed a larceny streak? Later, over supper with Bonnie and her husband, we all had a good laugh over the events.

The following day a photographer and reporter from the Sault paper asked to interview me. I was walking across the lawn outside the Sault Star on my way to the reception desk when a voice rang out. "Who do you think you are, wearing a Seaforth Highlanders badge?"

I swung round to confront my gruff-voiced challenger. The belligerent words belied the beaming countenance. I was startled that someone could so readily identify the regimental badge that had been my dad's in World War I and which I wore in my Tilley hat.

Ian Mackenzie thrust out his hand. "My father was a Seaforth Highlander too," he told me. He was delighted that someone was rooting for the Mackenzie clan and promised to ensure publicity for a famous fellow clansman like Sir Alexander Mackenzie. Later he took me for lunch downtown, and over first-class cuisine we exchanged memories of the "auld country" and exaggerated our success in the "new" one.

After lunch we crossed the road to City Hall where Ian introduced me to the mayor, Joe Frescati. Ian and Joe were good friends, Ian having been Joe's campaign manager at the last election. Joe congratulated me on my voyage thus far and wished me success in crossing the big lake. He presented me with memorabilia and literature on the historic city.

Because of his adamant stance in defying the Franco-Canadian Society by refusing to build a French high school, Joe had become a controversial figure. Ontario Premier Bill Davis, self-styled champion of French rights, had flown up repeatedly to "reason" with the mayor. Joe was painted as anti-French by the media over his stance to ensure taxpayers' money was used competently and not squandered on the altar of federal/political posturing over francophone rights. The hullabaloo generated great political fodder for the forthcoming Ontario election.

It did not surprise me to hear election results showing the Davis government had gone down to a humiliating defeat with the election of an NDP government. During my travels along the Ottawa Valley and beyond, I had been astonished that in every tiny hamlet, village, or small town, feelings ran high against the Liberal government. I found similar strong bitterness in the Soo. A general air of despondency was the result of the near-shutdown of Algoma Steel that had sent hundreds out of work. This was in marked contrast to the prosperity that I found in later years when I passed through the city.

During a walkabout of the city with Ian, we visited the historic Sault waterway. Completed in 1895, its purpose was to provide an all-Canadian water link between Lake Superior and Lake Huron. This major project marked a key step in the evolution of Canada's Great Lakes-St Lawrence shipping route. The first lock, destroyed during the War of 1812, was built in 1798 by the North West Company, intended for canoes and small bateaux.

For many years Canada declined to build another canal, relying instead on the nearby American lock constructed in 1855. However, following the humiliating experience in 1870 when the *Chicora*, a vessel that had served as a blockade runner in support of the South, was refused entry to the lock, construction began in 1889 for an all-Canadian route.

Across the channel from the once-formidable rapids lies Whitefish Island, the heartland of the Ojibwa nation. The Bawating, or "People of the Rapids," as they were called, settled here nearly 2,000 years ago. Now a national historic site, the island has become a popular spot, particularly the Attikamek trail, which in Ojibwa means "Caribou of the Waters," in reference to the whitefish. This beautiful trail winds through South St. Mary's Island, skirting the ancient rapids and the remains of an old dam and powerhouse. Ojibwa fishermen once came for miles to harvest the bountiful food source by dipping nets in the rushing waters while manoeuvring birch-bark canoes among the eddies and pools.

Missionary Pere Galine recorded in his 1670 journal: "The river forms at this place a rapid so teeming with fish ... that Indians could easily catch enough to feed 10,000 men." From the forlorn faces of the fisherman I passed below the rapids, this is clearly no longer the case.

It was now early September when the lake can be unpredictable. Considering the serious blistering to my eyes, it seemed prudent to end my trip until the following spring. While this was disappointing, I was buoyed by the knowledge that some 1,200 kilometres lay behind me. No doubt there would be many more serious challenges, but the mistakes I had made were turned into experience. Such experience had impressed on me the necessity of keeping a good weather eye. It was also time to think seriously about a better quality tent, sleeping bag, and backpack stove and a more efficient spray cover.

While my progress that first summer of 1990 was limited, nonetheless I felt confident about persevering. I was learning my own limitations. Besides, adversity really introduces a man to himself. Travelling across the vast stretches of Lake Superior next spring was going to test all the physical, mental, and spiritual resources I possessed. However, that was a long way off. It would be fun planning routes and checking out new equipment through the long winter.

PART 2

THE SECOND YEAR 1991

FROM SAULT STE MARIE TO LAKE WINNIPEG

Getting ready to face the icy high rollers on the vast inland sea of Lake Superior is a high-anxiety time.

The dreaded Grande Portage, "mother of all portages," demands determination, muscle, and a plentiful supply of mosquito repellent.

4

Paddling the Inland Sea

My departure from Sault Ste Marie in the spring of 1991 was a media event. No doubt Ian Mackenzie of the *Sault Star* had something to do with that. Joe Frescati, the mayor, not one to miss a photo-op, was at the press conference on the waterfront. The CBC television interviewer made a great deal of the fact that Lake Superior was unbelievably dangerous, many ships having sunk in the terrible storms that frequently arose. "Experienced captains have pronounced it more dangerous than the North Atlantic!" Working up to an enthusiastic pitch, he reminded viewers that the *Edmund Fitzgerald*, a huge ship, had taken its entire crew to their deaths at the bottom of that inland sea.

This was live television, and my face was falling all the time the interviewer continued to paint a dismal picture. He pointed a disdainful finger towards my "flimsy canoe," with the implication that my attempt to cross the lake was naive and doomed to failure if not certain disaster. I had done my best to keep up a bold front, but his profound pessimism got to me. I felt like agreeing with him: I should probably pack up and head home.

Fortunately the mayor came to my rescue with encouraging words: "John has come this far. It's likely he can make it across the vast expanse of Superior. Of that I have no doubt."

Later, my heart thumping with excitement, I prepared to launch *Spirit of Mackenzie*. Joe Warmington followed me down the beach, telling me that he had recently completed a series of articles on the ships that had gone down on Superior. In some ways it seemed he had written my obit already! He had obviously done a lot of research and knew what difficulties lay ahead. I took his advice seriously and was touched when he asked me to call him when I reached Thunder Bay.

I paddled vigorously along the shore and it didn't take long before the huge mills of Algoma Steel faded behind my stern. The spring air was invigorating, and while the sun was shining, it was distinctly cool on the water. The water temperature in early June was a frigid six degrees. Certainly, capsizing didn't bear thinking about. One doom-and-gloom expert said before I left, "You've only got five minutes before hypothermia sets in. After that ... you ain't worrying!"

I concentrated on steering a course towards Batchawana Bay. At this early stage leaving the Soo, my head was midway between the poles of tranquillity and terror. The particular hazards that presented themselves directly affected my confidence. My belief in my abilities as an adventurer ran from grandiose on placid days when the lake was an idyllic millpond to cold-belly fear and a sense of impending doom when foul weather turned the lake into a tumultuous hell.

Some bays on the great lake are as much as 80 kilometres across, so it is essential to carefully evaluate weather patterns before setting off. My experience as a pilot proved useful in this regard. However, most of the distances I tackled were in the range of 10 to 25 kilometres. But I could still get caught halfway across a wide bay. When the mirror-like surface took on a few frowns, gradually but insidiously turning to two-metre waves, I would pile on the coal to reach shore before Superior's famous high rollers put in an appearance.

The big lake has an abundance of good camping spots, usually located on sandy beaches or islands. But landing could be tricky. From a few kilometres away, a beach could look especially inviting after a hard day's paddling. On closer approach it often had rough surf and rock ridges that could rip the canvas bottom out of my canoe. To avoid this, I adopted a specific landing procedure. As the surf swept the canoe towards the rocky shore, at the last moment I would leap out and lift the bow up and over the obstacles, all the time hoping my feet would stand up to the abrasive rocks. After I got the canoe to shore, vigorous towelling was necessary, followed by a run to get my circulation going. A fire finally restored warmth to my limbs.

Launching was also tension laden. It required a well-thought-out procedure to get my heavily laden canoe into breaking surf and high-topped waves. First, I would search the beach for logs, selecting two or three small, well-rounded pieces to slip under the canoe at different spots. After placing a towel, dry socks, and shoes under my seat, I would patiently scan the waves until I judged the turbulence to be manageable. Heart racing, I would then roll the canoe on the logs into the water, all the while steadying it to prevent it being turned broadside to the incoming surf. Jumping aboard and keeping the bow dead centre to the waves, I would paddle furiously, then pause for a few seconds to tuck the paddle under my arm and towel my legs to restore circulation. After only a couple of minutes in the freezing water, my legs would be painfully numb. I prayed that cramps or muscle spasms would not occur.

Finally, with the canoe on course and safely out of the surf. I would pull dry socks over my chilled feet. What a marvellous feeling! Obviously the process was fraught with near-calamity at all stages, but it worked for me. Hypothermia and capsize were averted and I managed to avoid serious harm. This process for safe arrival and departure from Superior's beaches reminded me of the old adage about flying: "Any fool can fly a plane, but it takes a pilot to land it."

In spite of such challenges, Lake Superior is a magnificent body of water, and canoeing across it is a privilege and a joy. To really appreciate the lake's pristine wonder, you have to paddle across it as native peoples and early European explorers did. Crossing the unspoilt waters of Old Woman Bay, I searched the huge granite canyons along the shore for the old woman's face that's supposed to be visible 200 metres above the water. Awakening on a clear, crisp morning on a northern beach that has rarely seen human footprints, I felt marvellously alive. Sometimes tears ran down my cheeks in gratitude to a Creator who could devise such magnificence.

Frequently I saw the tracks made overnight by deer, moose, lynx, bears, and sometimes wolves. Such tracks were just outside my "boundary" spoor. I collected my urine during the day and would sprinkle this carefully around the camp before retiring. So far as I know, it worked well.

One evening on a sandy beach near Wawa, a young Iroquois man summed up aptly the remarkable beauty of the big lake. Aware I was on a reservation, my first stop after pulling my canoe onto the beach had been the Chief's house. Sensitive to the knowledge that the white man has paid scant attention to native property rights, I always made it a point of seeking out permission from the First Nation's elders or the Chief.

This reserve presented a distinct contrast to many Indian reservations. Neat lawns surrounded bungalows with pretty gardens, many driveways sporting late-model cars. Children played hide and seek around the carports, shrieking with laughter. The Chief turned out to be an attractive 40-something woman. She readily gave me permission to camp on the beach. When I commented on the evident prosperity of the reserve, she said that a few years ago drinking had been banned. Those who wanted to continue to drink had to leave. The result of this draconian law was plain to see: the community not only appeared well cared for but the people seemed content.

I returned to the beach to prepare supper. Later, a young man came and asked if there was anything he could do for me. "We saw you a couple of days ago when we were fishing on Old Woman Bay." In the bright glow of the mellowing sun slicing through the pines, we listened to the waves lapping on the shore. It is a sound peculiar to the big lake that you don't hear on other inland lakes or even on the ocean.

He lit up a cigarette. "We sell our whitefish in the Soo for a dollar a pound," he continued softly. "Barely pays for the gas to drive there and refuel our boat. In the fall we hunt for moose which keeps us going all winter. In summer, it's the fishing and out on the lake all day. Old Woman Bay is our favourite spot."

Then, with an expression somewhere between awe and admiration at the sun setting over the vast expanse of the lake, he contentedly exhaled a puff of smoke. "We don't make much money, but we sure live like millionaires!"

We sure live like millionaires. His words in that magnificent setting struck a strong chord in my heart. I was moved by this distilled wisdom of an ancient heritage. His words remained with me throughout my journey. They caused me to reflect how we often fail to appreciate gifts that the Great Creator has endowed us with. Immersed in our petty problems, we don't know the value of what we have until it is gone. Placed in a situation remote from material things, we are forced to look into our hearts for answers.

Whenever I get an attack of the "poor me's," I take comfort in one special piece of Ojibwa wisdom: "Sometimes I go about pitying myself, and all the time I am being carried on great winds across the sky." This saying usually brings me out of the pity pot. Although it seems paradoxical, it is often within problems that we discover our greatest blessings.

On the shores of Superior I came across the remains of stone kettles used by young braves hundreds of years ago. At puberty they were sent out into the wilderness by the band elders to contemplate and meditate on the profound mysteries of earth, water, sky, sun, and moon, as well as to gather spiritual strength in contemplating the mystery of life. One way to get in touch with your spiritual self is to head off into the wilderness in a canoe. Despite the claims made that solo canoeing is some sort of bizarre death wish, Bill Mason knew intimately that wilderness meditation is vital in aligning our personal spiritual compass. In solitude you are never lonely because you have searched for the Great Spirit in your own heart.

From vast solo experience in the wilderness, Bill Mason knew the bountiful spiritual catharsis granted by nature to a wounded spirit, freeing it from the confinement of its ego cage. This process comes about through the healing power of nature for those who risk everything by wrapping themselves in its embrace. For me, life without risk isn't worth living. Each of us is a wilderness that is only partially explored. Consequently, we never know exactly what we will find: certainly, some great and moving experiences, as well as some frightening but spectacular ones, along with the peace and tranquillity of pleasant rest spots. Our own personal belief system is a guide for survival in the wilderness. It tells us how to follow our own spiritual compass and to orient ourselves to life's waypoints. The longer we spend in the wilderness, the more comfortable we become with it. For my wounded spirit, having lost not just a job but a vocation that was my whole life, I can witness to the wondrous healing power of nature's balm for brokenness.

One blustery day on the lake a faint whitish shadow on the horizon became my point of reference for 25 kilometres. Gradually it became identifiable as Lamb Island lighthouse. For me the lighthouses sprinkled along the rocky vastness of Superior's treacherous shores hold a special place. Their tall, white shape offers a welcoming beacon to wayfarers and a reassurance that all is well. It was comforting to know that shortly I would reach a safe haven.

About two kilometres from the light, I could see an out-building perched on the rocky bluffs, likely the keepers' home. What kind of people lived there, I wondered. When I was a boy living near the Moray Firth in northern Scotland, I used to love visiting the beautiful lighthouses along that rough shoreline. Invariably, the keepers were kindly, and always ready to show a kid around and explain the workings of the light. At Lossiemouth, the huge lighthouse was 10 kilometres from my home, a hefty round-trip of 20 kilometres, but I thought nothing of it. The keeper would let me climb the enormous spiralling staircase to the top. There was a marvellous view of the coast from there, but it wasn't only the sea view that grabbed my attention. I had a grandstand view of aircraft taking off from the nearby bomber station. The huge twin-engine Wellington bombers would cross the North Sea, a mere 100 kilometres, to bomb the Nazi submarine base at Stavanger in Norway.

The airmen who flew these planes were my heroes. My dad often entertained the aircrew at our house. It thrilled me to see the shoulder flashes on these young men from every country in the Commonwealth. But it was the brevets on their breasts that thrilled me most: pilot, bomb aimer, wireless operator, navigator, air gunner. How I longed to be old enough to wear their uniform and fly.

The airfield was strictly forbidden to civilians, but I used to sneak in over the barbed wire and play in the aircraft. I knew the names of every plane that flew in the U.K., and most of the German ones. At twelve, an inveterate Blitz kid, I could even recognize the type of aircraft from its engine sound.

Setting off one day along the beach for the lighthouse, I heard an aircraft taking off and knew it was a Wellington with a crew of five. The twin engines rose to a crescendo at the end of the runway and the plane slowly gained altitude. As I watched it climb, at about 200 feet, to my horror, the entire right wing fell off. There was an ominous silence as the motors cut out. The heavy bomber spiralled downwards, creating a huge splash as it hit the sea about three kilometres from where I was standing. Shocked, I stared at the outline in the water. It looked like the back of a huge whale. Thinking that I could somehow be of help, I swam out.

The tide was changing and the current was strong. When I reached the aircraft there were no signs of life. The pungent aroma of gasoline from smashed tanks surrounded me. My head reeled. Gasping for breath, I gulped huge volumes of gas-tainted seawater, retching violently. I was losing consciousness. As I started to sink beneath the waves, I felt an arm around my neck. At first I thought it was a rescue attempt, but the arm round my neck was throttling me. It was frightening. I remember kicking out. Whoever it was gave a gasp and let go. A short time later someone else placed a hand under my chin and held my head out of water.

The next thing I remember is waking up in the Air Force hospital and staring into my parents' worried faces. I was very lucky, since not only the entire crew lost their lives but so did a workman who, like me, had swam out to attempt rescue. Sgt. John O'Toole, my saviour, was an air gunner with the RAF. He had been in the pub when he heard the motors cut out and had dashed towards the beach nearby. Later, my mother corresponded with him, sending several food packages as well as socks she had knitted. We learned later he was killed in action in a raid over France

Behind the rocky cliff on which Lamb Island lighthouse stood, I made out the outline of a dock at the rear. I paddled into the small harbour, the wave heights diminishing almost instantly. Tying my canoe to the jetty, I made my way up the steep incline towards the red brick building, obviously a residence for the light keeper and his family. I hollered several times, but the entire complex was deserted. There was graffiti on the walls around the yard, but the dwelling was in excellent condition except for a pane of glass smashed above the door handle. The door was unlocked.

The living room had no furniture, but signs of the previous owners were very much in evidence. In fact, it seemed as if they would return any moment. The house conveyed an impression of people having left in a hurry. A child's broken and discarded doll lay on a bedroom floor. I picked it up, pondering how symbolic of the family's shattered hopes that broken and forlorn doll was. I felt like an intruder. However, it was unlikely the owners were ever going to return.

It would have been easy to unroll my sleeping bag in the living room, but the thought of using the home of people displaced and cast aside by an uncaring technology was distasteful. Behind the house a new generator whined, regulating the cycles of light. A helicopter would land periodically to do any maintenance checks necessary, its presence ringing a final closure on the need for a human presence on the island. Automation had taken over.

It was a relief to return to my canoe. Supper that night was rather melancholy. And later, as my tent flap closed for the night on this scene of disuse, I couldn't help wondering how the former residents were making out.

When I woke next morning, something was odd: there was no sound of birds, not even the raucous cries of the gulls. I pushed open the flap on a cold, clammy greyness, a real pea-souper. I stumbled through my morning breakfast routine, but it was like playing blind-man's bluff. The thought of falling over the edge of the dock into the icy water wasn't pleasant.

It was a situation I had never before confronted. Superior's unpredictable rolling fogs were going to tax all my skills. Like great blankets rolling across the water, they would appear out of nowhere, dropping a thick curtain, enveloping everything in a misty embrace that penetrated the thickest clothes. While the damp is unpleasant, what's worse is the distortion of perception. Not being able to see is bad enough, but the lack of normal sounds like birds or the lapping of waves has disturbing effects on the psyche over time.

Cheered by a second cup of coffee, I reminded myself to be thankful I was on Lamb Island instead of roaming helplessly around the big lake. However, as the first day passed (a very long one, as I didn't leave the dock area for fear of stumbling into the water) I fervently wished I was off the island. I had deliberately chosen not to take a watch or a radio with me, and with no way to observe the sun, I had no idea of time passing.

The second day passed as miserably as the first. Reading by flashlight in my tent, I was feeling claustrophobic and trapped. On the third day of my island incarceration, I knew drastic measures were called for. God only knew when this miserable fog would lift. I sketched out my recollection of the area around the lighthouse as I rigorously perused my charts. The hell with it! It was canoe-launching time, fog or no fog. I felt buoyed by having come to a decision, but as I made my preparations to leave, gnawing anxiety set in.

It was relatively easy heading across the narrow bay to the other side, compass in hand, using dead reckoning. I'd used this form of navigation for years when flying. But it rapidly became clear that navigating on an enormous fog-shrouded lake in a canoe was a different kettle of fish. As I groped my way along the shore, my compass readings seemed incompatible with my intuition of where I should be.

But I knew from experience that it was essential to trust your instruments. In a plane, failure to trust your instruments leads within a few minutes to an uncontrollable situation. You can be upside down and spinning to the ground while clinging tenaciously to the illusion of flying straight and level. In my canoe it could mean travelling far from land far out into busy shipping lanes

Plan B was to cook supper and sleep in the canoe. This is not quite as drastic as it sounds. The fitted covers on my craft made a cosy shelter from the wind and rain. It was a simple enough matter to roll out my sleeping bag along the bottom of the canoe. An added bonus was that the gentle rocking would put me to sleep faster than a double Scotch. I had found this worked well for a couple of hours. However, what it would be like for one or two nights was something else.

I decided instead to stick unswervingly to a compass course, vowing not to allow myself to be sidetracked. While I had no concept of time, a peculiar phenomenon accentuated by the eerie quiet was that my senses were tuned to the soft shoosh of waves on the shore. I placed my paddle stealthily so I wouldn't miss a sound. In the stygian darkness, encased as I was in a damp cocoon, I couldn't even see the canoe bow. The fog seemed to grow denser, making it hard to distinguish reality from illusion. I recalled experiments on sound deprivation in which volunteers pleaded to be let out of soundproofed rooms after only a few hours. As I strained my eyes, shapes took on the appearance of trees and misty apparitions of boats and human figures loomed out of the fog, making my heart pound.

As the hours passed, I grew even more anxious. Enduring the fog and isolation on Superior ranks among the most challenging experiences I've ever had to face. At the same time, I was relieved to be on my own. Arguing over direction and navigation in a canoe under such conditions would be disastrous.

Just as I was preparing to bed down in the canoe, I caught a glimpse of the serrated top of a jack pine through the clammy mist. Relief flooded through me. I never thought scrubby old jack pine could look so appealing. A series of uneven shapes ahead revealed themselves as rocky outcrops. I picked my way through these ghostly lumps to an uneven shoreline. Leaping out, I lifting the bow onto the shore, levering it between two large rocks to secure it.

As I stumbled and slipped across my newfound rocky abode in search of a campsite, the visibility improved slightly. I realized my island sanctuary was in fact a guano-shrouded rock without a sandy beach or even a blade of grass. But at least it was a refuge from the wraith-like apparitions and misty tentacles that had engulfed me. Hop-skipping through the jagged rock, I found a flat area about the size of my tent. The trouble was, it was on the other side of the island from my canoe. Unloading my gear and leaping from rock to rock was no picnic. The tent overlapped the space by a couple of feet, leaving my legs dangling. But it was the stench from the guano that was unbearable. I was literally between a rock and a hard place!

In the morning there was a bit of a let-up in the fog. Since it could roll in again at any time, I decided to forego breakfast and launch immediately. I had no appetite for food anyway with the smell. A few hours later the sun made its first appearance. A breeze dissipated the last of the fog. A sprightly ten-knot wind sprang up, signalling that it was time to raise sail. Soon I was moving swiftly across the water, the bow dipping and rising, spray dashing in my face and running down my neck. It was exhilarating. I felt like I had just got out of jail. It was great to be alive. I wouldn't have changed places with anyone.

The great bank of fog had moved about 60 kilometres away on the horizon, but its lingering presence was still a threat. Aware of how dramatically conditions could change, I decided to find a camp as soon as possible. About ten kilometres ahead, I saw the outline of a wireless mast. These beacons, which could be seen from a great distance, never ceased to thrill me as they were reliable and welcome harbingers of a community. A glance at my map indicated that it could be Terrace Bay.

As I neared the east side of the town, the wind picked up to about 20 knots. I slid up on the beach and toppled forward as the canoe came to a screeching halt, inches from a reclining couple enjoying the sun. They gave me an angry glare, their afternoon ambience broken. Securing my canoe and gear behind some bushes, I headed into town. I had seen a Dairy Queen in the distance, and quickened my steps towards it. I was ready to kill for a butter-pecan sundae.

Terrace Bay was a pleasant five-kilometre walk from my camping spot. I decided to visit the information bureau – normally the last place I would visit, but with time on my hands, I thought it might be nice to catch up on a little local history. I learned that the town was named after the sand and gravel terraces left behind when glaciers receded about 20,000 years ago. As I cooled off in the air-conditioned office, one of the summer staff, Judy, a personable and informative Master's student in biology, told me she was working on the Slate islands. I had noticed this small group about 20 kilometres out from Terrace Bay, and actually considered stopping there.

Judy said that the islands' origins are of interest to international scientists, some from MIT and NASA. Intriguingly, the cluster is home to the most southerly herd of caribou in North America. Quite tiny in comparison to their northern cousins, these southern caribou are Ontario's largest herd. Speculation exists that there may once have been an ice bridge across from the mainland. Likely the caribou migrated there and were stranded after the ice melted. Somehow they adapted and bred.

But that isn't the only peculiarity of these islands. Judy explained that geoscientists have concluded they resulted from an asteroid strike. The stupendous explosion from this 30-kilometre wide space boulder liquefied the earth, which eventually cooled to form the islands. As a direct result of this cosmic creation, their flora and fauna are quite unusual. Due to the lake's cooling effects, Arctic and alpine plants have been found there. This is one of the reasons Judy chose the unique biology of the Slates as her thesis topic. Intrigued, I made up my mind to come back and explore them by canoe one day.

Returning to my campsite I found the beach deserted except for a man who seemed to be expecting me. A reporter from the local newspaper, he was curious that no one was accompanying me. After I answered his questions, he asked if I was aware of the cross-Canada trip planned to commemorate Mackenzie's bicentenary in 1993 by a group of 100 students from Lakehead University in Thunder Bay. These young people, he explained, were travelling from Lachine, Quebec, and re-tracing Mackenzie's voyages to the Pacific. They were being paid to paddle across the country in voyageur costumes, occasionally giving concerts at various locations. Presently they were in the Soo but would be heading into Lake Superior for a rendezvous at Fort William.

When I reached Thunder Bay, I learned that the article in the Terrace Bay paper describing my trip had caused a big flap, arousing the ire of the organizers of the government-sponsored million-dollar recreation of Mackenzie's voyage. They claimed I was stealing their publicity!

The soft sandy beach at Terrace Bay made a great camping spot, and I awoke next morning ready for action. Sensitive now to the fog hazard, I scanned the horizon, but it was a crisp, clear morning with no sign of the rolling menace. Since my next stop was Rossport, I was able to hug the shoreline. I had no intention of being marooned again on some guano-encrusted island.

For the best part of the day I had a nice easterly pushing me along. I lay back in the stern, feet planted firmly on the gunwales. Occasionally I had to use my paddle to maintain course or pull on the lines to hold the sail steady. There were a couple of islands about five kilometres east of Rossport, and I decided that's where I would call it a day. I was elated as I pulled onto the sandy shoreline of a rocky islet: 35 kilometres without paddling was great day's run.

Next morning I awoke to raucous screams of gulls fighting over some stew I'd spilled on the grass the previous evening. At least they weren't bears. After breakfast I paddled across the bay into the quaint hamlet of Rossport. I pulled my canoe out of the water next to a well-laid out camping area, then passed a pleasant hour gawking at the antique and arts-craft shops that line the main street. My steps led me to a pretty home that also functioned as a restaurant. A signboard announced its speciality: whitefish, my favourite. The hostess turned out to be a helpful neighbour minding the store for the proprietor. She insisted their whitefish was the best in northern Ontario. The supper, albeit expensive, surpassed all my expectations.

The cook suggested I might like to call on the Kennys across the road since they liked to meet long-distance canoeists passing through. After complimenting her on the meal, I strolled to the other end of town. On the way back I turned in at the Kenny residence. Mr Kenny greeted me warmly and invited me in. His wife handed me a cup of coffee, as I relaxed on the comfortable settee. A retired school principal, Mr Kenny told me he now spent his time as a guide-fisherman. Most of his trips were with experienced anglers from the United States who had been coming to Rossport for decades.

He told me about one client, a retired federal judge from Chicago who loved to fish the cold waters for lake trout. One year the judge brought some inner-city youths to Superior's wilderness on a camping trip. This proved so popular that each year he returned with more youngsters. Canoeing, fishing, and hiking worked wonders on these juvenile offenders. The judge noted a remarkable drop in recidivism. Many of the young people gained the courage and self-respect to break out of the ghetto crime culture and begin new lives. It was no surprise to me that these kids were coming to terms with themselves: the wilderness is a profound teacher.

Mrs Kenny announced – discreetly – that there was lots of hot water. I didn't need a second invitation to enjoy the luxury of a bath. It was wonderful to get rid of weeks of ingrained dirt. Feeling like a new man, I spent some time with Mr Kenny chewing over world troubles. Downsizing had caused local problems, he said, and many people in the community were finding it difficult coming to terms with a reduced income.

We talked until late, and the Kennys insisted I stay in the small trailer in their yard. It was luxurious compared to my usual camp spots. Next morning, Mrs Kenny called me in for breakfast. I was glad my feeble protests didn't dissuade her. They had been hosts to several long-distance canoeists over the years, including Gary and Joanie McGuffin, a delightful couple who had travelled all the way from the St Lawrence River to the Beaufort Sea.

My stay in Rossport was a refreshing interlude, but I was keen to get back on the trail. Unfortunately, the weather didn't look promising. As I bade them farewell, my hosts urged me to stay another day. I was touched when Mrs Kenny clasped my arm and said she would pray for my safe return, as she had for other travellers on the dangerous North Shore.

I quickly gathered my gear. If things got tough, I would take shelter on one of the islands scattered around the lake. Out on the water, the sky grew progressively more sombre. It would have been easy, not to mention smart, to return to Rossport, but I stubbornly continued on my way. Several hours' paddling later, a huge rock reared up ahead with a sloping ledge leading down to the water like a gigantic ramp. By now the skies were black, so I decided to stop. Unloading the canoe at the bottom of the slope, I carried it about 30 metres to the top, returning for the rest of my gear. It was now nearly pitch dark, and I was seriously alarmed. The wind had risen to enormous speeds, whipping the lake to a frenzy. A downpour hit, and lightning flickered wildly amid a pounding barrage of thunder. I watched fascinated from my perch: this was truly one of Lake Superior's amazing sound and light shows.

But as the waves leapt higher, my rocky sanctuary didn't feel as secure as it had appeared at first sight. I was grateful that the canoe and gear were well above the angry waters – in fact, as far up the rock face as it was possible to climb. But my sense of security plummeted as the wind rose. Shrieking like a demented banshee, it raced along the shore. Trees bent double before it as if in supplication.

The canoe with all my gear in it was swinging wildly around on the cliff face, threatening to take off and plummet into the waters below. I flung myself in to add further weight to arrest its gyrations. Whenever the wind dropped, I made a mad scramble to grab up loose rocks and place them in the bottom of the canoe.

By now the waves were dashing up the rock face. The enormous rollers bowled along while the wind continued to accelerate. The lake was a fearful spectacle. Then, incredibly, the wind changed direction 180 degrees. In an instant the giant waves were flattened, like hay in a field. It was an astonishing demonstration of the vast power of enraged natural forces.

I could easily understand how Ojibwa legends arose about the power of mighty manitous, like Misepeshu, the Great Horned Lynx, who could stir up the lake to a frenzy and drown people. The only time it was safe from this tyrant was during winter freeze-up when he was trapped in the depths. The Ojibwa frequently made offerings of tobacco to appease Misepeshu. I was almost sorry I'd quit smoking.

My vantagepoint high above the lake was like being a spectator at some gladiatorial tournament in which manitous unleashed awesome weaponry, locking in savage combat to see who could match the other's stupendous feats. But as time passed, my anxiety grew of having to spend the night on this exposed rock. Fortunately, late in the afternoon the wind abated. Tentatively, I launched my canoe, heading for a larger island close by. I set off, hugging a lee shore to avoid high rollers. Just before nightfall I was relieved to be making my way into the small bay of a tiny island in the Rossport archipelago.

The following day the seas were confused but manageable. Cruising past a rocky island where the day before I had watched the cliffs being covered with spray, it dawned on me these cliffs were over 20 metres high! Those tales of high rollers on Superior were not tall tales at all. Bill Mason, swamped one day in his canoe on Superior while filming, found from photographic measurements that the heights of the wave tops were some sixty feet! And at the lighthouse on nearby Battle Island, Mr Kenny had told me, during a great storm in 1977 waves smashed the lantern in the lighthouse an incredible (37 metres) 133 feet above the water!

5

Portage from Hell

Cruising near Nipigon about 15 kilometres offshore, I was startled when a powerful motor launch suddenly appeared off my starboard bow. The occupants were wrapped up in yellow foul-weather gear as if plying the Arctic ice-fields. When I hailed them with a wave of my paddle, they turned and pulled up close behind me. Boaters have no clue how easy it is to tip a canoe with their wake. I signalled frantically to them to back off, and they retreated a short distance.

The vessel turned out to be a coastguard launch. "What the heck are you doing so far offshore?" someone shouted.

I hollered back that I frequently used headings that took me well offshore. Actually, hugging the shore is hazardous. High rollers travelling the enormous distance across the lake pack a fierce punch. As they meet land, they create enormous turbulence, resulting in dangerous waters just offshore.

The throbbing of powerful diesels off my stern as the launch paced me was making me very nervous. A crew member said they had heard about my trip from a newspaper article and were concerned for my safety since leaving the Soo. I assured them I was okay. It was a great relief when they finally wished me luck and sped off. While I appreciated their concern, tipping into Superior's frigid waters gives you only three minutes in the water at 4-6 degrees Celsius before hypothermia sets in. If you're wearing a wet suit, extend that to 18 minutes. Let's face it: there's absolutely no way anyone is going to fish you out of the water alive in the wilderness of Superior in early spring. In any case, the patrol area for the coastguard extends well over 1,000 kilometres between the Soo and Thunder Bay. Even if you triggered an emergency radio beacon, the chances of a pick up would be remote.

Rounding a rocky inlet one day, the dramatic outline of Sleeping Giant appeared in the distance about 40 kilometres ahead. It was an impressive beacon for the city of Thunder Bay, just around the massive cliff overhangs of Cape Thunder. The remarkable rock formations along the escarpments are considered by the Ojibwa to be creations of the manitou. Certainly, the giant figure atop the mountain resembles a sleeping man with his arms folded across the chest. The giant figure forms enormous cliffs that rise over 250 metres, considered the highest in Ontario. Ojibwa mythology says the sleeping giant is Nanaboozho, a revered manitou and great teacher of their nation.

Thunder Bay and Cape Thunder derive their name from the thunderbirds, or Animikeek. These great eagles are the deadly enemies of Mishepeshu, the sea serpent, and the frequent roar of thunder is the sound of their voices warning humans to get off the lake when they are about to enter combat. The two opposing spiritual forces, good and evil, represent the balance of the natural world of water and air central to Ojibwa tradition.

As I neared Cape Thunder, rain suddenly came down in torrents. Fortunately, a small hamlet appeared a couple of kilometres ahead, with a scattering of houses around a much larger building. This was Silver Islet, at one time the largest silver mine in Canada. I decided to stop in for lunch.

After pulling my canoe onshore, I strolled towards what looked like an old general store. Inside, cottagers were milling about enjoying themselves, and someone handed me a huge plate of strawberries and cream. I had arrived just as they were having a strawberry festival, they told me, and invited me to make myself at home. As I meandered around, a man engaged me in conversation, telling me he was a newsreader for CBS Newsworld. He appeared perplexed that neither his name nor his appearance failed to register. I told him I didn't watch TV.

Seeing through the window that the rain had stopped, I took my leave of the friendly group. I decided to head for Cape Thunder, 40 kilometres from Thunder Bay. My enthusiasm was tempered by knowing this was a treacherous area for boaters. Southwest or northeast winds predominate, producing steep and chaotic seas on Cape Thunder. The bizarre interaction of channelled winds crossing the mountains outside the bay and mixing with lake winds sets up a swift current and high waves. Unusual geological formations in combination with the weather produce some very odd hydraulics. During electrical storms, the pyrotechnics around Thunder Bay have been cited "as the grandest representation of the end of the world."

Rounding the cape I was awestruck at the huge cliffs towering above the water. The grandeur of this panorama seeps into your very bones, infusing you with humility at human insignificance in the face of nature. It was easy to understand how the aboriginal manitou mythology of

Lake Superior and its mountains could have arisen.

Then the lights of the city of Thunder Bay were twinkling in the distance. My goal was in sight. The perils of the 1,000-kilometre waterway from the Soo were behind me, and I felt a great sense of accomplishment. My journey across the great lake was almost at an end.

That night I gazed through my tent flap at the glistening lights on the horizon. It was almost a month since I'd left the Soo. I recalled the doomsday scenarios of a multitude of dire fates that would befall me. Well, here I was in one piece. I had been well aware that the water temperature was low and one accidental tip would be catastrophic. I had countered this threat by double-checking routes when crossing large bays and being especially vigilant about weather.

Despite many anxious moments behind me, my goal now lay ahead. My confidence was bolstered that I could make it all the way across the country. I had crossed Superior's icy waters in the face of constant prevailing nor'westerlies by taking it one day at a time. I believed in living fully, and never fearfully or rashly. Life without risk is surely meaningless.

It was now the last week in June, and the early morning had that crispness that makes you feel good and sharpens the mind. Soon the sun lit up the huge expanse of Thunder Bay. As I stood basking in it, the lake's mirror-like surface perfectly reflected the nearby mountain. I thanked God that I was living in a beautiful country where it was still possible to head off into the wilderness paddling my own canoe.

About 10 kilometres on I saw a pleasant little cove with fine sand that looked like a great spot for breakfast. A mug of tea in my hands, excitement gripped me as I looked across the water to Thunder Bay. But as I washed the dishes, my angst started to rise. Should I take the long trip around the edge of the bay, which was safe but could take a couple of days? Or should I chance the treacherous waters and powerful currents by heading directly across?

Checking that the canoe was properly ballasted, I slid it into the water and pushed out. I checked once more to ensure that the spray covers were buttoned down, my extra paddle was positioned for easy access below my legs, and a life-jacket was within reach. Cold drinks, chocolate bars and various snacks were in a pack behind me.

I hugged the lee shore, scanning the horizon. The wind was gentle, about 10 kilometres from the east, and the lake was calm. My destination looked so close, deceptively so. I continued to procrastinate over whether to head directly across or move around the bay. Deep inside a voice warned me to be cautious. The wind was rising, and the waves that had been gently lapping onshore were now slapping against the rock.

Unexpectedly, a gust of wind carried me out into the open lake. At this point I could have turned back with a few thrusts of my paddle. But caught up in wild exhilaration, I paddled towards the city dead ahead.

The bow bit into deepening troughs and the canoe swung up and down like a teeter-totter. But there was no way of turning back into the wind without risking an upset. I just had to tough it out. At least the wind seemed to be holding steady at about 10 knots, and the waves weren't too hard to handle. A little while later the wind fell and the waves subsided further. I could see a huge freighter about eight kilometres away making its way towards port at a high rate of speed. Soon it disappeared from view.

About 20 minutes later the canoe was suddenly slammed hard over to one side. The stern swung violently to the right, then hard to the left, almost catapulting me into the water. I felt like I was in the grip of a giant whirlpool. It was ridiculous, but I actually thought a submarine must have surfaced close by.

By some miracle I did not capsize. My heart pounded madly at my near escape. Later a coastguard officer suggested it could have been wake from the freighter, despite the distance. The odd hydraulics within the bay can exacerbate the effects of turbulence from a large ship. The heavier the vessel, the greater the effect, particularly on a small craft like a canoe.

The wind had now risen again. I decided to make for the aptly named Welcome Islands, about 18 kilometres due south of Thunder Bay. Pulling up on a beach, I threw myself on the sand, exhausted. But after a short nap I arose refreshed and made lunch. Invariably my lunches were soup, and the occasional luxury of bread, followed by several draughts of Tetley tea with biscuits and honey. This gave me renewed energy for the afternoon paddle, without the lassitude that follows a heavy meal. Sitting on the side of the canoe, sipping piping hot tea and looking across the bay to what used to be called Port Arthur, I felt confident this would be my last stop.

To be sure of the weather and wind conditions, I hiked around the other side of the island. A freshening breeze was turning into a stiffening 15 knot wind. I decided to camp and head out early in the morning, cheered by the thought that my next stop would be the big city.

Checking the sky at dawn I saw wisps of cirrus cloud. That was unusual so early in the day. I decided to launch in any case, figuring I could make port before the weather became unmanageable. But an hour later, with Thunder Bay dead ahead, the wind had increased and waves had built up to about two metres. The high rollers thrust me forward, lifting the canoe high as it soared over a crest. The rapid and steep descent into the trough that followed scared the hell out of me. My speed made it vital to rigidly maintain direction. I couldn't even risk a glance behind to check the weather, as it would cause me to veer dangerously.

The wind was still increasing. The headlong roller-coaster ride continued. All my efforts were concentrated on maintaining the bow in an unerringly straight line. Even a slight deviation could mean capsize. Occasionally a rogue wave came at me from the side, turning the bow and thrusting the beam directly along the high rollers. I rode the crests, clinging with both hands to the gunwales, terrified of falling overboard. I used my paddle only to control direction. Riding down a wave felt like plunging to the bottom of a well, straight into the depths of the lake. Somehow, magically, the bow would once again rise and bear me aloft up the crest of another gigantic roller.

The wild Valkyrie ride became an erratic helter-skelter. Not for the first time I breathed a prayer of thanks for Cree workmanship. My canoe is about five metres (16 feet) long, but some waves I slid down were almost perpendicular. They must have been more than five metres in height!

At the top of one particularly large wave, I saw thin wisps of smoke directly ahead. I realized it came from a freighter getting ready to leave port. As it manoeuvred onto the lake, it soon lay directly in my path. Obviously I was in the middle of a shipping lane. Coldness gathered in my belly. The huge ship was facing me bow to bow. As we drew inexorably nearer, like the mouse and the elephant, I gazed spellbound at the bridge towering above me, knowing there was no way they could see me.

Because of my experience the previous day with the phantom turbulence, my apprehension mounted to fever pitch. How strange life is, I thought: a short time ago I was panicking about ending up in the icy depths, and now this great freighter towering above me was the new menace. The throb of its huge motors heightened my sense of impending disaster.

If the wind and waves hadn't been so belligerent, I could have changed course and paddled swiftly away. But turning broadside meant instant capsize. I found myself gasping prayers, making desperate plea bargains with the Great Spirit: "Please God, get me out of this." I raised my paddle in a forlorn effort to catch the attention of someone on the freighter.

Suddenly, when it seemed nothing could stop the great ship from churning me into fish food, it made a 90-degree turn to the right. It was simply moving to a new berth! I'd been handed a reprieve at the last minute. Madly euphoric, I screamed to the elements bawdy songs from my Air Force days. The wind and high rollers were still fraught with danger, but my immense relief at the averted catastrophe reduced their threat.

The city marina lay a few short kilometres to my left. Frustratingly, there was no way to alter course without putting myself in jeopardy. I continued ahead, which meant passing the city entirely. Off to my right, about 15 kilometres east of the city, I could see floatplanes taking off. Bowling along with the 25-knot wind at my back, it looked like the floatplane base was going to be my port of call.

Drawing closer I could make out a long ramp down to the water. I was headed for it at breakneck speed. Carried on the back of a high roller, *Spirit of Mackenzie* swept about 10 metres up the concrete ramp, then came to a grinding halt. I was catapulted forward onto the spray cover, arms and legs flailing.

The receptionist from the base had seen me from the office and stood gazing bemused as I lay spread-eagled across the canoe. Hysterical with relief, I roared with laughter.

"Is there anything I can do?" she asked.

Certainly it wasn't one of my better landings, but anytime you can walk away from near disaster, it's okay.

Despite my unimpressive entrance, the staff were most helpful, allowing me to store my gear and canoe in their compound. I called a taxi and sat in the waiting room nursing a cup of coffee. It felt wonderful to be freed from Mishepeshu's malevolent embrace.

With no campgrounds nearby, I decided to spoil myself by checking into the downtown Sportsman's Hotel. After a shower and meal, I called Ishbel. She was thankful to hear I was finally off the lake and relieved that the waterways before me were relatively manageable.

My arrival at the lakehead was a milestone, not only because it signified the halfway point. It convinced me that I could probably make it to my final goal – to reach Bella Coola for the bicentennial celebrations of Mackenzie's feat of 1793. I was more confident my physical abilities would stand up to the arduous voyage across Lake Winnipeg, the North Saskatchewan, the Athabasca to the Peace and then down the Fraser to the coastal mountains. I was less certain about the 250-kilometre mountain trail to Bella Coola. Anyway, while I certainly had qualms, my confidence was buoyed at having put some 2,500 kilometres behind me.

Few cities in Canada have such a spectacular view from the shorefront as Thunder Bay. The Welcome Islands with the Sleeping Giant lying behind make an impressive vista.

In the centre of this thriving northern city lies the Nautical Centre, a first-class marina with footpaths meandering through well-tended gardens. It was a pleasant change to gaze out from the promenade instead of the confines of a canoe.

It's strange, I reflected, how the same fear that can paralyze us can motivate us to rise and face an overpowering threat. Fear seems to serve as a catalyst for what is termed courage. Courage does not mean the absence of fear, merely its conquest. This is the only conquest we make when facing challenges in the wilderness. It is vanity to think we can "conquer" this river or that mountain; what we can conquer is our inherent fears, by coming to know who and what we are. This search for self has driven humankind into the wilderness since the mountains cooled.

At sunset a kaleidoscope of hues flickered and danced across the water. Still relatively undiscovered by tourists, the lake here has a wild ascetic beauty, tinged with an icy coolness even in mid-summer. Those qualities drew large numbers of Icelanders to settle in the city over the years, to work the lumber camps lining the shores. Suddenly overcome with weariness, I turned back to the hotel. It was a fabulous luxury to slip between sheets, and better still to be free of anxiety with no challenges to face the following day.

I awoke late. After a brief walk I returned to the hotel for breakfast. In the dining room I was conscious of stares. The reason became apparent on picking up the local paper. There was my picture splashed on the front page. As I sat down, a diner at the next table greeted me with a cheerful "Good morning." We struck up a conversation, and it turned out he was a coast-guard captain and a most interesting man. He told me he had participated in many rescues on Superior's tricky waters, including several aircraft crashes and numerous small-craft Mayday calls. I had found it surprising that despite the large numbers of recreational craft, particularly sailboats, plying Lake Huron's North Shore, few seemed to venture into Lake Superior's waters. Remarkably, in the enormous distance between the Soo and Thunder Bay, the only craft I came across during a month's travel was a coast-guard launch.

After breakfast I strolled through the town, stopping in at a barbershop. Revitalized, I spent time browsing in the library and window-shopping at the mall. When I returned to the hotel later that day, a message awaited me. I called the local number, and almost before I gave my name, an irate voice informed me I was speaking to the coordinator for the official Mackenzie Cross-Canada Voyageur Canoe Route. She went on to explain that this venture involved 100 students paddling across Canada, following the route Alexander Mackenzie travelled in 1789 to the Beaufort Sea and in 1793 to Bella Coola on the Pacific. "Everyone involved in this event has worked hard to make the re-creation a success," she told me.

Puzzled at what this had to do with me, I tried to interrupt. She continued indignantly: "All of our plans are being thwarted by you!"

When I asked her how my attempt to follow Mackenzie's route

could be hindering their million-dollar enterprise, she retorted primly, "Because you're stealing all our publicity." The media was focusing on me because I was a lone canoeist. It wasn't fair that I should be the recipient of all this attention since it distracted from the official expedition. I was astonished that she considered me a threat to their event. Taken aback, I asked for specific details of my "unwarranted interference."

A story in the Soo paper, she said, had mocked their "government sponsored million-dollar show with 100 paid student crew paddling in heritage plastic canoes, the latest in high-tech nav-aids, GPS, cell phones, and accompanied by a huge trailer truck." The article continued, "By contrast, here is an old-timer using an authentic Cree-built canoe with only compass and charts, no sponsors, using his own financial resources, yet beating them to the punch!"

She quoted another story in the Terrace Bay paper that divided its front page in two. On one side was a small picture and report of the "official" expedition; on the other was a big picture of me beside my canoe headlined: "Lone Canoeist's Epic Journey on Superior."

Amused at the storm in a teacup, I told her I was unaware of any of these news stories since I was constantly on the trail. She then put forward an outrageous demand. "Would it be possible for you to wait in Thunder Bay until the Voyageur expedition arrives, since you're compromising our entire enterprise by stealing our publicity?"

Stung by her comment that I was "stealing" anything, and incredulous that she had the gall to make such a request, I retorted that my schedule was my own affair and I would leave when I was good and ready.

It became clear later that the media were indulging in wry humour and a little bit of a spoof. This likely arose from Joe Warmington of the *Sault Star*. Joe had implied several times in stories that the Voyageur brigade had still not "caught up" with me, giving the impression that this was some kind of race. Of course the Voyageurs were organizing exhibitions and dances at various towns and villages along the way. And certainly any suggestion of a race was ridiculous, as their canoes were manned by eight to 12 strapping 20-year-olds, and they covered at least 70 kilometres a day compared to my 18 to 20 kilometres.

I found it highly amusing that the Ottawa-subsidized Voyageur Expedition considered my venture a "threat." But like most federal grants, sponsorship is dependent on the media beating the drums for government concern over Canadian heritage. My presence on the scene put a spoke in the wheel. I was a definite embarrassment.

My resources were meagre, my subsidy consisting entirely of my Canada Pension. I had no other backing and was solely my own man. It really made me appreciate my independence. It's the old story of who pays the piper: when you take government money, the bureaucrats demand their pound of flesh.

The plastic canoes of the "official" Mackenzie expedition had no relation to the original birch-bark canoes used by the Voyageurs. Surely it wasn't beyond the capabilities of a university like Lakehead to build their own canoes as part of the project? Old Fort William, right on the university's doorstep, boasts a birch-bark canoe construction site! This would have given the canoes a touch of authenticity, but more importantly, would have demonstrated inclusiveness to First Nations people.

Old Fort William, a reconstruction of the original North West Company fort at the mouth of the Kaministiquia River, is an outstanding attraction of Thunder Bay. The original fort was located at Grand Portage, about 50 kilometres south, but following the Treaty of Paris, when the continental boundary lines were redrawn, the territory was ceded to the United States, and the company had to look elsewhere for a base. The Nor'westers built Fort William, named after Company Chief William McGillivray, on the present site in 1804. Through the years the fort fell into ruin, until it underwent extensive renovation in the 1970s.

It now has a first-class museum and one of the continent's best fur-trade interpretation centres. Chief librarian Jean Morrison, an authority on the voyageurs, has gathered an extensive collection on the fur-trade era. She gave me permission to use the library and also asked if she could have my canoe for the museum when I had completed my cross-country journey. While it was nice to know she had confidence in my abilities, I told her it was still early days.

My visit to the fort coincided with a city press conference to announce several new programs funded by federal and provincial grants. Fall elections were on the horizon, and the mayor was making a speech citing the administration's achievements. I was introduced to him at the reception afterwards. He asked if I had seen the city and kindly volunteered to give me a tour. As we drove around old Port Arthur, he pointed out interesting areas and unusual architecture, and noted that while the great northern port is known widely as a key terminal on the St Lawrence Seaway route for grain handling, plans were underway to diversify and attract new industry. My heart sank when I learned these plans would include waterfront hotels, a monster tourist-ship terminal, and a casino.

After a sojourn of several days in Thunder Bay I set course towards Grand Portage, Minnesota. Grand Portage was the terminal depot for the voyageurs travelling from Montreal. It was also the terminus for the

Northmen, the *hommes du nord* who travelled by canoe from the Athabasca country via the Athabasca, Saskatchewan, and Winnipeg rivers, then crossed Lake Winnipeg and Lake of the Woods. At Rainy River they would deliver their furs and pick up the goods the voyageurs had brought from Montreal.

Eric Morse in *Fur Trade Canoe Routes of Canada Then and Now* notes the great rivalry that existed between the Montrealers and the Northmen, who travelled using the smaller but more manoeuvrable *canots du nord*. Derisively they termed the Montrealers, *mangeurs des porc*, or pork eaters, on account of the pork rinds which they chewed on during their travels.

The lengthy Grand Portage bypasses the rapids, steep waterfalls and gorges of the Pigeon River. Consequently, each voyageur, carrying two 40-kilogram (90 pound) packs, or *pieces*, tethered to a tumpline around his forehead, humped these great loads some 14 kilometres up a steep path climbing over 200 metres (660 feet) to Pigeon Lake. When men were in short supply, each voyageur had to carry a total of six or eight *pieces*! Mackenzie himself commented on the men's stamina and perseverance. He noted wryly that company horses and oxen had initially been tried on the hellish trek, but that even the animals were unable to perform this laborious task!

My two-day, 50 kilometre trip along the lakeshore was uneventful, thanks to glorious weather. At Grand Portage the original North West Company stockade and buildings are now a national monument, administered by the U.S. National Park Service. In contrast to Fort William, it is somewhat of a poor cousin. U.S. forest rangers run the historical site with a minimal budget.

Some of the many buildings reconstructed from the period include the Great Hall and a kitchen and warehouse, all enclosed by a stockade. Park employees wearing historic costumes staff the buildings. Dedicated members of the Minneapolis Historical Society have furnished a museum and large house depicting the fur-trade era. It was in the Great Hall that the Nor'westers, almost exclusively highlanders with names that read like the roll call from the battle of Culloden, met to discuss business affairs. Then it was time to celebrate with a dram in true highland-style victories over their bitter rival, the Sassenach Hudson Bay Company. Because of its initials, the scornful Nor'westers derisively termed the company Here Before Christ.

The skirl of the pipes filled the air as native girls danced with Scottish partners. The rafters rang with chorus upon chorus of old voyageur songs and tall tales of the harsh life in the *pays d'en haut*. The voyageurs ran up debts at the nearby company store, got drunk at the local whorehouse, and picked fights with each other. When things got out of hand, they were chucked into the "butter tub" overnight, a run-down privy that served as a jail.

Despite the museum's valiant efforts to portray eighteenth-century voyageur traditions, the lack of historical awareness by the student guides acting out the part of figures like Radisson, La Verendrye, Mackenzie or Fraser was painful. One student playing the role of Mackenzie, laudably anxious to learn all he could about Big Mack, questioned me for details. Americans have little knowledge of Canadian history in general, so it is understandable that their portrayal of key Canadian historical characters carries a Yankee spin. This impression was reinforced later when I read of plans to build a large casino and lodge next door to the fort. I found it distasteful that such rampant commercialization would be allowed on a site designated as a U.S. National Monument. Presumably plans will include appropriate "heritage" themes like the "Great Nor'westers Hall of Roulette"!

The chief ranger let me camp close by the heritage trail so I could make an early start. Time was critical, as it would probably take me all day to reach the summit. The trail itself has been left as close to the original as possible. The voyageurs talked incessantly en route about this fearful portage, terrifying novices with hair-raising tales. This was a portage that either broke or made a voyageur. During the height of the fur trade, rough wooden crosses lined the edges of the trail in clusters of as many as 30 men who had succumbed to stroke, heart failure, or strangulated hernia from their enormous burdens.

Anxiety began to gnaw at my innards. This was the first time I had felt uneasy confronting a land-bound obstacle. After a restless night camping under tall pines, I rose at sunrise. Hoisting the canoe onto my head, I took my first steps on the mother of all portages. The 200-metre (660 feet) ascent was straight up for 14 kilometres through swamp lined with thick brush. It had rained the previous day, and the muddy track was plagued by voracious mosquitoes, blackflies, and sandflies that nipped constantly at my ankles.

The first few kilometres were not too bad since I was fresh and the morning air was cool. Further on, I would leave the canoe by the side of the trail and head back for my two packs. Although it entailed a double carry, it gave me some respite from carrying the canoe. In fact it was a glorious relief to travel back downhill empty-handed. I repeated this process of doubling back ad nauseum, the sweat running off me like a leaky faucet. My progress up the incline was painfully slow. The bow of the canoe collided with low-hanging branches, swinging it violently to one side so that I slipped and slid in the mud. Fallen trees were major obstacles, and tree roots lay in wait like land mines, cunning traps for the unwary. In an instant I was catapulted sprawling along the muddy track. Sometimes I ended up in a patch of stinging nettles.

Most of this bone-jarring climb was through deep mud. At one point, with the canoe on my back, my feet slid from under me. As I lay prostrate, the weight forced my face into the mud. As it oozed into my eyes, mouth and ears, the winged devils swooped in for the feast. Finally I was able to push the canoe to the side and ease myself out.

Over and over I asked myself whether it was worth it. Tottering along from one muddy foothold to the next, a heavy pack threatening to tip me back down the steep trail, I lost track of time. This portage qualified for inclusion as one of Dante's Seven Circles of Hell.

Hysteria overtook me. I was suddenly convulsed with laughter, remembering my Air Force training, when we had to climb all sorts of obstacles under very difficult conditions. Clad only in pants and vest, we swung along ropes across a stagnant swamp, rifle over our shoulders. Once I got stuck in the middle with not enough swing on the rope to get me to the other side. Just then my belt broke, and my pants slipped down. I clutched the rope with one hand while striving desperately to retain my dignity with the other.

A group of women on their way from shopping stood watching my predicament through the wire fence. As my pants continued their relentless descent, they hurled insults and ribald comments: "Give us another show, love!" With a groan, my face crimson but honour intact, I let go of the rope and sunk to my neck in the slime.

But military training was kindergarten compared to this tortuous ascent. No wonder the voyageurs used to say that it was easier to climb to heaven than to Pigeon Lake! All at once, I realized the light was fading. Since I had set out before dawn, the whole day from sun up to sundown, about 18 hours, had been spent stumbling, falling, and cursing the mosquitoes along this trail to hell. I hadn't even thought of eating. All my energies had been focused on this miserable foray in the bush. Who was it that spoke about the romantic era of the fur trade?

At last I reached the summit. I was tired, hungry, aching in every muscle, badly bitten and mud-caked. But I was not defeated – I could now truly identify with the hardships of Mackenzie and his intrepid voyageurs two centuries earlier.

I didn't have the strength to put my tent up but just threw it on the ground and crawled inside, mud-encrusted clothes and all. An assortment of bloodthirsty insects followed me in. I felt like I had run the gauntlet with 20 men beating me with baseball bats. Despite the sharp rocks digging into my back, I fell asleep at once.

The sun was well up when I awoke tired and sore. Fumbling in my muddy packs for my first-aid kit, I spent most of the morning putting cream on the bites over my face and neck. Eventually I managed a cold breakfast, which worked wonders for my morale. Again I donned my packs and trudged towards Pigeon Lake.

As I loaded the canoe preparatory to launching, it felt great no longer having to hump all this gear over a rocky mountain trail. This respite was short-lived, as in the 600-kilometre paddle that follows the Border Lakes route along the international boundary to the Lake of the Woods, there are more than 40 portages. But it was some consolation to know that none of them was anything like the portage from hell now behind me.

6

Paradise Lost

O ne advantage of travelling Superior had
been the freedom from the heavy physical
labour of portaging. That was all changed now. I hardly finished one
portage and re-packed when it was time to unpack and shoulder the
canoe once more.

Heading along the inland traverse, the weather patterns changed
dramatically. I was used to wearing heavy clothing on frigid Superior.
Now I was constantly discarding layers. And unlike on Superior where
cool temperatures kept the bugs at bay, the mosquitoes gave me no peace.
They were unrelenting on the water as well as ashore. Frequently, I threw
down my paddle, cursing my winged tormentors and scratching my
ankles. Even when my frenetic swatting reduced dozens of the kamikaze
varmints to a single fly, the lone surviving demon would continue to
torment me, unconcerned by the fate of its colleagues. It was a losing
battle.

I was also astonished that small lakes could pack such a punch. The
northwesterlies arose in the early afternoon, whipping them into a frenzy
of whitecaps. The wind constantly changed direction as high outcrops
along the shore blocked the gusts. This made it hard to maintain any
direction for long. As well, the many islands and peninsulas made
navigation difficult.

On South Lake, wind speeds reached 80 to 100 kilometres. After a
few hours, I hauled up onshore, bone tired. I made the most of being
pinned down by extending my lunch break well into the afternoon. I
watched the lake surface in amazement. At certain points where cat's-
paws stroked the surface, it looked like a field of white flowers.

When the wind fell, I hugged the shoreline, taking breaks when the
turbulence became too threatening. It was a relief to reach the end of
South Lake and prepare for the portage into North Lake. This portage
marks the continental divide. From here all the rivers run north to the
Arctic. For me it meant the end of upstream paddling since leaving

Montreal. From here on I would be going with the flow.

For the voyageurs the portage marked the end of their noviciate canoemanship. They now graduated into the esteemed ranks of *hommes du nord* and were recognized as members of that intrepid breed. But the perils of the waterways from Montreal, including the wrath of Superior's Mishepeshu, were minor compared to the hazards facing them as they ventured towards the fur-rich regions of Athabasca territory.

The rite of passage for initiation began when the *gouvereneur* or senior guide cut a cedar bough and dipped it in ditch water like a priest at the baptismal well. The candidate would kneel before him. The branch was held high over the canoeman's head, water cascading down his face as he received the "blessing." The audience would cheer lustily, reminding him that he had to stand a round of drinks. The ceremony concluded as the candidate swore allegiance to the code of ethics of a true Northman. This meant never to kiss another voyageur's wife and never to allow an "unqualified" voyageur to pass the portage. This directive applied especially to the degenerate "*mangeurs de porc*" from Montreal! The whole business was taken very seriously. A new graduate acquired an air of superiority that reflected an astonishing "single belief in his supremacy as a north western voyageur."

Alexander Ross recalled a conversation he had in 1855 with one old voyageur, long retired from the rigours of the fur trade:

> I have now been over forty-two years in this country. For twenty years I was a light canoe man ... no portage was too long for me; all portages were alike. My end of the canoe never touched the ground till I saw the end of ... [the portage]. Fifty songs a day were nothing to me, I could carry, paddle, walk and sing with any man I ever saw ... No water, no weather, ever stopped the paddle or the song. I have had twelve wives in the country; and was once possessed of fifty horses and six running dogs, trimmed in the first style. I was then like a Bourgeois, rich and happy: no Bourgeois had better dressed wives than I; no Indian chief finer horses; no white man better harnessed or swifter dogs ... I wanted for nothing; and I spent all my earning in the enjoyment of pleasure. Five hundred pounds, twice told, have passed through my hands; although now I have not a spare shirt to my back, nor a penny to buy one. Yet, were I young again, I should glory in commencing the same career again. I would spend another half-century in the same fields of enjoyment. There is no life so happy as a voyageur's life; none so independent; no place where a man enjoys so much variety and freedom as in the Indian country.

It was about six kilometres from the height of land portage to Little Gunflint Lake, but I humped my gear across the portage and headed out across North Lake. Then, somehow, I managed to get lost and had to backtrack a humiliating 10 kilometres. How had I managed to get lost on a postage-stamp lake, yet had crossed the enormous expanse of Superior without any navigation problems? This was not the only time on the Boundary Waters Route that my ego took a dive.

Crossing Gunflint Lake was a trying experience, though it did provide relief to my aching arms and muscles after the portage. But after Superior's relative tranquillity, I found the incessant noise hard to take. From morning till dusk the lake reverberated to the roar of motor boats of all shapes and sizes. Because of the many roads leading into the park region from Minnesota, most of the boats were huge high-powered cruisers loaded with camping and fishing gear. Cases of beer were piled high over the gunwales. Several times I was swamped by wakes. I was glad now I hadn't removed my spray covers. Originally, I had figured they would be unnecessary traversing the small lakes.

Near the west end of the lake I pulled ashore close to a cluster of buildings with an extensive array of slips. A large sign advertised it as Gunflint Lodge. When I went in, I was struck by all the moose heads and fish trophies adorning the reception area. There was no question that the clientele took their hunting and fishing seriously. I felt out of place in my old army pants and jacket, since most of the people milling in and out of the reception area wore fashionable outdoorswear.

The coffee-shop waitress turned out to be a student from McGill. We exchanged trivia with a nostalgia that only Montreal exiles understand. When I was about to leave, she told me that the cook would like to meet me.

Jean, another Montrealer and an avid canoeist, was doing her Master's degree in hotel management. Thrilled at learning I had paddled all the way from Montreal, she begged to hear some of my adventures along the trail. Before I could begin, she set down on the table a mountainous plate of roast beef and fries. I managed between mouthfuls to convey some idea of my transcontinental trip. Several off-duty staff joined us at the table, a delightful and appreciative audience. When I left, they came out on the deck to cheer me off.

It was a short paddle to Magnetic Lake, so-named because of large iron deposits in the area that can cause huge errors in compass readings. Luckily, I didn't find it necessary to use my compass and crossed the lake without mishap. Most of my days were now spent in portaging rocky trails, frequently booby-trapped with tree roots. The rapids were easily run, except for one or two occasions when I got hung up in white water on a rock or shrubs. I somehow managed to extricate myself without dumping. At Gneiss Lake I portaged through mud and slime to my knees. The traverse took me ages. As I leaned panting against a tree, I was chagrined to learn from a passing canoeist that I had missed a much easier route.

The portage trails and waterways were becoming crowded with wilderness tourists. At one portage, I incredulously watched a scene right out of an old African safari movie: a young guide leading four burly males portaged all their canoes while they reclined in the grass swilling beer.

I was glad to leave the yuppie adventurers behind. I was especially disenchanted at the lack of sensitivity of my fellow voyageurs. Supposedly embarked on a wilderness experience, they jostled each other to be first on the trail, their canoes loaded down with an unbelievable assortment of food and drink. It was great relief to find a good camping spot a few kilometres down the trail and hit the sack after a frustrating day. I was exhausted by the unending portages, biting flies, and sweltering heat. The blistering sun had left my face swollen and puffed.

In the morning I headed out early for Saganaga Lake, figuring I'd stop and cook breakfast at the next portage. Although the canoe was heavily loaded, I decided to run the rapids. This nearly proved my undoing: it turned out to be a lively trip downstream. I bashed against rocks a couple of times, and on one occasion turned completely around.

The wind rose unexpectedly to about 80 kilometres, and the wave caps were flecked with foam. Though it was only early afternoon, I put up the tent and caught up on some sleep. By the time I woke, it was coming on towards evening, too late to launch. I passed the time by taking an inventory of my food supplies. I generally tended to err on the side of caution, so there was ample for two weeks. Besides, I could easily get more near Rainy River or Fort Frances.

Next morning, after a short paddle down the lake, I found myself pulling into a Canada Customs station. The officer introduced herself as Mary Ellen Cooper, and we spent some time chatting. A part-time customs officer during the summer, most of the time she wore another hat as a hydroponics expert and owned a store in Thunder Bay.

She was quite a raconteur and had me in stitches with some of her experiences at the customs post. "One day we had this couple… of all the odd sights I've seen here, this for sure was the most bizarre. A canoe about 16 feet long pulled up. The man was wearing a business suit and the woman had on a tight flowery dress. They looked like they were on their way to some wedding. The canoe was laden with five or six suitcases piled atop one another. But that wasn't all – there were two large dogs aboard, one at the front and the other at the rear." She chuckled in recollection. "The whole shebang went wiggly-waggle down the lake. That was the last I saw of them."

Saganaga Lake was wider and longer than other lakes along the

Boundary Region, so it was no surprise when a wind whipped up the lake. It reminded me of the big storms on Superior. Once again I was wind-bound for the day. I made the best of it by pulling into the shelter of a cluster of islands and making myself a nice lunch of mushroom soup, beef stew, and biscuits and honey, washed down with copious amounts of billy tea. Reclining on my sleeping bag I picked up a book my daughter had given me, a suspenseful William McIlvanney detective novel set in Glasgow. It proved a painless way to pass the time.

Cache Bay, at the edge of Quetico Provincial Park, was my first port of call next morning. Registration was mandatory at the ranger station there, and camping fees were required. I found this unsettling, having never paid fees until this point. The historic voyageur trails just happened to lead through this area, as they had over 200 years ago.

At the long government dock with Ontario and Canadian flags flying, I could hear squeals of children playing in the garden. It was a pleasant surprise to meet the rangers running the station. The Puddicombes, Peter and his wife, Janice, had heard on the radio about my trip and knew I would be passing. Both are avid canoeists and could tell me first hand about the tricky waters that lay ahead. Peter said with a broad grin, "There isn't any question you're an authentic voyageur, so I guess we can forego the usual fees."

Later, heading towards Monument portage, I was thrilled to realize I was entering Quetico. Some years ago on TV I watched one of the superb NFB documentaries on this pristine wilderness filmed by Bill Mason, and for years I longed to visit it. Even the name enthralled me. My anticipation was enhanced by having travelled such an enormous distance to get here.

I paddled enthusiastically across the threshold into Quetico. Sadly, it wasn't long before the boorish behaviour of my fellow travellers dashed my fantasies. The next several days I spent paddling across numerous small lakes, running rapids, navigating tricky fast water, or manoeuvring around waterfalls. Heading towards the portage on Carp Lake, I met a fellow traveller with a canoe on his shoulders coming along the trail. He rested the canoe against a tree, puffed out.

"You'd better watch yourself going down those goddamned rapids," he advised me. "I smashed my canoe and lost all my supplies a few years back, hung up on a bloody great rock. There's four big ones spaced out like a diamond just inches below the surface. Just as you're through the white-water, when you think you're home free, they appear right at the bottom. If you miss the first one, the last bastard will get you for sure."

Later, after I'd hauled my gear up the steep trails, I was able to see from an eagle-eye perch high above the swirling waters the huge rocks hidden under the surface. But for my meeting with the Good Samaritan along the trail, any one of them would have dumped me.

Prairie Portage is the gateway to Basswood Lake. It's one of the busiest locations on the entire route as there is road access from the east shore of Moose Lake to Ely, Minnesota. It was Saturday, and packed with weekend vacationers. The lake reverberated to the sound of marine outboard engines, from the tinny two-horse motors on aluminum canoes to the roar of 3,000-horsepower speedboats. Everywhere it seemed there were canoe transporters laden with baggage roaring across the lake. All were filled with testosterone-charged canoeists eager to come to grips with the "wilderness experience" and in the process taking on any ornery critters unlucky enough to get in their way. Clutching massive quantities of gear, the throng spilled across the portage trail jostling each other to grab their share of ambience. One young girl, plainly wishing she were elsewhere, was scolded by her parents for not enjoying herself.

I stared aghast at the scene. My disillusionment was reinforced by an opinionated fellow traveller astonished that I was travelling alone. "You must be out of your mind!" he cried. "Don't you know there are all kinds of predators in the forest, and the rapids are deadly? It's criminal to travel alone in the wilderness." I was too surprised at his vehemence to offer rebuttal.

Just before Basswood River I took a wrong turning, again adding an extra 10 kilometres onto my journey. When I finally got my bearings, a sudden a strong northeast wind arose, sending black thunderclouds scudding across the sky. A solid grey curtain gradually enveloped the lake and distant hills in a cold drenching rain, soaking my clothes and sending rivulets down my neck. It was infuriating – I could have been warm and snug in my tent instead of slugging it out against this tempest.

I had cause to be again thankful for the spray covers. At least my supplies were dry. I swore that in future I would use my compass and chart faithfully, since trusting to judgment in this region was impossible. Even the voyageurs had a difficult time finding their way along the Boundary Lakes region. I was also having a tough time in the sweltering heat. My eyes and face were now badly swollen. Likely just plain weariness had played a role in my going off the trail.

I decided to run the rapids near Basswood Falls. This turned into a brisk run bouncing through wave crests coursing through the channel. In contrast, the Wheelbarrow Rapids were relatively straightforward. But occasionally I made a halter around the mid-thwart and hauled *Spirit of Mackenzie* on a long rope through the turbulence. It was easier than humping it over craggy portages.

Leaving Quetico, at the Lake La Croix ranger station I met ranger Joe Meaney and his wife, Vera. "The coffee's almost perked. Sit yourself down," Vera told me. "We heard you were coming through and were looking out for you." Once again I marvelled at the accuracy of the bush telegraph. Joe, who had paddled a kayak to Montreal for Expo '67, told me to call in at Atikokan. His brother Don, who lived there, made magnificent paddles carved with the XY Company emblem. Since this was the insignia of Alexander Mackenzie's own company, I looked forward to getting one. Vera insisted I stay for lunch in a tone that wouldn't accept refusal. It was difficult taking leave of this hospitable couple, but they understood I was anxious to get some distance on the trail.

I picked up supplies at the Neguaguon Lake Indian Reserve. In these remote areas food prices are high, but I was still taken aback at $4.25 for bread! A Beaver floatplane was tied up at the government dock. Ted, the pilot was sitting on the dock plainly bored, pleased to have some pilot-to-pilot chit chat.

"I've been cooling my heels for the best part of two days waiting for two American canoeists. God only knows where they are now." He had arranged to meet them late afternoon the day before, but they still hadn't shown up. He offered to take me for a checkout ride on the aircraft. I was excited to finally get an opportunity to fly in one of these great planes. However, just as we were starting out, the canoeists showed up. Deflated, I watched as they loaded an incredible amount of gear on board the Beaver, hitched their canoes to the floats, and took off. Next day as I was travelling towards Namakan Lake, an aircraft swooped low over my head and waggled its wings. It was Ted's Beaver giving me a salute. I was cheered by at his gesture, some compensation for missing out on my flight.

Making passage from Namakan Lake into Rainy Lake meant a portage at Kettle Falls. However, at the store in the village a young aboriginal fellow suggested that going via Bear River was a good shortcut. Heading down that narrow river I found it choked with high grass, making paddling tediously slow. Just as I was beginning to kick myself for taking this route, the grass thinned out, and I found myself in the Canadian Channel. I was elated at having bypassed the falls and wondered why I had doubted the directions. Since the white man came to North America, hasn't there always been an Indian to show him the way?

Coming down the Canadian Channel into Rainy Lake on this beautiful morning in early August, I felt great. Hauling heavy packs over never-ending portages and constantly running tricky white water had brought me to the peak of physical fitness. My high spirits were tempered as I headed down the lake. Houseboats the size of small ships meandered about while high-powered boats with skiers in tow zigzagged across the water. I had to be constantly vigilant to avoid being run down.

The lake was saturated with vessels. To add to the confusion, floatplanes were landing and taking off every ten minutes. The busy portage at Basswood Lake was nothing compared to the bustling throng of Rainy Lake. This was Coney Island, big time! Ramming my paddle deep, I made a desperate bid to flee to the wilder shore. After several hours of stiff paddling, I was free of the recreational war zone. The clamour had abated. By a stroke of luck, a northeasterly wind came up, and I hurriedly raised sail. This was the first time since Superior I had been able to take advantage of a wind at my back. In early evening I pulled into a little bay on the north shore among a cluster of islands, and set up camp for the night.

I had travelled 40 kilometres down the lake, placing me within reach of Fort Frances. The last time I had been in the town, I had arrived by ambulance following a plane crash in deep bush. Painful memories of that event now flooded me. I spent a restless night punctuated by disturbing dreams and was glad to rise at first light.

After an uneventful 20-kilometre paddle I tied up at a large dock in Fort Frances alongside several floatplanes. The signs said Rusty Myers Flying Service. Judging from the twin engine Beech 18, Beaver, and several Cessna 185 aircraft, business was flourishing.

Rusty Myers, one of the bush plane pioneers in this part of the country, had sold the business back in 1979. The new owner was Angela Korzinski. Angie kindly let me store my canoe and equipment at the seaplane base, giving me the freedom to head into town. It was getting late in the day, so I decided to pamper myself with a motel room. My body was caked with grime. A real hot bath would be luxury.

Walking along the main street, I passed the city hospital. I remembered walking dazed down this street eight years before after leaving the hospital, my clothes bloodstained and my face heavily bandaged. Waiting for Ishbel to drive down from Winnipeg, I had wandered the city like a lost soul. Over and over I asked myself how I had survived.

Some of the details were fuzzy. I recalled driving out to the small airport just outside Winnipeg where I kept my Piper Tripacer. I checked the aircraft as usual, being particularly careful to make sure the tanks were full. After filing a flight plan with the air-traffic control centre, I taxied out to Runway 24, ran up the engine, did my instrument checks, and took off. I climbed to 5,000 feet on a southeasterly, heading for Oshkosh, Wisconsin.

About an hour into the flight I passed above Lake of the Woods, dotted with islands in a sparkling expanse of water and sky, with unlimited visibility. Toy boats made streaks on the lake like tiny fry skittering across a pond. I scanned the instruments. Revs, OK, fuel, OK, mixture, OK, primer, OK, switches, OK. Everything just as it should be in a well-tuned engine, no problems evident.

Rainy River appeared below, an enormous convoluted serpent twisted around as far as the horizon. The motor purred contentedly. Master of a planetary view, I was suffused with contentment that all was right with the world. It was then that the engine quit.

A great coldness started at my toes. I scanned the instrument panel. Was it ice in the carburettor? Pull carburettor heat on anyway. Gas? Mixture control? My hands ran over the instrument panel, desperate to find the source of the problem.

Don't panic. Control column forward ... get her into a glide ... must maintain flying speed. Altitude now 3,000 feet.

Christ! I'd lost 2,000 feet already. What was the emergency drill? Still lots of time to think. Scan the ground for a landing spot. Nothing but an impenetrable forest of jack pines stretched limitlessly before my nose.

Now 2,000 feet. This plane glides like a tank. I was flying down the north side of Rainy River, seeing nothing that looked remotely like a landing strip. The glacial mass in my lower body glided upwards. Entering my chest, it threatened to choke me. Voices, initially murmuring, became a strident and mocking chorus in my head. "*You ain't going to make it!*"

I felt like the doctor had just told me I had inoperable cancer. Angrily, I jerked my head from side to side trying to spot a landing field. Nothing but trees. At 1,000 feet the trees loomed large around my line of sight. My hands flickered over the instrument panel. Despairingly I repeated the emergency check: ignition, gas, mixture, primer, de-icer, trying to bite down the panic threatening to immobilize me. I clutched at straws, hoping that somehow or other the bloody engine would start and all would be well.

The altimeter continued to unwind: 800 feet. I knew in the time remaining I must plan for a controlled crash landing. Controlled – what a joke! There were only huge spiky trees below, not an acre of clear ground, much less a field in sight. I wasn't far from the airport at International Falls but there was no way I could make that now.

Four hundred feet. I bartered with Providence. Please God, get me out of this. I swear I'll never give you trouble again!

God, please find me a landing spot ... Oh, shit. What's the point. I can't maintain flying speed. I'm going to end up skewered on those trees.

Going down. Two hundred feet. The voices were back. Brazenly they shrieked, "*Let go the controls. Just dive into the ground. There's no way you're going to make it. Get it over. Give up! Give up!*" The voices rose to a crescendo. One hundred feet. The airspeed was dropping drastically.

Almost in the treetops. My hands involuntarily pulled back on the control column in a futile gesture to gain height and steer away from the inevitable. The controls went mushy with an imminent stall. I was going to fall out of the sky in a sickening spiral likely ending in a fiery conflagration. I must put the nose down to gain speed.

What's the point? I'm going to die anyway.

Fifty feet. Now or never. I prayed for a cool head as all my senses screamed to ignore physics and pull back on the column to clear the trees. To give in to emotion made an uncontrolled crash inevitable. But the alternative wasn't any better – maintain flying speed in a crippled aircraft by ploughing through the trees and certain death pinned to the tops of these giants of the forest!

The polar chill reached my head. The phantom sirens sang their sweet airs of surrender. "It's hopeless. It's all over." It seemed to me they were right. I clenched my teeth and bit down fiercely on this alien force that was strangling me.

I sat upright in my seat, roaring "Die well!" I thrust the control stick forward to put the plane in a steep dive. It was a forlorn gesture, a moment in which the term "absolute humility" assumed new meaning. I surrendered, let go, and let God take over.

The slapping of branches against the fuselage beneath my feet made a fearful noise. I kept the stick forward as speed built up. Like the last ride of the Valkyries, the plane and I continued to slice through the top of the forest. I cringed, waiting for the finality of impact. And then, unbelievably, amidst that impenetrable mass of trees a clearing appeared.

I blinked in astonishment. Not much room, but a piece of earth I would kill for. I babbled my thanks to God as euphoria swept me. I had flying speed. As the ground reared up, I gently pulled back, lifting the nose, and held her there to lose speed to land. Not too long – I didn't want to run out of room and smash into the trees at the end of this tiny, wondrous airstrip.

The wheels of the aircraft touched down smoothly. Incredibly, I was on the ground. Released from the suffocating tension, my ego soared. I screamed in relief, "I made it. What a fucking pilot!"

The plane lurched at high speed over rough terrain. Suddenly, as the ground opened, it lost its wheels and spun over on its back as one wing sagged. My head smashed against the instrument panel and my body was hauled in all directions. The next thing I knew I was hanging upside down.

I'm not sure how long I was there. Gradually I became aware of a pinging sound. The smell of high-octane gas abruptly roused me. Terrified that the plane was going to erupt in flames, I struggled to release my safety belt.

Somehow I managed to find the door handle. It wouldn't open! I kicked at it wildly. Finally it opened a crack and I fell out. Dazed, sure the plane was going to ignite at any moment. I put as much distance as possible between me and the wreck.

As I stared at what had once been my plane, exhilaration flowed through me like a drug. I shouted at the top of my lungs, "Christ! Against all odds, I survived!" I felt like I had won the lottery.

Strangely, my head ached terribly. And though the sun was shining, I felt rain running down my face. Touching my face, I found it was drenched in blood.

My hands went to my breast pocket and I pulled out a cigarette pack, fumbled one out, and lit it. Inhaling deeply, I laughed hysterically. "Jesus, maybe I'm dying! What the hell, I'm going to have a smoke anyway!"

I felt very tired. Slumping to the ground, I thought I'd rest a while, then see if I could put a Mayday call out on my radio. That is, if it wasn't all busted to hell.

The next thing I remember is waking up in a hospital with a splitting headache. Someone was flashing a light in my eyes. "So, our intrepid airman is awake," a soft voice said. My eyes gradually focused on a nurse holding a sponge to my face. "We're just cleaning you up. Then we're shipping you back to Canada. You're in the International Falls hospital. They have more facilities in Fort Frances."

Crossing the border by ambulance next day, I was asked by Canada Customs my "reasons for entering Canada." Nothing is as imperturbable as bureaucracy.

On my way from the jetty to the hotel I came across posters advertising the Sir Alexander Mackenzie Canada Sea-to-Sea Bicentennial Expedition, which had just arrived. The expedition of students from Lakehead University was giving a performance in the park that evening. The concert turned out to feature old voyageur songs, supplemented with fiddle music of jigs and reels from the fur-trade era. The park rang with the cheers and tapping feet of the audience and soon dispelled my gloomy recollections of my accident.

Next morning I woke to azure blue skies and a mild crispness in the air. I portaged around the dam and launched my canoe into the 130-kilometre stretch of Rainy River toward Lake of the Woods. The river's name is derived not from the weather but from the French name Riviere de la Reine – "Queen of Rivers." One look at the water and I knew that taking fresh water on board had been a good move. In some stretches it was badly polluted. I didn't paddle more than a leisurely 20 kilometres that day, then pulled in to a stretch of inviting grassland to camp. This turned out to be a swamp inhabited by enormous mosquitoes and sexually active frogs that kept me awake all night with their courtship serenades.

Next morning near Emo, I was aroused from my reverie by a chorus of jeers and the splashing of many paddles. Several large voyageur canoes, each with between six and 10 paddlers, were furiously making their way towards me. As they drew alongside there were shrieks and catcalls. It was a contingent of the students from the Alexander Mackenzie Cross-Canada Expedition. From their good-natured banter it was evident they had been chasing me and were delighted to have finally caught up.

"What took you so long to get here?" I shouted. "How did you make out on those tough portages?" I added, knowing full well that they had detoured around the forty or so portages along the Boundary Route. "So much for your posters claiming authentic recreation of Mackenzie's continental trek!" From their sheepish glances, I could see this shot across their bows definitely hit the mark

"Get yourself some real canoes with that million-dollar government grant, not those plastic boats," I shouted.

After a further exchange mostly concerned with who would make it to Mackenzie's Rock in time for the bicentennial celebrations, the flotilla headed downriver. To my amazement as they paddled off, some of the party, following the example of their leader, Jim Smithers, dipped their cups in the water and drank. When I shouted warnings that the water was polluted, they merely shrugged.

The heat was stifling as the afternoon wore on. It was a great relief to pull into the little hamlet of Emo and make for the local Canadian Legion, Branch 98. As I gratefully quaffed a cool one, my eyes became heavy and I felt myself beginning to nod off.

"So you're travelling Mackenzie's route?" a friendly voice enquired. An elderly gentleman thrust out his hand. "Cameron MacKinnon," he announced. "All my folk came from the highlands. I recognized your accent the minute you opened your mouth."

He pulled up a chair and sat down. "I'm 79 now, but I travelled all over Canada in the Depression when I was young. It's nice to hear about somebody doing something for Canada and her history. I overheard you telling the waiter about Alec Mackenzie when you came in and wanted to shake your hand."

Being an incurable war buff, I enjoyed his story of how he survived the D-Day landings on Juno Beach as a member of the Canadian Division. I told him that my uncle in the Calgary Highlanders was wounded during that assault. I remembered his being transferred to Glasgow for treatment. He visited our house in uniform but wore the hospital blue pants indicating a wounded soldier.

Once he took me to the movies. When we arrived, the usual huge crowd was already waiting, a common occurrence in war-weary Scotland.

As we joined the rear of the queue, I was sure we would never get in that evening. However, the commissionaire spotted my uncle's blue pants and led us to the front of the line. "There's no way we let our D-day heroes wait out here in the bloody cold," he said.

Boy! I felt like royalty, my head swelling as we walked triumphantly to the front of the line. The crowd, recognizing the medals and blue pants, were not in the least resentful. Instead they applauded.

Cameron enjoyed my story and insisted on buying me lunch. We spent another hour shooting the breeze. It was difficult to tear myself away, but I had to find a camping spot before nightfall.

"I've a favour to ask of you," Cameron said, as he helped me cast off from the dock. "Would you send me a postcard when you reach Bella Coola for the 200th anniversary of Mackenzie's landing?" Seeing my surprise, he went on self-consciously, "Just so I'll know you've made it and you're okay." Touched, I assured him he was on my mailing list.

Camping spots along the river were few. The high grass and bulrushes seemed never-ending. Spots that initially looked possible turned out to be swampy with hordes of voracious mosquitoes. The chorus of frogs made sleep near impossible. When I reached the town of Rainy River, the river widened directly onto Lake of the Woods. This cheered me considerably. I was sick to death of the stale brownish water that changed to foamy white near hamlets as laundromats flushed directly into the river. I pulled out strongly into the open water.

Suddenly I was thrown forward. A number of sandbars surround a cluster of small islands called the Sable Islands, and I had run aground. It was time to get out and pull. Tying a line to the bow, I slipped the other end over my shoulders, straining like a dray horse. Thankfully, it wasn't long until deeper water when I was able to jump on board and paddle off.

Early one morning as I glided along the lake's mirrored surface, the sound of beating wings broke the stillness. Glancing up, I was thrilled to see masses of pelicans in flight. Their snowy wings rose and fell in metronomic cadence as they glided above the treetops. Squadrons of about sixty of these magnificent birds swept across the river in tight-knit chevrons, wheeling and soaring in displays of precision flying that would have shamed the most skilled aerobatic pilot.

Suddenly, out of the blue a growling roar intruded on this idyllic scene. With the precision of soldiers given a command, the pelicans turned north. Towards the centre of the lake, a vast flotilla of boats appeared. Their numbers continued to increase as boats of all shapes joined one vast armada. I was momentarily perplexed. Then it dawned on me: this was a recreational fishing expedition, U.S. style.

The poor bloody fish didn't stand a chance. There were boats of all variety, from aluminum outboards to enormous cabin cruisers capable of crossing the North Atlantic. All sported fishing gear, complex outriggers that looked like they were baited for tuna or shark. I pulled into a quiet cove for lunch to allow time for the fleet to disperse.

Later that day as I approached the hamlet of Nestor Falls, the wind rose, and the placid waters became menacing. Marching rows of waves about a metre or so from crest to trough lined up like guards on parade as I was battered around the lake. I couldn't make any headway. A gust blew me into a small bay with a large docking area, penning me like a stray sheep. Whitefish Lodge, a rustic sign indicated. About a dozen aluminum fishing boats were berthed in the slips. Tying up alongside them, I made my way across the neatly kept grounds to a large log cabin, centrepiece to a number of other similarly constructed smaller buildings.

"Anyone home?" I shouted. There was no response. Stepping inside, I found myself in a large dining room. The walls were covered with trophies of bear, moose, and muskie, bass and pickerel of all shapes and sizes. Dining tables for groups of four, six, and twelve were set with gleaming cutlery and quality dinnerware. "Hi there," I called loudly, and walked to the kitchen at the far end. It was empty.

Puzzled, I left the building and made my way to several smaller cottages. All of them were open, but of guests there was nary a one. Hearing a whine from one of the outbuildings among the trees, I walked towards the sound. The door opened on a maintenance workshop with a generator humming away, but no maintenance personnel.

It didn't make sense that the tables were set, all doors in the buildings were open, and the generator was unattended. Walking back to the dining room, I sat down at a table and poured myself a glass of water, consumed with curiosity.

I was shocked out of my socks when a voice bellowed through the screen door, "How you doing, fellah!"

I scrambled to my feet as a man staggered in. The door slammed behind him, the noise reverberating around the empty room.

Walking unsteadily towards me, he sat down. "Feel like a little drink?" he asked, his speech slow and indistinct. He didn't seem the least put out at my presence. "You stay here as long as you like, buddy, no problem. I'm the boss here. There's lots of cabins. Just pick one." He threw his arm around benevolently.

"Thanks all the same, but when the weather improves a bit I'll head out," I told him. It was plain he wasn't capable of processing what I was saying. Thinking some caffeine might bring him to his senses, I went to the kitchen and put the percolator on. I had figured initially he had been boozing, but his breath had no odour of alcohol. Also, he ignored the bottles in the dining room's well-stocked bar.

He told me his name was Bill, that he lived in St Paul, Minnesota, and that the lodge belonged to his father-in-law. "He's a miserable SOB and doesn't appreciate me. Would you believe? He has three more lodges scattered around. Got all kinda money. Thinks he's a big shot. Made me manager, but he keeps on sticking his nose in." Bill's voice rose. For a couple of hours I listened to a recitation of his problems.

I didn't really understand what he had against his father-in-law, but it was plain Bill was running the business into the ground. Few tourists, or serious fishermen, would want to spend their vacation in a camp run by someone with a serious addiction problem. But with the weather unsettled, there was no way I could hope to find a camping spot this late.

Bill insisted I use one of the cabins. I felt uncomfortable about staying in the camp with such an erratic individual. When I asked about the generator, he seemed indifferent to my suggestion that it should be checked out. I decided the best course was to fetch my tent from the canoe and set it up in a grassy area close to the dock.

I passed a restless night and rose early in the morning resolved to get underway. It was raining and the wind was rising, but there was no way I wanted to stay a moment longer. I was uneasy about leaving Bill on his own but figured he must finally have got to bed. There was really nothing I could do anyway. Hopefully, he would come to himself later in the morning.

As I paddled towards Sioux Narrows, my mind was in a flurry of emotions. The weird experience at the lodge had left me thinking about the large number of American-owned lodges around northern Ontario. Having visited quite a few in my travels by canoe as well as by floatplane, I never failed to be surprised by the deep southern accents from Georgia, Alabama, or Tennessee, even in remote and sparsely settled areas of the province. I remember in the late 1950s a scandal about the way the Ontario government was auctioning off government land. Somehow large tracts of prime land seemed to end up in American hands at auctions where Canadians were conspicuously absent.

The voyageurs had endless difficulties navigating their way around the Lake of the Woods. Now I was experiencing the same frustrating problems. My previous adventures in Lake Superior's tricky bays were trivial in comparison. One hot, humid afternoon I paddled lazily down the lake with one eye open, heading north for Sioux Narrows. To my embarrassment, instead of the shortcut I planned on, I ended up putting on a gruelling 35 kilometres on an easterly route that took me nowhere!

I drew comfort from Eric Morse's observation in his book that the voyageurs seem to have got lost more often in Lake of the Woods than in all the other miles of their long journey put together. I had not considered just how essential marine charts would be. I was using topographical charts, which don't provide enough detail for tricky regions like Lake of the Woods.

Kenora finally came in sight. Floatplanes were taking off and landing from all directions, dozens of aluminum boats skittered everywhere, and large tour boats packed with tourists plied the waters. Near the huge muskie carving that advertises Kenora on the highway I paddled through Rat Portage into the Winnipeg River. This portage, one of the busiest in the northland, at one time resounded to the lilting songs of ebullient voyageurs packed into dozens of canoes bound for Athabasca country. Then the river was a magnificent waterway lined with spectacular falls and violent rapids. The giant whirlpools from the Dalle Rapids in particular swallowed many a *canot du nord*. Today dams have tamed it, and the free-flowing river is no more.

I knew this country quite well, as I used to fly into Kenora on weekends when we lived in Winnipeg. It was a great vacation area for Winnipeggers. The profusion of lakes made it a mecca for fly-in fishing lodges and gave a big boost to the local economy. I learned to fly floatplanes at the Kenora Flying Club. Some of the club's pilots were remarkably skilled. Sometimes on a bet they would fly at zero feet over the water, then set the aircraft down in landing mode and bounce their wheels off the waves in an incredible display of precision flying.

The last time I'd been at the airport was in 1979, as one of several volunteers taking part in a search for a missing flyer, Ken Leishman. Accompanied by a nurse, he had been flying a patient from Red Lake to Thunder Bay for treatment when his Piper Aztec disappeared from the radar about 200 kilometres north of Thunder Bay. Several searches in the thickly wooded country were unsuccessful. It was unlikely anyone would survive long in the cold December nights.

But Ken, an experienced, dependable pilot, had lived through many crashes in the wild bush country of northern Ontario. It was hard to believe that he hadn't survived this one also. Sadly, the plane was found in early spring. There were no bodies in the wreckage. Bone fragments were later found, indicating they had been thrown into the bush by the impact or dragged there by animals.

I had first heard about Ken when I was a volunteer visitor at Stony Mountain Penitentiary just north of Winnipeg. At that time he was doing a stretch for robbery. His love of flying and desire to become a pilot struck a resonant chord in me. He was turned down for Trans-Canada Airlines, which figured he didn't have the education to make a good pilot. Never one to let an obstacle stand in his way, Ken robbed a bank to buy his own plane!

His exploits read as if they were based on the Scarlet Pimpernel. He had been catapulted to fame in the late 1950s when he and members of his gang stole the gold bullion being delivered at Winnipeg airport, the first-ever robbery at an airport in Canada. He stashed over $400,000 in gold bars. Most of it was recovered, but one bar worth about $60,000 remained unaccounted for.

Prison authorities boasted that they finally had his number. They claimed there was no way he could make a break from their new high-security complex. Ken could never resist a challenge. His escape from his "escape-proof cell" had the makings of a Houdini exploit. He stole a plane and disappeared across the border in the biggest jailbreak in Canadian history.

He achieved the attention he craved. The public's admiration for him arose mainly from the fact that he never used violence. Even hard-bitten policemen had a soft spot for him. The general adulation was so great that everyone hoped that he would stay free. However, the authorities launched a massive manhunt, and ultimately he was caught and returned to jail.

After his release Ken became a successful businessman, even becoming president of the local service club and only narrowly bested for mayor of the bustling community of Red Lake. Intriguingly, the town was renowned as Canada's foremost gold-mining town, a factor causing many folks to shake their heads, knowing Ken's penchant for the metal. Heather Robertson remarks in her book *The Flying Bandit* that he lived his life like a movie. His crimes were brilliant moves in a chess match with police. He became a celebrity, a folk hero, a modern Robin Hood stealing from the rich to give to the poor. He was such a legend that many refused to believe he had been killed in the crash in Northern Ontario, thinking he had somehow escaped and was living in luxury in South America.

North of Kenora the river is dotted with cottages and a profusion of "No Trespassing" signs. I clenched my teeth at the roar of high-speed boats that left my canoe rocking in their wake. Fortunately, it wasn't long before the densely populated area gave way to open country. Despite a number of dams that feed power-hungry Winnipeg, the river does have stretches resembling something close to its original wild state.

Paddling swiftly along, I breathed thanks to be leaving civilization. While there is some pretty country left on Lake Superior's shores, all through Lake of the Woods the heavy emphasis on recreational tourism and "wilderness excursions" hit a jarring note with me. I was used to solitude and jealously coveted the ambience that comes from canoeing in areas of wild or sparsely settled country. I still had not recovered from my shattered illusion of a Shangri-La named Quetico. Europeans consider Canada the last wilderness, but the relentless impact of a global tourist industry is jading even the most remote areas of our country.

Passing under the bridge that crosses the Winnipeg River near Pinawa, home to the Pinawa Nuclear Research Facility, brought back many memories. I knew this stretch of the river well, having spent some vacation time on it canoeing and fishing. I laughed aloud recalling one fishing expedition with my son Grant near Pinawa. We were standing fishing from the top of a very large rock that sloped down to the water. With my weather-beaten Tilley on my head, and my favourite old corncob stuck in my mouth, I was relaxing, waiting for a bite.

Suddenly, something tugged at my line. "Jeeze, a big northern Jack!" I cried. Then, still upright, I was pulled slowly but relentlessly down the rock. Like a stiff marionette, I slipped into the water, clutching my rod, hat on and pipe still clenched between my teeth. Grant convulsed in laughter as my head bobbed in the water and the big Jack took off.

PART 3

THE THIRD YEAR 1992

FROM LAKE WINNIPEG

TO FORT SMITH

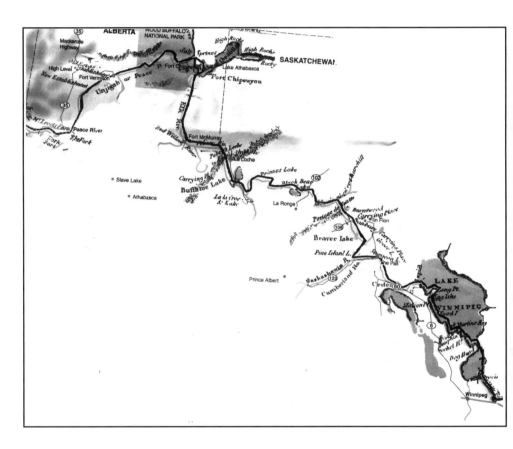

As disaster strikes on the mean waters of Lake Winnipeg, *Spirit of Mackenzie* is down but not out.

Along the muddy shoreline of the Saskatchewan River, a paddle serves as a convenient anchor.

Master fisherman and host Colin McKay with the author in front of Colin's fishing boat at his riverside cabin resort in Grand Rapids, Manitoba.

An aerial portage provides a swift getaway out of the territory of La Loche's "mad bandit."

7

Bears Galore

As I prepared to set out for the third year on the trail of Mackenzie in May 1992, the anxiety I was feeling reminded me of my first day on Lake Superior. There are no roads running up the isolated east shore of Lake Winnipeg and almost no communities other than remote native reserves. To travel this sparsely settled area, I picked up a huge supply of food, enough for about six weeks: 60 assorted packets of "boil-in-the-bag" dehydrated chicken, beef stew, and macaroni and cheese. These were supplemented with sardines, soups, six loaves of bread, and a bag of apples. For the first time I carried drinking water as well as soft drinks.

Being able to use my friend Ron Clay's cottage, conveniently located on the Winnipeg River, was a great help in getting organized. I carefully repacked all my supplies into boxes, covering them tightly with plastic. *Spirit of Mackenzie* was sporting newly painted canvas as well as a custom-made spray cover, giving her the look of a kayak. I also had a new paddle, beautifully carved from B.C. stikine by an artisan in Perth, Ontario.

Formed from shallow Lake Agassiz, Lake Winnipeg was created by Ice Age glaciers and takes its name from the Cree word meaning "muddy waters." A storage reservoir for a river system that includes the Saskatchewan, Nelson, Red, and Winnipeg rivers, it is the third largest lake lying entirely within Canada. Only Great Bear Lake and Great Slave Lake in the Northwest Territories are larger. Lake Winnipeg covers 24,387 square kilometres, and is 416 kilometres long and between 32 to 110 kilometres wide. Its very shallow depth makes it extremely challenging for small craft. Eric Morse considers it "neither canoe country nor vacation land."

The storm-tossed surf produces a desolate tangle of fallen trees along the shoreline, an impenetrable barrier for the canoeist. At times the shore is broken with small sand spits that give some respite from the constant hammering of surf. Unlike Lake Superior, renowned for its high rollers, Winnipeg's waves are steep fronted and choppy. The voyageurs detested the lake because its water is unfit to drink. However, its position provided a key route for both the Hudson's Bay Company and the Montreal-based North West Company

Despite all I had read about its treacherous waters, I was frequently caught unawares. The old voyageur route favoured the west shore, as this provided some let-up in the prevailing nor'westerlies. But in studying maps over the previous winter, I decided to take the east shore. One reason for this decision was the number of risky traverses on the west side. For exactly this reason the Hudson Bay Company preferred to use York boats. These sturdy craft, similar to a Newfie dory, were seaworthy enough to make the long exposed crossings.

The Canadian Shield sets the boundary at the east side, and some interesting islands and granite outcrops contrast the boring terrain to the west. But a principal reason influencing me to follow the east shore came from the traumatic experience of my friend Jerome Orange. The young teacher from France whom I met on the Ottawa River was retracing Mackenzie's voyage to the Arctic. He wrote to tell me he had capsized and nearly drowned in the frigid waters of Lake Winnipeg's west coast.

"Make sure you stick to the east side, John," he warned. "Everything was okay until I was rounding Wicked Point. A wave hit me from the side and over I went. The water was bad."

On my first day out the sun rose to a clear sky with no sign of cumulonimbus or other weather warnings. Ron, unusually quiet, helped me push the canoe into the water. "God, you've got enough grub here to feed a regiment!" he burst out. "Not only that, but it's more like gourmet cuisine than wilderness food." He nodded at my Breton crackers, yoghurt and cans of Coho salmon. He was right. In the first few days I indulged in luxuries, knowing before long it would be porridge and bannock ad nauseum.

"Thanks for everything, Ron." We shook hands and I prepared to shove off.

Then unexpectedly, almost shyly, he asked, "Would you mind if I said a little prayer to ask the Lord to look after you?"

I was deeply touched. Religion and spirituality are usually taboos with guys. But I was anxious to get all the help I could, and we bowed our heads together.

Heading across the bay towards Elk Island, I thought about Ron's moving concern for my safety. He knew well the dangers of the lake. But all the clouds had disappeared, and with the sun shining and a fresh breeze springing up, my sombre mood dissipated. It was time to set up sail. Detaching my new button-down spray cover, I lashed my paddle to the mid-thwart and secured the cover with cord to the top of the paddle.

At once the wind filled the material, bowling me across the water. A great advantage of the arrangement was that I could control the amount of sail and easily dismantle it when the winds became too high.

Elated at my progress, I began to relax. After all, this was my third summer on the water. I knew from experience that the first day was always one of nervous anxiety. But while difficult challenges faced me, I had gained a lot of skills over the past three years. Regaining those skills on the trail would take a little time; I needed to be extra cautious in these early days. No amount of caution, however, could have prepared me for the disaster about to overtake me.

After an easy sail across the bay I was paddling up the east shore with lots of time before sundown to find a camping spot. The beaches were covered in thickly tangled brushwood as far as the eye could see. I must have travelled five kilometres looking for a place to pull up, but eventually a small sand-spit free of tangled trees revealed itself. There was just enough space to pitch my tent and park the canoe. I was careful to haul it well out of the water.

After taking out my sleeping bag and personal pack, I fastened the spray covers, leaving my stores well protected from weather. I rarely took food into the tent. Pleased that the first day had gone so well, I settled comfortably into my sleeping bag and looked over my chart, planning tomorrow's route. Soon I drifted off to sleep.

Crackling flashes of brilliant light woke me up – that, and a peculiar odour I couldn't quite place, probably ozone. A terrible thunderclap that left my ears aching finally drove me from my bed. Through the tent flap, the lightning revealed a frightening sight. While I had set the tent up about ten metres from the water, as far up the beach as possible, the waves were now lapping under my nose! The wind howling across the lake was driving rain hard against the tent, billowing it like a parachute.

One of Lake Winnipeg's malevolent idiosyncrasies is its ability to completely rearrange the shoreline. This was now happening on my tiny piece of beach. I struggled into my clothes as water ran over my feet into the centre of the tent. In a few minutes it and my gear would be carried away. Shoving everything I could into my pack, I rushed outside, dumping it as far from the lapping water as possible.

Terrified the canoe might have blown away, I was relieved to see it was still there, lying on its side. I could only glimpse it now and then through the driving rain, but the angle at which it was lying didn't seem quite right. A lightning flash revealed a sickening sight. The spray cover had been torn back, and the interior was filled to the gunwales with water and sand. My food supply had been swept away! In shock, I lashed some rope around a thwart, securing this to a water-soaked stump. I dragged the tent away from the water and tied it down too.

The wind speed rose close to 100 kilometres. I huddled shivering in the tent, praying it would abate. Waves lapped hungrily at the door, while the pounding rain lashed the tent into a wet sack. Rivulets of water running down the walls gathered on the floor. My sleeping bag was sodden, and there was nowhere to place it that wasn't wet. Finally a pale dawn arose on the storm-tossed waters, and I went out to stretch my aching limbs.

The grey light revealed a dismal scene. The entire sand spit was completely rearranged. My beautiful canoe appeared to be a basket case. It had turned over about 60 degrees, partially disappearing into a sandy pit created by the waves. Tightly packed pebbles, sand and dirt filled the canoe, putting enormous pressure on the frame and bulging the sides. At least two ribs were broken. Adding to this calamity, all of my six-weeks provisions had been swept away.

Not quite. Tucked near the bow I made out one box of dried food that appeared intact. But all my fresh water supplies had gone. This was not the full extent of the calamitous turn of events, however. My paddles had disappeared! Likely they had been swept out on the tumultuous seas that continued to batter the shoreline.

This was a major blow. I struggled to stop my rising panic. Without paddles I was marooned on the meagrely inhabited east shore of the lake. Possibilities for help were almost non-existent. I had flown over this area many times in a Piper Cherokee out of St Andrew's airport outside Winnipeg, and knew that only impenetrable bush and muskeg lay to the east. On the west a tiny spit of shifting sands fronted an enormous lake. North and south were massive entanglements of trees and bushes seeming to weave a continuous wall along the beach. I braced myself from giving in to pessimism. Having weathered other tough situations, I was well aware this creates an emotional dithering that wears you down.

For the moment I refused to think about the loss of my paddles, turning my attention instead to organizing breakfast. Fortunately, I had some provisions – most of them being soup. Enough for a week, or maybe longer, if I strictly rationed my meals.

I moved the tent closer to the muskeg and as far from the water as possible. The rain had ceased for the moment, but the presence of massive cumulonimbus indicated the storm would likely continue. Without fresh water, I would have to find a way to filter the algae-choked lake water. Some large trees blackened from fire lay nearby. I scraped the charred bark off into a cooking pot and picked out as much of the wood fibre as possible. I pounded away with a rock until I had ground it down into a fine black powder. I then gathered small pebbles. From the first-aid kit, I took several gauze dressings, then cut a plastic bottle in half to provide a filter funnel. I planned to use three filters – coarse, medium, and fine – to get rid of as much of the contaminants as possible.

As the primary filter for the raw lake water, I used a sock. The second filtration was through an old chamois cloth. Fortunately, I had several plastic bottles that served as filter funnels when the sock or chamois cloth or gauze dressings were placed around the lip. I filled the dressings with washed sand, pebbles, and carbon particles for the final filtration process.

After pouring raw lake water into the first filter, I was delighted to see it steadily lose its brownish sediment. Beaver fever was unlikely, but I was concerned about toxic fungi. This would have been the last straw. Normally I used water for boiling my food in aluminum foil packets, as well as for making tea. In fact, the same water after heating my food served for tea, hot chocolate or coffee. The final product appeared okay and didn't taste unpleasant.

Watching the water trickle through the funnels, I felt childishly pleased with myself. When there was enough for a pot of tea, I set up my backpack stove and carefully boiled the water. In the damp confines of the tent the tea tasted like nectar. It warmed my insides; the heat from the stove warmed up the tent. My morale zoomed and I began to feel more confident about facing my predicament as a castaway.

Late in the evening the seas appeared to be moderating. Moving the tent had been a good idea as the inside eventually dried out, allowing me to lay the sleeping bag on top of my ground sheet. Sleep wasn't too bad during the night, but next morning the storm was raging as vigorously as ever. I was desperately anxious to get out and start removing the silt and rocks from the canoe. Sediment was pouring into the hull with each wave, creating serious structural stress.

When the storm abated in the mid-afternoon, I grabbed a saucepan and headed out to do battle. The work was backbreaking, as the silt was packed tight. I had to scrape and push the saucepan down like a spade to obtain a decent scoopful. It took me ages to remove about half of the silt. As I sat back to admire my handiwork, the wind suddenly rose. A big wave surged over the canoe, filling it up again to the gunwales with sand, pebbles, and rocks!

Disgusted and weary, I headed back to the tent. The wind continued to rise and the seas again grew violent. Waves over two metres high dashed up the beach, breaking up the packed sand and creating fresh rivers that flowed inside the tent. Exhausted from shovelling, I could make only feeble efforts to try to stop the flood invading my living quarters.

The storm lost strength in the evening, allowing me to get the tent dried out once more. It felt good to no longer stare mesmerized as the water level increased and dry floor space decreased. Except for one pair of pants and a sweater, my clothes were sodden. I headed out once more with pan in hand, attacking the packed muck in the canoe. After I'd got half the silt out, I combed the skies anxiously for signs of better weather. My heart sank. The wind was stiffening.

Scraping and dumping at great speed, I kept one frantic eye on the build-up of waves – to no avail. Once more the canoe was swirling in lake water. Chucking the pot away angrily, I stumbled once more for the tent. I was astonished not only at the ferocity of the weather but also that it could continue from one day to the next with only mild respite. I had been stormbound many times, but it had always been possible to take a stroll along a beach or rocky outcrop and stretch my legs. This marine desert was akin to solitary confinement, a tiny Devil's Island. Lake Superior had been dangerous and sometimes frightening, but this was offset by its sheer magnificence and pristine scenery. Lake Winnipeg, on the other hand, was a spiteful child constantly in tantrums, a malevolent body not to be trusted.

It was now my third night trapped on this narrow strip of beach, and the storm was still lashing the shore. There was no way I could start digging out the canoe again. Everything I had attempted thus far had ended in failure. I wondered whether I hadn't exceeded my own capabilities.

Shaking off this negativity, I concentrated instead on a plan to get the hell off this ghastly piece of beach. Perhaps I could jury-rig something to help turn the canoe over. There was lots of wood and some rope. However, the weight of all the debris in the canoe as well as the unequal strain of the rig could cause the frame to fracture, even break in two. The jury-rig was definitely a last resort.

Another grey morning dawned, but at least the waves were more settled. Spurred on by fear that the weather might deteriorate, I started digging around the canoe to make it easier to turn over, should I manage to free it from the load of muck. On this, my fourth attempt, I could appreciate how Sisyphus felt, spending eternity pushing a rock uphill.

With one eye on the waves, I toiled like a gold-fevered miner sniffing pay dirt. My heart started to race. I was almost scraping the bottom. Was this was going to be my lucky day? As if in response to this optimistic thought, the manitous set up a mocking cacophony as the wind increased. I couldn't believe this rotten bastard of treacherous water!

Dashing around to the other side of the canoe and grabbing it in the middle, I heaved with desperate strength. It lifted halfway. I paused to get my breath. A sense that I was fighting a losing cause started to overwhelm me. Biting my lip, I strained with maniacal fury to turn it over. There was a loud crack – the sound I had been dreading. But the canoe was over, by God. I stood panting, exhausted, fearful but exultant. I had done it!

I hauled her away from the quickly gathering waves. I could see two or three cracked ribs, but overall the damage didn't seem so bad. My relief was overwhelming. Time to celebrate! I brewed some tea, my confidence bouncing back now that the major problem was settled.

Then the old gut-wrenching worries returned. How was I going to launch without paddles?

After savouring the last dregs of my brew I walked down the water's edge, wading in to avoid the tangled brush. I soon realized how irrational the hope was that I was nursing of finding a piece of wood that could be shaped into some sort of paddle. Sifting through a motley collection of branches, deadheads, and other paraphernalia, I found nothing remotely resembling paddling material.

About two kilometres later I figured it was a hopeless quest. On the point of turning back, I caught sight of a familiar shape at the edge of the beach. As I drew nearer, my eyes opened wide until they were the size of organ stops.

I gazed in awe at what lay on the sand. There before me were two paddles! Incredibly, not one – two paddles, side by side as if placed there by some jesting manitou! Amazingly, they were MY paddles.

Tears ran down my cheeks. Defying all known laws of mathematical probability, the paddles had been carried out to sea by a storm lasting three days, drifted around on this enormous lake, then washed up on the same beach. Conceivable, albeit improbable, but just possible, a case could perhaps be made for one paddle. But it defies all logic to think that two unattached paddles could meander together in this storm-bound waterway, then return to the same patch of beach they had disappeared from three days earlier. I sank to my knees.

A miracle? For me it was unquestionably divine intervention. I blurted out grateful thanks.

I clutched the paddles to my chest as if they were priceless articles of booty. I was now free from the threat that had hung over my head of being left to die on a miserable spit of sand. I leaped and danced along the beach, bawling out vulgar ditties from my student days.

After washing the final dirt out of the canoe with my trusty pot, I repaired two of the broken ribs using duct tape. I then launched into the lake to check if any other damage had occurred that could result in leaks. She was bone dry! Paddling back to the beach, I started to load up.

With my food supplies so drastically reduced, this was going to be a light load. The chart revealed the hamlet of Manigotagan nestled in a bay near Clements Point. This small community was the last place on the road from the south. It should be possible to pick up more supplies there.

The canoe was partially in the water, loaded except for the tent. Hurrying over to start dismantling it, I pulled down the poles. Reaching around the other side, I walked straight into a large brown bear!

With the brisk easterly blowing he hadn't picked up my scent. We both stared at each other. I don't know which of us was more astounded, this lumbering giant or myself. In the microseconds before my brain could begin to process the threat, I wasn't even scared. The bear reared up, at least six feet tall!

Then, remarkably for such a large animal, he pirouetted like a ballet dancer, swivelling around. When he had completed this movement, he lumbered off into the muskeg. Despite the highly charged situation, it was quite comical. Then my heart started pounding, adrenalin going into fast-forward. In one lightning move I grabbed the tent and poles, threw them into the canoe, and shoved off, paddling like all the banshees in hell were chasing me.

Reflecting on my narrow escape, I realized how lucky I had been. There had been nowhere to run from the bear – impassable muskeg in front of me, entanglements to the right and left, the water behind. Once again a helpful deity had seen me through.

Anxious to take advantage of moderating weather and a steady wind, I set off down the lake at a fast clip, pulling onshore only for a brief lunch and a coffee break. As the sun started to set, I was delighted to find a spot on a nice flat rocky area with real trees. What a relief it was to set up camp on solid ground after the muddy waterhole of the past three days. After cleaning the tent, I laid it out to dry along with my clothes. It felt wonderful to be free of omnipresent dampness. I crawled into my sleeping bag liberated from the fear that I might die on this godforsaken shore.

The sun was shining brightly through the tent fabric as I awoke. It was a magnificent day, not a cloud anywhere, the water as tranquil as a garden pond. After being wind-bound for so long I was anxious to get back on the lake. It was a pleasure launching on such a beautiful day with the elements all at peace.

My revulsion for the lake diminished. Sigurd Olson had it right when he stated in *Lonely Land*, "As with most expeditions into the wilds when we have endured storms and rapids, cold and sleet and sometimes lack of food, it is ultimately the good things we remember, not the bad."

Well rested, I paddled strongly and before long was surprised to be passing the navigation beacon that marked the small bay leading into the fishing hamlet of Manigotagan. Pulling up to the dock, I tied up and headed for the local general store across the road.

It was a small store with limited supplies. Those available were not what I wanted but would have to suffice. It was nice to have bread again. I also bought corn flakes, drinks, coffee, and jam. Food prices escalated the further north I travelled. When I asked for Magic Pantry's Boil-in-a-Bag, the clerk said. "Sorry, we don't get much call for that kind of thing." No dehydrated supplies were available, and I was forced to buy huge cans of Irish stew. I detested cans because of their weight and bulk. The empty cans cannot be buried because of the danger they represent to wild animals. Wolves especially may be unable to extricate their jaws and end up starving. But leaving empty cans in the canoe presents a major security threat as they generate odours that attract animals, particularly bears.

Still, it was great to have supplies of any kind and I no longer was afraid of running out of food. The storekeeper – "Just call me Don"– told me supplies were available at Berens River, about 100 kilometres further north. "My daughter runs the store there," he said. "Just tell her you spoke to me." Bloodvein Indian Reserve, only about 50 kilometres distant, also had a small store

Don drove me to a campsite about two kilometres down the road and promised to pick me up in the morning and help me load the canoe. At night the rain came on. In the morning the tent and ground were waterlogged. It was still raining when Don appeared with his pickup. As I was leaving, he told me he had a cabin at Hollow River Indian Reserve and offered me the use of it. It was a thoughtful gesture but I politely declined as I wanted to make up for lost time. I found such generous hospitality was the usual custom the further north I travelled, especially in aboriginal communities.

Before I left I called my wife from a public phone. I called Ishbel whenever possible to let her know that all was okay. She had a map of the route and knew exactly where I was at any given time. At the time she was manager of a nursing home in Sharbot Lake, Ontario, but she told me that she could pick up some supplies of Magic Pantry in Kingston and forward them to me at Berens River. I kept quiet about my recent ordeal, and we talked instead about family gossip.

Leaving the deep bay at Manigotagan behind, I entered the lake, immediately taking advantage of a brisk southwesterly wind to get my sail up. Soon I was bowling along at a steady clip. Southeast of the great bulk of Black Island is a small spit of land with a beach marvellously free of flotsam entanglements. First appearances indicated it would make a good camp: the sand was firm and there were lots of shady trees. It was late afternoon but the sun was strong. After I had the tent up I brewed a cuppa and sprawled under a tree to catch up on reading Peter Newman's

Caesars of the Wilderness. I opened a chicken supreme for supper from my last half-dozen Magic Pantry meals, figuring I would use them up before starting my "iron rations."

I watched the sunlight slowly fade across a calm lake. Despite my reservations about this treacherous lake, I was impressed it could appear so beautiful. Waterfowl of all kinds, including Canada Geese, flew overhead. Great masses of white pelicans, my favourite birds, soared and zoomed above the lake. Tiny Arctic terns were darting everywhere. Cormorants raced past, their wingtips barely clearing the waves.

In the morning I noticed a variety of tracks around the beach area, most of them from small animals. Considerable stripping of the bark from a number of trees also indicated the presence of moose or deer. As I paddled out from camp, three bald eagles flew overhead, their white tails flashing in the early morning sun.

I was sorry to leave, but despite the labour-intensive task of making and breaking camp, I made it a practice never to stay more than one night at any place. There were occasions when I regretted having to move on. But I had developed a strict routine and disciplined myself to "working" a 12 to 16 hour day, seven days a week. It was almost a welcome relief whenever I was wind-bound – provided it didn't last too long. I tended to look on it as a holiday from canoeing.

Passing Black Island, I was delighted at the incredible profusion of islands. Usually they meant good camping sites. Past noon it turned incredibly hot. In early days my face had taken a beating from the sun, but with a very powerful sunscreen supplemented with a scarf and hat, I was now prepared. However, sweat was running from every pore. Pulling alongside a rocky islet I hauled the canoe into the shallows and went for a swim. It felt wonderful. My anxiety about this malevolent lake began to slip away. Refreshed, I paddled towards a distant group of islands. Skirting several, I chose one from the enormous selection, setting up camp under some trees.

Next morning I woke up to the tent shaking as wind battered my campsite. Within a few hours the weather had abated, and the seas were relatively calm. Taking advantage of this window, I got underway, but by early afternoon the wind rose steadily again. As the wave heights increased dramatically, I headed for shore.

It was a good move. The temperature dropped rapidly as cold weather fronts went through, one after the other. Unsettled conditions prevailed through the rest of the day, and there was no abatement in the wind by sunset. Once more I marvelled at the patterns of western weather. It seems ready to clear, then the wind intensifies; sometimes it maintains its ferocity, with occasional lulls, for days at a time. Ruefully I realized I would have to rearrange my schedule to fit the weather. This meant more night paddling, which I didn't relish.

The following day started well with a clear sky. But in the afternoon the wind again forced me to set up camp near Loon Narrows ahead of my daily schedule. The beach was strewn with debris, but I was pleased to see a large outcrop of Canadian Shield. Checking the ground over briefly, I set up camp on a huge rock flattened at the top and lying between dense thickets on either side. Approximately 15 metres long by 8 wide, it overlooked the water. The one snag was lugging my gear up the trail to the top. Hauling the canoe well up the beach I secured it to a tree. After setting up the tent, I was ready for my brew-up. Rummaging for my stove in one of the packs, I knelt on the ground, unwrapping the newspaper that kept it free from damp and protected other items in the pack from gas. As I started to prime it, I was startled by several loud snorts.

Looking up I was astonished to see a black bear shuffling across the rock towards me. His shoulders were hunched. In full attack mode, he was ready to charge. And I was the chosen victim!

I reacted by shouting and waving my arms. He was not intimidated and barely slowed. This guy wasn't shy and he was certainly experienced. About five metres away, he stopped and faced up to me. His stance was belligerent. The sight of him standing his ground scared the hell out of me. Surprisingly, he wasn't nosing around for food. This spot must be his favourite patch of territory. I watched him, my heart pounding. Grasping the stove and paper to my chest, I moved slowly backwards, fumbling with one hand in my shirt pocket to find my lighter. I had no idea how far back I'd retreated. I was acutely aware the outcrop ended in a sheer drop of about 15 metres to the water and rocks. Even if I survived the fall, the least I could expect would be a broken leg or arm.

The bear was sizing me up, uncertain how big a problem he was going to have with me. Evidently he made up his mind I was a pushover and started to advance.

My fingers closed on my lighter at last. I prayed that the wick wasn't damp. Then I turned up the fuel lever on the stove and thrust it outwards the full length of my arm. The bear was now about two metres away. I prayed fervently the stove was primed enough to light but not too much or it would spout only a tiny flame. The gas hissed, spewing out a fine spray of naphtha gas.

The bear caught the scent at once. Sniffing loudly, he shook his head derisively, then continued his shuffling advance. I flicked my lighter with one hand, the other poised with paper above the stove. There was a sudden whoosh and a streak of yellow flame leapt outwards. The paper caught immediately. When it was burning fiercely, I threw it at the bear's face.

The effect was dramatic. He stopped in his tracks, reared up like a spooked stallion, then turned aside and ran swiftly down the track towards the beach. My enormous surge of relief gave way to arrogant bravado. I was enraged. The paroxysm of aggression and desire for revenge that swept me was so overpowering that if there had been a stout club at hand I would have pursued him! I resorted to chucking rocks in his direction. "Take that, you big bastard!" I roared after him. I felt a surge of wild elation at having turned the tables.

But I couldn't wallow in self-satisfaction at having frightened him off. This victory was only temporary. He could return anytime. Fortunately, there were great piles of driftwood lying around. Grabbing up all the dry pieces for kindling, as well as huge logs, I piled them in a heap. Dousing the wood with a few drops of my precious stove fuel, I lit the bonfire. Soon flames were leaping into the sky. I kept several long dry pieces close at hand ready to plunge into the flames should the bear make a sudden reappearance.

About an hour later, in the encroaching darkness I saw him emerge from a clump of trees near the beach below. Although he stared across the water at me for a long time, he made no move to cross towards my camp. It was the last I saw of him.

That night I relinquished the comfort of my tent and sat close to the fire. Fortunately, it didn't rain, but I kept watch all night, stoking the flames. I guess I fell asleep a couple of times since I awoke to find the fire burning low.

Packing up next morning, I kept my stove and a wad of paper close at hand. To my relief I saw no more bears on the prowl. Easing away from the beach, I wondered again why this particular bear was so aggressive. Later I learned there was a berry shortage, causing normally shy bears to become mean. Possibly the response was territorial. The area where I was camped may have been a good source of young shoots. and he was ticked off at me for intruding. I was very thankful I happened to be priming the stove when he made his house call. I didn't like to think what would have happened had the stove and paper not been readily available. This brought home to me once again the fact that having some means of defence immediately on your person at all times is the only effective bear strategy.

The suddenness of the attack indicated that the bear might have been stalking me for some time before he made his move. A rifle would have done me little good, besides being an annoying encumbrance to lug around. Many people consider it a tenet of faith that you are protected by a rifle, and it is difficult to convince them otherwise. But experienced aboriginal hunters I met across the country disagreed. Several of these professional bear hunters pointed out that firing a shot into the skull of a bear, unless with a high-powered rifle using titanium-tipped bullets, is useless. The shot is easily deflected due both to the rigidity of the bones and the angling of the skull at about 45 degrees, like armoured plating on a tank. This makes penetration almost impossible. A shot in the heart also has its difficulties since the bear's multiple layers of fibrous tissue are extremely tough. Even if you are a good shot and have the balls to stand your ground and face up to the animal, it takes a cool head and considerable courage to confront an angry bear while efficiently loading and firing.

To make things worse, should you end up wounding the animal, you are now confronted with a savage maddened killer. In my limited experience, when a bear surprises you, there's no time to look around for a weapon. Unless you have a weapon on your person, or near enough to grab, you are plumb out of luck. All that's left is to try to devise some stratagem like playing dead, rearing up to make yourself taller, or banging on a pot and yelling. Native friends convinced me that such strategies depend not only on the circumstances but the species of bear, environment, time of year, food sources, and so on. After my experiences on Lake Winnipeg, I made sure I always had my lighter and paper in my shirt pocket.

The Narrows, a tiny five-kilometre wide stretch between the east and west shores of Lake Winnipeg, suddenly pulls apart as the lake swells from 40 to 100 kilometres wide at some points. Rounding Doghead Point under sail, I was making terrific progress with a strong southeasterly pushing me along. Suddenly the bow dug deeply into a wave trough and in the gusty wind became almost uncontrollable. I was afraid that my canoe might porpoise when the bow plunged. But making such good time, I was reluctant to take down the sail. I kept my fingers crossed that all would be okay. On such occasions I was grateful to the Cree nation for a craft that had the toughness to handle big waves.

Pulling into the mouth of the Bloodvein River, I made for the small village on the Bloodvein Indian Reserve. Tying up at the dock, I headed for the store. My face fell at the sparse supplies. The shelves looked distinctly forlorn. A young girl pointed out a few cans of corned beef and stew, and some jaded cornflake boxes. Apart from soft drinks, there was little else.

Outside I was struck by the community's desolate appearance. Garbage littered the street and it seemed nobody was around. Finally I spotted a man sitting in the open on an old chair in a vacant lot. I strolled over to introduce myself. "Hi, there. Things pretty quiet around here, eh?" I called out as I approached. "So where is everybody?"

My query was greeted with a long pause. The man was about 75 or so, with a distinct tremor in his hand and a frail appearance. He didn't seem in the least surprised to see a stranger. He answered in a thin reedy voice, "Oh, there isn't anybody around yet. I'm just waiting for someone to sober up to take me to the clinic for treatment. Everybody is hung over now, but they'll likely come and take me down there." This was said in a non-judgmental tone. "I get treatment twice a week for my problem. It's Parkinson's disease."

The wasteland around me was like a war scene in the Middle East. Burned-out cars littered the street. The old man's words set amidst this stark scene affected me deeply. Dear God – waiting for someone to sober up to take him to the doctor. His simple uncomplaining logic reflected all the tragedy of alcohol and the Indian reserves.

Not all, I thought, recalling the delightful reserve near Wawa on Superior's shores where booze was banned, children romped in playgrounds, and an aura of well-being permeated the community.

I have never been able to eradicate the image of that forlorn old man. It sticks in my throat that we have the hypocrisy to blandly ignore Third World conditions on our reserves, yet point the finger at other countries to criticize their human rights record. Some years ago, volunteering at Stony Mountain Penitentiary near Winnipeg, I was shocked to learn of the disproportionately high native incarceration rate – at that time nearly 70 per cent of the population in provincial institutions. I shall not forget listening as native men and women recounted their horror stories of alcohol-induced abuse, incest, gang rape, suicide and family breakdown. Alcoholism is astronomically high on Manitoba reserves. Sensitive to native issues, I have tried to help the community when possible. I was delighted during "aboriginal days" at "Stony" to participate as an invited guest during sacred ceremonies. On several occasions I was honoured to take part in sweat-house spiritual events.

Crossing the huge expanse of Bloodvein Bay, the ferry between Matheson Island and Bloodvein honked in salute as it passed close by, scaring the life out of me. With the weather so good and the winds fair, I was able to haul up the sail for a couple of hours. Overnighting at Rabbit Point near Princess Harbour, I was off next day across the bay to Split Rock Point. Fresh winds came up again from the southeast, and I had an exciting sail for more than ten kilometres.

Further along the lake at Catfish Point there was a large fish processing plant. I changed direction to check it over. The manager,

David from Riverton, was especially knowledgeable on Lake Winnipeg history. He told me about finding several flint-heads on the beaches. Researchers at the University of Manitoba placed their age at some 2,000 years.

The previous year someone had stopped by at the plant sailing a replica of a miniature Viking ship about five metres in length. The man, an amateur historian, was working on a theory that Vikings came to Lake Winnipeg. He intended heading towards Norway House, then by a series of lakes towards the Nelson River to Hudson Bay, to check out the feasibility of his theory. It is difficult to believe that a voyage down the fierce Nelson River could have been possible without canoes. Albeit it was not impossible, since the Hudson Bay Company had great success with York boats, clumsy large craft similar to Newfie dories. But manhandling these heavy, unwieldy boats through rapids was exhausting, and they had to be dragged or winched over numerous gruelling portages.

A man I met at Catfish Creek I shall not readily forget. His ancient tattered clothes, topped by a battered cloth hat, were set off by a great bushy beard and unkempt straggly hair down his back. He would certainly have raised many an eyebrow even on Portage and Main. But appearances are deceptive, for he was an inspiring and unique character if ever there was one. "Old Sasquatch," as he was termed by everyone at the plant, was a remarkably resilient man embraced and healed by wilderness.

Like too many former vets from World War II, he had holed up in squalor in a room on Winnipeg's skid row. His life was a lonely existence between pension cheques, the tavern, and oblivion. Befriended by the manager of the fish processing plant at Catfish Creek, he finally found the courage one day to put his wasted years behind him. Leaving his squalid existence, he set himself up in a disused 100-year-old cabin close by the plant as his summer residence. Incredibly, he stayed there throughout the formidable Northern Manitoba winter.

Sober now for years, he enjoys a life with many "friends" – bears, wolves, coyotes, fox, beaver, pelicans, even a bevy of mallard ducks! Any form of life is welcome at his cabin. Animals sense that he is a friendly presence and that the area around his cabin is a sanctuary. He will not allow anyone to shoot them. Having no electricity, he cuts his lumber and pulls it by sled to the cabin. Harsh winters with temperatures of minus 50°C do not bother him. He has found not only sobriety in the harsh Canadian wilderness but also peace and a life of spiritual fulfilment. What more could one want?

I've often thought of Old Sasquatch and the contentment he found living out a spartan existence in the north. Henry David Thoreau had it right:

I went to the woods because I wished to live deliberately to front only the essential facts of life and see if I could not bring what it had to teach and when I came to die, discover that I had not lived. I wanted to suck out of life deep and suck out all the marrow of life, to live steadily and spartan like as to put to rout all that was not life.

When I asked how Old Sasquatch got his name, David laughed heartily and told me. One day a young rookie pilot on his first trip up north in the supply plane flew into camp from Winnipeg. The camp was deserted as all the men were out fishing. Searching around for someone to help him unload, he came round by the log cabin and walked straight into the old guy. He happened to be "talking" to one of his "friends," a large black bear. Terrified, the young fellow raced back to the dock and took off fast. Later, when the manager called Winnipeg to find out what happened to the plane and supplies, the dispatcher said that the pilot came back highly agitated. He swore he had actually seen a Sasquatch talking to a bear!

After making my farewells, I was walking to my canoe when there was a shout from one of the buildings. Furiously beckoning from the cookhouse was a figure in white, Jim, the native cook. "You've got to try my speciality," he insisted, handing me a package. "It's a bannock burger, Indian style," he said, laughing. "Try it for your lunch. You'll really enjoy it."

Nibbling a corner, I was impressed. Bannock is a great Indian dish, but with sausage it tastes delicious. I stuffed it in my pack. I was touched by the wonderful hospitality and sorry to be leaving such friendly people. Sometimes it gets lonely on the trail, and it brings joy to the heart to meet people who share what little they have. The salt of the earth, such individuals make life worth living.

8

The Longest Crossing

The weather turned sullen as I left Catfish Creek. During my crossing of Pigeon Bay the clouds lowered dramatically. The winds rose and soon were shrieking at about 80 kilometres per hour. By the time I drew into a beach, the lake was a mass of foaming white. It was impossible to even think of trying to get the tent up. I hauled the canoe well out of the water and inserted myself between the packs by wiggling furiously under the spray covers. When I closed them over my head, it was like being in a cocoon.

I dozed off, awakening to find that the wind had dropped a bit. The temperature had also plunged drastically. I learned later that at Berens River it had fallen to minus 3° Celsius and there was snow on the ground.

Leaping out of my sleeping quarters, I had the tent up in no time. With the stove hissing away, the tent was soon comfortably warm. I brewed up some tea, grateful that my supplies for the "cup that cheers" were still intact.

By early afternoon the lake was still choppy – dicey, but manageable. I decided on launching immediately. The trip became quite precarious at times as the canoe was thrown around by the unpredictable wind. Berens River, though in sight, would have to wait till tomorrow. I made a mad dash for a landing on Pigeon Point, a small spit of land not far from the Berens River Indian Reserve. That night it turned bitterly cold again. In the morning a brisk north wind made for a chilly ride. However, two magnificent bald eagles that swooped down almost on my head made up for it.

Berens River, a mere 10 kilometres off, should have been an easy trip. However, the best-laid plans often go awry, and a squall line came up and blew me all over the lake. With the wind dead in my face, I was exhausted trying to maintain direction. If I rested my aching arm even for a moment, the wind pushed me back, and I had to paddle frantically to get back on course. Eventually I spotted a tiny rock about a kilometre ahead, covered in spray. I was desperate to take a breather, but it was difficult to make progress. If the wind turned me around, I would be blown back to my starting point, now several kilometres behind me. Angrily, I plunged my paddle deep, at times rising to a standing position to get forceful thrusts. Ever so slowly that rock came tantalizingly closer. Even when I was within a few metres I didn't think I was going to make it. My arms had no feeling. But that slimy rock, about two metres high and a metre wide, was a haven.

Thankfully, I swung the canoe around broadside to it. The wind pinned me safely against it and I let my arms hang limp.

Deep in the confines of my day pack I discovered half a Mars bar I had forgotten about. I devoured it, relishing the sweet chocolate filling my mouth. About 20 minutes later, my energy renewed and the squalls abated, I headed across the bay and set up camp.

As I pulled into Berens River early next morning, my eye was caught by a sign advertising breakfast at the Berens River Lodge. Bacon and eggs. Yummy! I tied up at the dock and headed down the road. It felt good to exercise my cramped legs. After an excellent breakfast, the lodge owner, Jack Clarkson, came over and introduced himself.

Jack, a bush pilot pioneer, was interested in my trip and we spent some time discussing various topics including local politics. He told me that because of the high oxygen content of the water, Berens River had the finest fishing in the province. "People come from all over Canada, the U.S and Europe to our lodge." He pushed his chair back and got up from the table. "Why don't you take a break from camping and stay? On the house, of course, glad to have you."

It was an invitation I couldn't refuse. When I left to get my overnight gear, Jack added, "By the way, the teachers are having an end of term party tonight, and you're welcome."

After wilderness camping under quite primitive conditions, the comforts in the lodge were overwhelming. I revelled in a hot shower, sloughing off the ingrained dirt from my body, making me feel like a new man. When I came downstairs the party was in full swing. I wandered around talking to people and answering questions about Mackenzie. It was pleasant, but I was so used to isolation that I found it hard to take in the loud music and shouted conversations and soon headed upstairs. It felt wonderful slipping under the sheets of a beautiful soft double bed. Still, I found it hard to get to sleep. My body took a while to adjust to the soft life.

In the morning I went to check at the post office for a package from Ishbel. She'd promised to forward a new supply of Magic Pantry. To my delight, it was waiting for me. I was elated. I called her from the phone outside to let her know that I'd received the package and gave her my route up to Grand Rapids. It felt great to make contact with home. I explained that some native fishermen on the lake had volunteered to pass on messages, so if she got a call from a strange guy, she would know what it was about. We spoke for a while about our grandchildren, particularly the triplets, and it was nice to hear that all was well on the domestic front. Of course I didn't mention my harrowing experiences on the isolated sand spit or my bear encounters.

Glen Woodford, manager of the local Northern Store, gave me a tour of Berens River. The community depends heavily on fly-in tourism. Later he invited me over to his place for supper. T-bone steaks were on the menu, a real treat in isolated communities up north.

The Northern Store is a large chain operation throughout much of northern Canada. It functions on a marketing principle that acknowledges links to the old North West Company. The Nor'wester stores flourished in bitter competition with their fur trade rivals, the English-run Hudson Bay Company. In contrast, the North West Company was comprised almost entirely of Scots, most of them proud veterans of Bonnie Prince Charlie's defeated army at Culloden, bonded by ancient clan ties. The company amalgamated with the Hudson Bay Company in 1821. In 1990 the company changed its corporate name to the North West Company, and the trading name of its retail operations to the Northern Company. Considering the deadly enmity between the two companies, each plotting to take over the other, this move must have had the Nor'westers rolling in their graves with glee.

The Northern Company uses a flag similar to that used by the old North West Company. As I was leaving, Glen presented me with a flag and a Tilley hat. I told him I would fly the flag from my stern as the old Nor'wester voyageurs did. "Just hope you don't meet any Bay men on the waters," he cracked as I paddled away.

I was determined to put on a power push this year and reach Peace River by fall. I would then be well positioned for next year's final objective, Mackenzie's Rock, near Bella Coola. I wanted desperately to be there for the bicentenary anniversary of Mackenzie's landing of July 22, 1793.

About 100 kilometres further north, the wind in my face, I struggled to maintain course towards Poplar Point, hugging the shoreline to take advantage of the windbreak. Conscious of movement above me on the hilly craggy shore, I was amazed to see a lynx sprawled on the grass about two metres above the water. He seemed unperturbed at my presence, an almost mischievous grin on his face. His attention was focused on two ducks swimming below him. Like a big pussy-cat, he pawed at the grass as if beckoning the ducks to come up and play. The wise ducks played the same game, swimming just within reach of his perch, then quickly swimming away, knowing he dared not jump in the water after them. Eventually the lynx gave up. It was a truly theatrical performance.

A Mallard swam almost across my bow with two little ones. She took off with the babies threshing the water wildly behind her. A few kilometres further along, two otters, always inveterate show-offs, surfaced right beside me, turning over on their backs and demonstrating incredible gymnastics. It cheered me no end meeting animals on the trail (with the distinct exception of bears) – a kind of wilderness camaraderie.

A little further on I passed a large bald eagle dead in the water. It looked like its neck was broken. Possibly it had been diving to attack the ducks and miscalculated the water depth. I came across many such birds. Eagles seem to have a propensity for this kind of flying accident. As many as 40 per cent don't survive their first flight. Since the mature eagle is able to spot fish from hundreds of feet above, it is likely that eyesight in the young eagle develops slower than other faculties, influencing its ability to perceive depth. But even experienced seaplane pilots can fly straight into the water when glassy water conditions prevail. This phenomenon occurs when the water is dead calm with no visual cues to determine depth. Some pilots drop an object like a cushion to create ripples on the surface.

One of my concerns travelling the eastern side of Lake Winnipeg was that sooner or later I would have to cross the huge expanse from east to west to reach the Saskatchewan River. I intended to cross at the shortest distance when safe passage could be made. Long Point, 60 kilometres south of Grand Rapids, is a great spit of land that stretches out like a pointer into the lake on the west side. It has a lighthouse, ideal for navigation if I was caught out in darkness. This is the shortest route to Poplar Point, 50 kilometres distant.

I was dreading this passage. Jerome Orange had written from France to warn me of the dangers. He told me that in October 1991 he capsized near Long Point, spending five days marooned on the beach recuperating from hypothermia and shock. "Take great care, have patience, stay close to shore," he warned.

The prairie winds roar across this wide expanse. If I got caught in them, they would blow me all the way back to the east coast. There were no sheltering islands. But, I thought hopefully, it was almost the end of June and there should be a good weather window. All I had to do was wait patiently, as Jerome had advised, and study the cloud formations. "If in doubt, get out" was my motto.

Eventually the outline of George Island became visible. This was where I would be heading when I was sure the weather was okay, en route to Long Point, now about 50 kilometres on the other side of the lake. The weather was calm, but I decided to call it a day. I did myself proud for supper that evening, selecting Salisbury steak from my Magic Pantry stores, along with tomato soup and bread. Dessert was mixed fruit cocktail, topped off by digestive biscuits with honey and (naturally) Tetley tea. Walking along the beach afterwards, I felt a lot more confident. It's curious how a good supper can allay an attack of nerves.

But next morning the weather was misty and rainy. I decided to stay put in camp. It was the same in early afternoon. Bored to tears, I decided to line the canoe along the beach towards Marchand Point, about six kilometres away, my stepping-off point for George Island 15 kilometres offshore. Lining was my usual procedure in fast water and rapids, but I never thought I would have to haul the canoe along a lake. It was exhausting, and I was glad when I reached a tiny cove that looked like a great camping spot. The weather was fine now. I sprawled on the beach, nursing my aching body.

There was a roar overhead and a Piper Cherokee zoomed low over the waves. I could see by the paint it was pretty beat up. It was only about 50 feet above me, apparently heading towards a landing about five kilometres across a large bay. I wondered what on earth it was doing in this isolated part of the country. I climbed to the top of a small mound to see if I could spot an airstrip. There was some indication of one about seven kilometres away. Thoughtfully, I made my way back to camp.

In a flash the penny dropped. About eight years before, the Aviation Interfaith Ministry, a Christian group for people in aviation, used to meet at the Winnipeg International Airport once a week. One evening I listened to a talk being given by Milt Menzies, who represented a Christian foundation called the Shantymen's Association. Shantymen provide spiritual help to those in dire straits. The name comes from Depression times in the Dirty Thirties when thousands of homeless men lived in shanties – cardboard lean-tos – around cities in the U.S.

Milt Menzies' mission was to aid disadvantaged youths from the Saultaux First Nations. A senior captain with Air Canada, he gave up an interesting career to become a Shantyman. The association provides no funds. His wife, Wendy, joined him. The couple built a summer holiday camp for abused native children up north. Milt has an old Piper Cherokee in which he travels around the outlying reserves. The area where I saw the plane land just might be Milt's camp.

Jumping into the canoe, I headed across the bay. Hauling the canoe up onshore, I looked up to see a man emerging from a large building about 100 metres away. Intuitively, I knew it was Milt. "Milt Menzies, I presume," I shouted.

Startled, he looked towards me, then burst out laughing. "Good heavens. Where did you come from?"

Milt told me he was setting up the camp for summer and had just flown in from the Saultaux reserve at Fairfax further south. "You've got to meet Wendy. We'd love you to stay for a meal."

After a delightful supper, the three of us spent a pleasant evening discussing their work. Milt was delighted to hear that on a recent Air Canada flight I had taken to Los Angeles, some of the cabin crew were members of the Winnipeg Aviation Fellowship. They plied me with treats and prior to landing invited me into the cabin to take in the sights. There I discovered the captain was also a fellowship member! It was one of the best flights I've ever been on. My special treatment prompted a fellow passenger to ask, "How come they're giving you the royal treatment? Are you a VIP?"

As I took my leave, Milt said a prayer for my continuing safety on the lake. Crossing the bay towards my own camp as the sun was setting, I pondered the remarkable coincidence in meeting with this dedicated couple who have found fulfilment in the remote Manitoba wilderness. It takes remarkable individuals to walk away from a comfortable lifestyle to live on meagre resources while following a spiritual discipline. Unfortunately, before I left, I learned that Wendy had cancer and was receiving treatment in Winnipeg.

During the night a tremendous storm came up. Violent winds shook the tent, and the fly flapped madly. In the morning the lake was a boiling fury. Fortunately my canoe was well away from the beach, tied to a tree. I checked repeatedly to make sure the tent was secure and well pinned down. I was pleased there were no leaks despite the intensity of the driving rain. In fact, with the stove hissing merrily away for morning tea, it was most comfortable.

In the afternoon the winds increased to over 100 kilometres. Waves dashed to the door of the tent. Cuddled in my sleeping bag with several interesting books, I didn't mind what was going on outside. Besides, since I couldn't go to "work," I might as well enjoy my holiday. This happened so frequently it was becoming routine to accept that I would be stormbound one day out of three.

The storm continued into evening and then into night for a second day. The following day the wind dropped for an hour or two in early evening, then increased again. I walked along the beach, pleased that I could at least stretch my limbs and blow away the cobwebs of my enforced isolation. I was shocked at the violence of these storms, particularly when I contemplated crossing this huge expanse of lake with no possibility of sheltering islands. It was a thought I found myself brooding over. I was not too concerned about the initial crossing to George Island, some 15 kilometres due west. It was the great unknown beyond that worried me.

On the third morning my prayers were answered. The sun rose on a gentle lake. Elated, I hurried to get the tent down and packed the canoe. With a benign following wind, I arrived at the island early in the afternoon. A big ship appeared to be anchored almost on the shore as I drew close. Its brilliant red and white colour indicated that it was a coastguard vessel, likely checking on the buoys and other navigational markers along the lake. With the shallow waters and shifting sandbars, navigating these shores must be a constant hazard.

I made camp about a kilometre along the beach from the ship. No sooner was the tent set up when I heard the sound of a motor. An all-terrain vehicle with huge balloon tires came roaring across the beach towards me, and the driver jumped off and thrust out his hand. "Jeeze, we don't see many canoes on this lake. Frank Gnitzinger, pleased to meet you. I'm the chief officer on the CCGS *Namao*. That's the tub you see along there." He pointed towards the ship. We chatted a while as I explained the purpose of my trip. As he was about to leave, Frank extended an invitation to dinner.

I washed, shaved, and walked down the beach. It seemed strange to be going out to dinner in the middle of nowhere! I was curious to see that unlike most coastguard vessels, this one had a flat bottom. That explained why she was able to beach onshore, probably a necessity for these treacherous waters.

Boarding was not easy. A very long wooden ladder leaned at an angle of 45 degrees against the bow. As I rose steadily higher, the ladder kept bouncing. I was sure I was going to miss my step. What a joke that would be – surviving this bloody lake and then breaking my neck falling off a ladder!

"Permission to come aboard, Captain," I shouted towards the wheelhouse. A cheerful wave beckoned towards the bridge. I felt like a bum in my mud-caked clothes, more so when I walked into the fastidiously clean control centre where the sprucely dressed officers awaited my arrival. The floors gleamed, the polished brasses shone.

"Welcome aboard. Vic Isidoro, captain of the *Namao*," a friendly voice greeted me. The captain showed me around the wheelhouse, explaining the various duties of the navigator on the ship. When he asked me about my trip, I explained my route from the Winnipeg River up the east coast during the past week and also my destination on the west coast of the lake. He looked concerned about my crossing such a large chunk of lake in an open boat. My heart did somersaults as he pointed to a chart. He then took a pair of dividers and plotted the most direct course to Long Point on the west side. It was an incredible 55 kilometres. However, I breathed a sigh as he went on to say that there were two islands, Sandy Island and Cannibal Island, about 30 kilometres west of George Island.

As we sat chatting in the wheelhouse, Captain Isidoro asked for my home number. A moment later he handed me the radiotelephone. Ishbel answered immediately, surprised to hear I was calling from a ship. All was fine, and our triplet grandchildren, now almost two years old, were in great shape. She promised to send me some more Magic Pantry dinners to general delivery at Grand Rapids.

The captain gave me a tour of the ship, then led me to the officers' wardroom for dinner. Around the table sparkling glassware and gleaming cutlery were laid out on starched white tablecloths. I really felt out of place in my sweaty, grubby clothes, but no one seemed to mind. The friendly officers plied me with questions, making it clear I was considered their guest of honour for the evening!

A steward in whites handed me a menu and poured the wine. The soup was delicious, as were the grilled lamb chops, mint sauce, boiled potatoes and carrots that followed. Dessert was strawberries and ice cream, followed by coffee and cognac. I found the contrast with my primitive living conditions surreal – indeed, almost overwhelming.

Eventually, stuffed to the gills, I took my leave, offering profuse thanks to my hosts. When I complimented cook Bill Persity on an excellent dinner, he told me to hold on and returned a moment later with a bag of fresh bread. I had mentioned to the steward at dinner that the one thing I missed was a fresh loaf. This spontaneous gesture was in keeping with tradition that those serving at sea share with one another.

The next day I made camp at the other side of the island. Two of the *Namao*'s crew came round on their ATVs to give me a send-off. They handed me a package with a picture of the ship signed by all the crew. I was sorry to be leaving such a warm-hearted group. I would not forget their wonderful hospitality.

At sun-up next day, I headed for Big Sandy Island. It was a long haul, but it was a magnificent day and I struck out vigorously. The weather looked okay and I felt confident all would be well. A short time later, a nor'easterly wind rose to about 15 kilometres, and I decided to put the sail up. Soon I was moving briskly across gentle waves and looking forward to a smooth and safe passage. After an hour the wind dropped abruptly and I dismantled the sail. My great fear was that a norwesterly might start up, forcing me to battle heavy winds and giant waves.

My heart sank as the wind freshened. I paddled briskly, but the wind increased. Rising up in the canoe, I thrust my new stikine paddle deep. Following one very deep thrust there was a mighty crack, and the handle broke in two. I fell forward, landing on the spray cover. There was another great crack as the wood frame supporting the canvas cover caved in. The canoe rocked alarmingly from side to side. I was almost thrown into the water. It was a damned close thing. Picking myself up carefully, I grabbed the other paddle.

Fortunately the wind dropped, giving my nerves a break. Adhering rigidly to compass and map, after a long, strenuous paddle, I saw Sandy Island ahead through a warm haze. A pleasant little cove on a pebbly beach looked like an excellent place to stop.

After making camp, I took a stroll towards the other side of the island. To my surprise a large fishing boat was tied up at the dock. A weather-beaten man in his sixties was fixing nets. He didn't seem startled to see a stranger. "Come on aboard," he called out heartily. " I just put the kettle on. We'll have a cuppa tea." He stuck out his hand. "I'm Raymond Valiquette from Poplar River Indian Reserve. Actually, really Black River close to it."

Raymond's boat, made of steel with high flared bows to ward off ice floes in the spring, looked capable of handling all weather conditions. "Yeah, she's a pretty tough old gal, no doubt," he agreed, pleased at my appreciation of his boat. After some thirty years on the lake he had a fund of interesting stories.

"The biggest problem we have is the competition – those goddamned cormorants. They dive down deep, cutting and slashing among the whitefish, grabbing one but wounding two or three in the process which die later. Bastards are a pain in the neck, wasting good fish. Then those assholes in government tell us we're over-fishing."

I was astonished when he said that last year a group of irate fishermen had defied the government, which forbids any culling of the birds. Armed with shotguns, they killed over 25,000 of the competitive cormorants! As I took my leave to explore the rest of the island, he invited me back for supper. "Whitefish, naturally. We've got lots now." He grinned.

Towards evening I made my way back to Raymond's boat. Two young Indian men were busily cleaning the decks and greeted me as I stepped aboard. Raymond had the whitefish already cooking, and we sat around chatting and drinking tea until supper was ready. He said he was leaving the next day for his home base.

He was concerned about my long haul across the lake to Long Point. When I told him how my paddle had broken, he chuckled. "It wouldn't have broke if an Indian had made it!" I reassured him there was no way I was going to leave the island until a good weather window and a nor'easter appeared to help me along. After one of the best whitefish suppers I've eaten, we shook hands and I promised to send a postcard from Grand Rapids.

Next day the weather was poor and I spent the time fixing the cradle for the spray covers. The following day was similar. On the third day of my island stay I didn't get much sleep and rose very early. The weather looked like it might be okay. From a rocky outcrop I scanned the horizon, repeating my weather watch every hour. The sun was now up and the seas were still calm as a millpond with no wind, but that didn't mean a thing on this malicious body of water. I spent more time agonizing over whether to leave than for any other challenge on the trail. My stomach was in knots.

I decided to compromise. I would head out to approximately the halfway point. If it looked like the weather was turning nasty, I would make a 180-degree turn back to my island haven.

This trip was much more dangerous than any open crossing I had made. It was 30 kilometres from Cannibal Island to Kiche Point light at the extreme end of Long Point. This was predicated on my travelling in an unwavering line with no deviation for current or wind. There was no safe haven en route. I spent some time organizing my paddling for a very long day. My food supplies I placed strategically around me so that I could reach them easily. The stove was fuelled and ready between my legs so that I could light it and, with painstaking care, brew up some tea or make some soup. This is a tricky thing to do on a canoe while underway, but over the years I had become quite expert.

Three hours later the water was still tranquil. It was possible to lay my paddle down and relax while having something to eat. The spray cover top served as a useful table. Never before on this lake had I been able to get away with this sort of relaxed behaviour.

The exceptionally serene weather continued. By mid-afternoon it was baking hot and I was dripping with sweat. My eyes were sore and my head ached even although I wore sunglasses. Then, unexpectedly, the wind started to rise. I struggled to stifle an anxiety attack at the thought of facing a strong nor'wester. I was now approaching the point of no return. Fortunately, after about an hour, the wind dropped.

My course was northwest but I somehow became convinced Kiche Point light lay further north, so I inadvertently assumed a northerly course. Despite paddling strongly towards what I figured was the coast at Long Point, the outline did not get any closer. Doubts nagged me. It was likely a mirage. I had experienced this phenomenon several times paddling westwards when the sun was strong and the water calm. I'd spent hours steering a course to nowhere. Obviously there was no landmark on the horizon, just a tantalizing illusion! Always trust your compass and your chart, I berated myself as I turned further west.

The sun was almost down. The thought of being stuck out on this perfidious lake in the dark galvanized me, and I paddled like hell. Suddenly, straight ahead, a beacon flashed across the water. The white light vanquished the oncoming darkness, giving me an unmistakable fix to home onto. I was thrilled. My course was now bang on target. No question that dead ahead lay the light on Kiche Point.

I'd left at sun-up to arrive after sundown on Yankee Independence Day, after paddling some eighteen hours – like Wrong-Way Corrigan for some of that time. I didn't have an ounce of energy left to look for a camping spot. I simply headed for the lighthouse and hauled my canoe up the rocks and out of the water. Every bone in my body ached. I got the tent up in a half-assed way and threw my sleeping bag inside. It was sheer bliss slipping into sleep.

It seemed only minutes later that I felt my head being nudged. Sleepily, I pulled away from the tent fabric, wondering why my face was wet. Just as I was drifting off again, I heard a growl. A coyote? A wolf? Shuffling sounds indicated it was a bear.

Shit! Not now. My numbed brain remembered my previous encounter. Fire – where's my lighter? What to burn? In the pocket of the tent I found a plastic bag that I used to wrap my books. Grabbing it, I tried to light it. Outside the tent door I could hear pawing and shuffling. Incredibly, another growl came from the rear of the tent. There were two bears outside!

Holding my lighter to the plastic bag produced no flame but a stream of pungent smoke. I cursed my stupidity in not taking precautions for bear encounters. I held the smoking bag to the tent door. This produced a loud snorting and sneezing. After that, blessed silence. The fellow at the rear must have joined his buddy, because I heard no more activity.

Risking a peek outside, I saw no sign of movement. I was puzzled to find my face was sticky, then realized it came from the bear's saliva as he licked my face through the tent.

With no more plastic bags or anything else to burn, I went out to the canoe and brought in my backpack stove as well as a pot and some spoons. These would make an unholy racket should my unwelcome guests decide to return.

Next morning I awoke stiff and every bone aching and my face burning. Disentangling myself from my bed, I heard shuffling and snorting. Through the tent flap I saw a black bear walking into camp. Grabbing a pot and a spoon, I leaned out, banging like the clappers, shouting and screaming at the top of my voice. It worked – the intruder high-tailed it into the bush. I reminded myself to pick up a whistle at the next hardware store.

Forgoing breakfast, I didn't even take the tent down but chucked it into the canoe and launched. All around my campsite was a profusion of bear scat. Just my luck to set up camp at their fishing hole!

A short piece down the lake I saw a boat parked on the beach. A young aboriginal fellow was sitting beside it cleaning fish. Hauling up my canoe, I stopped to chat. He looked amazed when I told him I had crossed over from the east side.

"Sonofabitch, man, you took a very big chance. That can be a real bitch of a lake. I'm Albert Campbell, by the way, from Grand Rapids."

He figured I must have paddled 50 kilometres across the lake. Albert was a very friendly guy, a cousin of First Nations Assembly Chief Ovide Mercedi. He volunteered to call my wife to let her know I would soon be in Grand Rapids. As I was leaving, he handed me a whitefish. I tucked it well under the spray cover to keep it fresh.

After only a couple of hours paddling my body was protesting. My legs were stiff and cramped. Yesterday's marathon crossing had worn me thin. It was time to find a nice beach and take a day off. I spotted a hard-packed stretch of sand and several shady trees – just what I needed. Resting, reading and a stroll along the beach occupied my day. It felt great to be off the lake, relaxing like a tourist.

Incredibly, next morning I again awoke to a cacophony of snorts and grunts. A young black bear was snuffling around the canoe. I could have kicked myself, suddenly remembering the whitefish I'd put in there. I'd meant to cook it for last night's supper. Fortunately, after a steady drumbeat on the pot and lots of yelling, he took off.

Later, rounding Sturgeon Point, I followed my usual routine of scanning the horizon on either side of the canoe for weather clues that might indicate trouble. All was serene, a lovely day. But something was strange. It was quiet, peculiarly so. Gulls – in fact, birds of any form – were conspicuously absent. No fishing boats plied the lake. It didn't make sense: they should be taking advantage of the fine weather.

I pushed this anomaly aside and continued on my way. The sandy beaches changed abruptly to a continuous rocky shore. I felt wind rustling my neck. The significance of this finally hit: the wind was from the south! When I stopped paddling to turn around, I gaped in dismay. Just a few kilometres behind me, the sky was filled with wispy dark clouds. A squall line!

Before my eyes the waves grew taller. Rollers swept the canoe towards a shoreline of jagged rocks. There wasn't even a tiny spit of sand to crawl onto. I turned the bow in a desperate bid to head out into the lake, away from the dangerous pull driving me towards shore.

The winds, shrieking like a coven of malevolent manitous, quickly built the waves to an astonishing three metres. It seemed ludicrous to have survived a great traverse of the lake only to be battered to pieces on a ragged beach. Concerned that my canoe would be porpoised and over-ended, I quickly gave up my attempt to strike out and lined up horizontally with the shore. The waves sent me up and down the troughs like a roller-coaster. I paddled furiously, hoping against hope that the interminable line of rocks would end.

Once again I had put myself in a very difficult situation. I could easily have landed on a beach before the storm came up. Now I was battling a line of squalls that threatened to blow me out of the water. The story of my life: from relative tranquillity to high-stress terror. Would I ever learn?

My eyes swept the shore, desperately searching for a break in the rocky fortress. My arms ached from deep-thrust paddling and from contorting my body to balance the canoe's rolling. Suddenly I saw a break in the rock line. A small sandy cove opened up dead ahead. Eureka!

At the first lull in the waves, I turned the bow 90 degrees towards shore. Occasionally a rogue wave changed direction, thrusting upwards at the bow and making the canoe rear like a bucking bronco. The rollers from behind snared me in the surf. I fought to maintain direction as the canoe raced towards the opening. The entrance to the cove was only about six metres wide.

I swept past two giant rocks guarding the entrance. The storm noise abated instantly. I was now paddling over a stretch of barely rippling water. The cove was protected by high rising ground and trees, almost isolating it from the lake.

I tossed my paddle high into the air and threw myself spread-eagled on the sand. A glorious sense of freedom coursed through me. Once more I thanked the Great Spirit for deliverance.

I was still aching when I rose late next morning. It was a calm, clear day as I launched. After several hours of paddling, I turned past a headland. My chart indicated it must be Scots Point. This was an unexpected revelation. It's wonderful to find that you're further along than you thought and really boosts the morale. So it was today, as I swung around the point and into the Saskatchewan River. I was sure it would have taken at least another two days. To be finally free of this temperamental body of water felt like getting out of jail. I had reached the continental halfway mark!

From this river I would paddle down the Churchill, the Clearwater, the Athabasca and then the Peace to the mighty Fraser, and finally hike across the coastal mountains to the Pacific. I was filled with emotion, as Mackenzie was when he passed through.

Reaching this great river, the gateway to Western Canada, was an accomplishment that thrilled me to the core and I shed a few tears. It was a major milestone on in my pilgrimage across Canada's vastness to Mackenzie's Rock.

Passing under the impressive bridge that spans the river at Grand Rapids, I searched the high terrain along the banks for a camping spot. On the right bank was a billboard: "Riverview Cabins Fishing Camp, Colin

McKay, Host." I pulled in. No one was about but the soft grass was so inviting I sprawled out gratefully. Later, I set up camp and had a cursory look around but failed to find the owner. Sleep came very easily that night.

I awoke refreshed, my muscles no longer aching. It was a lovely morning, and a stroll along the riverbank with the air smelling sweetly was a great way to start the day. Looking down from the tall embankment, at the point where the Saskatchewan River flows into Lake Winnipeg, I wondered what it must have been like when Mackenzie first saw it, a fearsome sight as it plunged 200 metres in a foaming cataract of awesome power. Sadly, it was now tamed for hydroelectric power.

When I lived in Winnipeg I learned from my native friends how the building of the power dam created irreparable harm to a fragile ecosystem. The huge project also caused enormous upheaval for the aboriginal population. Their ancient fishing, trapping and hunting pursuits were disrupted. The headwaters of the lake, formed when the Saskatchewan was diverted, resulted in a vast body of water, considered globally as the tenth largest man-made lake, but a treacherous one. The constantly fluctuating water levels create serious marine hazards with deadheads and trees lurking just below the surface. In grudging admission that they hadn't quite got it right, Manitoba Hydro paid out a paltry $5,000,000 as compensation for the economic and social damage done to the band.

"Good morning." The booming salutation shook me from my reverie. Turning, I saw a well-built native man in his fifties walking across the lawn. "Colin McKay. Heard all about you from Albert Campbell." It never ceased to amaze me how the bush telegraph works. Everybody knows about you.

I asked Colin if he minded me using a patch of his grass. "No problem. But you ain't going to stay here. You're going to have a cabin," he announced, as if it was all settled. "That one up there," he said, pointing to a pretty log cabin at the top of the hill.

I protested that I didn't mind tenting on the grass. In fact, I preferred it, since I found it hard sometimes to adjust to civilized comforts. Colin was insistent. To reinforce he meant what he said, he grabbed the canoe under one of his huge arms and deposited it on the lawn outside the cabin. He was obviously a guy who didn't take no for an answer.

The cabin had a fridge, stove, bathroom and kitchen with all the dishes and cutlery one could use as well as a nice double bedroom. After weeks of living rough, it was great luxury. I brought in my gear and Colin sat at the table while I brewed us some coffee.

"You're a very lucky guy to have made it from Poplar Point in a canoe. I worked on the lake all my life fishing until I bought this camp, so I know what it's like. I never heard of anyone crossing it in a canoe. She's a real mean bastard. Stay here, rest up." He raised his hand to forestall my feeble protests. "There's no charge,"

I poured our coffee into two giant-size mugs. Colin relaxed in an old Lazy Boy. Sipping reflectively, he told me, "Not long ago, we saw this guy in the water just off Wicked Point. His canoe had tipped about five kilometres offshore. It was late October, lake starting to ice up. Unbelievable anybody would be in a canoe that late this far north. He was in pretty bad shape with the cold. I brought him here and he stayed a week or so to get his health back. Nice young man. Frenchman. Jerome was his name."

I was stunned. "Jerome Orange?"

"Yes, that's him."

Here I was meeting the guy who had rescued Jerome! What an incredible coincidence to be actually staying at the same place as Jerome following his narrow escape. I explained to Colin how Jerome and I had met.

"I remember he carried a Bible," Colin said. When I told him it was also listed on my mandatory equipment, he smiled: "It happens to be mine too. There are no atheists on fishing boats on Lake Winnipeg."

"Or among long-distance canoeists!"

Colin was delighted to learn I had heard from Jerome. He was amazed by the news that Jerome was now trekking through the Patagonia area of South America – a monumental hike of some 3,000 kilometres across the mountains.

As he was leaving, Colin showed me his boat parked in the grounds, a big aluminum twin engine with flared bows. He shook his head. "The fishing's never been the same since they screwed up the river in '65 with that monstrous diversion they call Cedar Lake."

Later I got to thinking about Jerome's misfortune. Wicked Point was named by the voyageurs. Like most of the names they gave to various areas across the country, it had significance. Many travellers had met their death rounding the point. The great Mackenzie himself had a lucky escape there after capsizing his canoe.

Downtown Grand Rapids was about a kilometre from Colin's camp. There wasn't much to the town, just a couple of gas stations, a restaurant, a large general store and a marina. I brought my broken paddle with me in the hope that it might be fixed. At the marine store the fellow looked at me scornfully. "It's a basket case," he said in disgust.

After I coaxed him a bit, he said. "Okay, leave it and I'll see what I can do. But it's gonna be just a patch job." Just so long as it held together, I pleaded.

Over breakfast in the restaurant, I met Garth Neel, an Anglican priest from Winnipeg. He was on holiday, staying at Colin's Riverview Cabins with his wife and two-year-old son. He told me that Colin and his wife Jean were a couple who tried hard to practise the golden rule. Since I was enjoying a freebie at Colin's place, I could only say amen to that.

I returned to the cabin and decided to work on my canoe. It was a dreadful sight, with mud caked along the bottom and side ribs. There was no way you could tell the colour for the muck. I leaned it against the cabin and turned the hose on, but the dirt wouldn't budge. I borrowed a brush, hot water and a scraper. Several ribs were cracked or broken, but I could only patch them with glue, fibreglass and the ubiquitous duct tape. Still, after a thorough cleaning and a spot of paint, Spirit of Mackenzie looked almost as good as new. Colin was impressed when he stopped by to invite me for supper.

His wife, Jean, welcomed me at the door. She had cooked fillets of pickerel caught that morning. Ice cream and coffee followed. Over coffee, Colin explained how the native population had suffered following the building of the dam. The diversion of the waters resulted in sheer chaos in the lives of the community, he said.

"It's not only that the artificial Cedar and Cross Lakes screwed up the trapping, fishing, and hunting. The lakes are very dangerous because of all the deadheads that rise to the surface, islands appearing out of nowhere. Boats run into them all the goddamned time. We've had deaths. Just a couple of years ago, an RCMP sergeant and three native people were drowned. We never found their bodies. When we complain, Hydro feeds us bullshit! They stole our life, our livelihood, then they have the nerve to throw us a pittance as conscience money."

After a pause he added, "It's not right. The earth doesn't belong to us. We belong to the earth."

Colin's melancholy tale of a government that that pays lip service to environmental concerns was one I heard across the country. It was also an unhappy commentary on Canada's failure to protect the rights of First Nations people. Despite countless lessons from numerous tragedies in the past, land treaties still continue to be sacrificed to political expediency.

Garth Neel had suggested I look up the pastor of the Anglican church in Grand Rapids, a man particularly knowledgeable about the local history. Next day I strolled along to the church, a pretty little building at the edge of town. Pastor Murray Wilt has worked with Métis and native members of Grand Rapids community for some time. After exchanging small talk, I told him one thing I'd noticed about the natives of Grand Rapids was their shyness.

He nodded. "That's pretty typical when you have a lot of child abuse.

They are confused, lost, desperately searching for their inner child." The problems of abuse and family violence were the same as most reserves. On a positive note, he said, the terrible cycle is now on the turnaround. "Young people are beginning to have a real interest in their heritage. The hope for the future is to break the cycle. In our church we now recognize Indian spirituality. Sweetgrass and sweat lodges are now incorporated into our service. This has had wide acceptance among the community, and we've been able to get people to come to church."

Later I stopped by the post office where I picked up another package from home with Magic Pantry supplies. Now there was no need to take on iron rations at the local Northern store. I could head out tomorrow if I wished.

Depositing my package in the cabin I headed down the street once again. A short way from the Anglican church, I came to the home of George Mercredi. I had met George at mass the previous day, and he had invited me for coffee and a chat. As we sat around the kitchen table, George told me that one time he had two dog teams he used for fishing on the lake during freeze-up.

"You don't have to worry about running out of gas when you've got dogs. They'll always get you home, even if you're sick. Not like a snowmobile." He told horror stories about people marooned on ice far from shore after a skidoo breakdown

He went on to tell me how proud he was of his son, Ovide Mercredi. Ovide worked diligently for the improvement of conditions on Canadian reserves. Eventually he had been elected Grand Chief of the First Nations. George was delighted when I told him his son was known across Canada for his criticism of government bureaucracy.

George reminisced about the time before the dam was built and of the ever-present roar of the rapids as the great Saskatchewan rushed down to meet Lake Winnipeg. "The river's voice was a factor in all of our lives." On the fateful day when the river was diverted, many were struck by the sudden silence.

9

Mud, Mud, Glorious Mud

While much of my five-year transcontinental adventure will dim with time, I'm unlikely to ever forget the mud and mosquitoes of the Saskatchewan River. Packed with brownish silt, the river winds serpentine-like around endless curves, in the process forming huge mud flats. This sludge effectively blocked all my attempts to traverse the high embankments to a more pastoral scene of fields, grass, and trees. Whenever a reasonable campsite appeared, it was a major undertaking getting the canoe and gear past the mud and tangled bush.

Mud clung to my clothes, crusted my face and hair, blocked my nose, and permeated my sleeping bag, eating utensils, food, toilet paper, soap, and razor. It pursued me relentlessly from the moment I pulled in to the riverbank, casting a pall over what used to be a great part of my day: quitting time.

Stepping from the canoe, I would sink to my knees in mud. Onshore, I searched for a spot in which the tent would not disappear into some slimy pit. Carrying gear from the canoe to the campsite created a quagmire. I longed for the Canadian Shield and the Ottawa Valley or the pristine waters of Georgian Bay.

I recalled the old Flanders and Swann hippopotamus song: "Mud, mud, glorious mud, there's nothing quite like it for cooling the blood." Certainly the hippo would have revelled in the delights of the Saskatchewan.

If I didn't grab for my shoes, they would disappear out of sight, and I could spend ages digging them out. Concealed roots lay in wait everywhere to topple me headfirst into the muck, especially when I was burdened with camping gear. Trying to find clean water for washing was futile.

There were no trees to tie up the canoe. Not even stumps remained along the riverbank. My standard arrival procedure was to push both paddles down into the mud at the bow and stern to pin the canoe in place while I unloaded. It was a challenging manoeuvre to balance everything for one mighty carry, since a return trip was unthinkable. Of course this meant that when the tent was secured, I was incarcerated. There was nowhere to walk to that wasn't a bog, and the mosquitoes made damned sure I remained in my tent.

No matter how hard I tried, the floor was layered with thick gooey patches. It was difficult not to bring it into bed. Getting in and out of the tent became a strategic undertaking planned with the precision of a military operation.

At Grand Rapids, George Mercredi had warned me that mosquitoes on the Saskatchewan were renowned as the most voracious in Canada. But I'd had to experience this myself to fully appreciate his words. With some familiarity gained during the past 3,000 kilometres on a variety of waterways, I thought I knew something about these bloodthirsty demons. I learned rapidly that the Saskatchewan is unique, and any prior encounter was mere kindergarten. My education on mosquito lore was about to reach an advanced level.

Early travellers like Mackenzie recorded their feelings about the "winged devils." Mackenzie makes more of encounters with mosquitoes than of episodes such as his canoe capsizing in white water or nearly being stabbed to death by an angry Indian. Some voyageurs drowned as they threw themselves into the water, driven to distraction.

One evening, having survived the great trek from canoe to camp across the wasteland, I was just settling down when I heard a distinctive pitter-patter. At first I attributed this noise to hail, but soon it became apparent it was something else. I looked up in horror to see the entire tent covered by millions of mosquitoes, their bodies blocking the light. Their battering on the fabric left no doubt they were enraged – they wanted to get at me! I had carefully checked the tent for any opening, but I could never be completely sure that they wouldn't infiltrate. I had been shocked to discover that smudge pots and even a powerful repellent spray were ineffective against them.

They pummelled the tent fabric for hours, the racket fearsomely synchronized with their high-pitched whine. I would be tormented into insanity if I dared venture outside. Lending credence to my claim is an account of the ordeal faced by men of the Northwest Mounted Police during their expedition to the Northwest Territory in the early nineteenth century. Henri Julien recorded their chilling experience:

> I myself have hunted in the interior of Quebec, and fished in the inland lakes of Ontario, and the visitations of these tormentors I then thought the most intolerable of nuisances, robbing me of fully half the enjoyment of my sport. But the Canadian mosquito is as different from his Manitoba congener as is the … civilized bug from the barbarian. As

soon as twilight deepens they make their appearance on the horizon, in the shape of a cloud, which goes on increasing in density as it approaches to the encounter. At first, a faint hum is heard in the distance, then it swells into a roar as it comes nearer. The attack is simply dreadful. Your eyes, your nose, your ears are invaded.

If you open your mouth to curse at them, they troop into it. They insinuate themselves under your clothes, down your shirt collar, up your sleeve cuffs, between the buttons of your shirt bosom. And not one or a dozen, but millions at a time. You can brush them off your coat sleeves in layers.

The mosquito of the prairie must be a distinct species in entomology. We had men among us who had traveled in all parts of the world, and who had been pestered by all manner of insects but they all agreed that nowhere had they seen anything to equal the mosquito of the prairie.

In the Mississippi valley, mosquitoes are warded off by a gauze net. In our Canadian backwoods [eastern Canada] the smoke of a big fire drives them away. But up here [the prairies], they would tear a net to shreds, and put out a fire by the mere super incumbent weight of their numbers. The best proof of their virulence is they attack animals as well as men. They send a dog off howling with pain. They tease horses to desperation. They goad even the shaggy buffalo as vengefully as the gadfly vexed the bull of Io.

Often in the evening, when our tents were pitched, and we went down to the nearest brook or rivulet to water our horses, hoping that this was to be our last work before turning in for a sweet night's rest, the mosquitoes would rise in columns out of the spongy soil under our feet and begin a regular battle against us. Our horses would rear, pitch and kick. We ourselves would be covered with scratches and blood. Our only refuge was to run our horses to their pickets, then hasten to throw ourselves on the ground, and cover ourselves up in blankets.

Invariably when the subject of mosquitoes comes up in conversation in southern regions, people smile condescendingly as if it's a trivial discomfort. However, when asked what was my greatest trial, unhesitatingly I would reply that it was the mosquitoes on the Northern Saskatchewan River.

The water volume in the river changed constantly, courtesy of the Grand Rapids dam, and my mileage for the day was meagre. Slogging against the strong current during 18-hour days, my morale sank when I looked back along the river to see the previous day's campsite still in view!

Bears were a constant presence along the riverbank – usually a mother with one or two cubs tagging behind. I had never seen so many bears roaming around, and it made me distinctly uneasy. The berry shortage the natives talked about on Lake Winnipeg was evidently widespread. Because of this, I made drastic changes in meal preparation. It was too risky to cook on shore. Preparing meals in the canoe meant I could shove off rapidly if shaggy guests appeared. In the morning I launched and then made breakfast. If there was a decent place to tie up, I stopped for lunch but usually cooked on board. Supper was eaten before I made camp. I thought of sleeping in the canoe too, but dismissed this as hazardous since there were no trees to string up food packs. Leaving food in the canoe was inviting disaster – bears would tear it apart

One morning the roar of a motorboat on the river took me by surprise. A powerful motor launch appeared around a curve. Drawing alongside, two young men quizzed me about the wildlife I had encountered. They were anxious to get some pictures but said that they hadn't seen any animals. Since they were zooming along in a noisy craft, their lack of sightings didn't surprise me. They were astonished when I told them that bears, moose, and deer were abundant. Bald eagles were common. Sometimes several pairs wheeled over my canoe. Muskrat and otters dived and splashed in front of the bow.

It was plain they figured I was an old sourdough from another era. I played along, allowing them to take a picture of me and the canoe. Before they took off downriver, they told me it was only another 20 kilometres to the province of Saskatchewan. My heart leaped: this would be province number four since leaving Montreal.

The volume of water in the river continued to increase, sometimes quite dramatically, turning a normal day's paddling into an endurance feat. The current became so overpowering that when I rested my arm for a moment after a heavy thrust, I drifted backwards. The weather turned sultry. Thunderstorms with heavy rain made the ground even swampier. To my delight I came across a patch of hard sand, a great camping site. It felt great to get a decent night's sleep with the floor of the tent on an even keel instead of skewed over soggy terrain.

I awoke very early, chilled by the mournful sound of wolves crying in unison. I was startled to see six young animals circling my campsite. Back among some trees a large grey timber wolf was keeping a wary eye on me. It was a mother and her cubs. The cubs I guessed to be about six months old. They were curious and ran around the tent several times. The adult continued to look on but made no move.

I took a few pictures but, anxious not to alarm the mother, I didn't attempt to approach the playful pups. Despite their harmless appearance, I recalled a trapper in Grand Rapids restaurant telling me he had seen wolves take down a bull moose. One of them would stop the animal by working its head, the other would grab at its hindquarters. "They're vicious killers, tearing out chunks of meat until the moose fell," he declared.

As I was having lunch, an enormous cloud of mosquitoes engulfed me. I threw everything in the canoe and paddled furiously away, pursued by the merciless foe. Fortunately a northeasterly wind came up, and for the first time in ages it was possible to raise sail. Soon I was speeding away from the bloodthirsty mob.

Just before Pemmican Point I pulled in to a piece of flat ground with some brown tufts resembling grass on it. It was only mid-afternoon, but I wasn't going to miss this prime spot. Some of the bushes had been pushed over and moose tracks were abundant, but I didn't pay much heed.

During the night the ground trembled and shook, startling me into wakefulness. Sitting bolt upright, I felt the tent vibrating. The snapping and crackling of underbrush made a terrific racket. It sounded like a herd of buffalo was outside the tent. After about ten minutes the noise started to fade. Through the tent flap the light of the moon revealed several large rumps disappearing into the bush. In the morning I found my camp was an absolute quagmire of moose tracks. All of them carefully circumvented my tent. I had been camped right on a moose migratory trail!

Pushing my way against the strong current was monotonous, but I was pleased to know I was now only a short distance from Cumberland House, once a key distribution centre for pemmican. This product fuelled all the Nor'westers' activities in the Athabasca country and beyond. Pulverized buffalo meat was mixed with tallow and berries, usually Saskatoon-variety blueberries, or whatever was available. It could be eaten raw, or pasted with flour and fried, or even cut up to make soup.

The Nor'westers swore by it, even went to war over it. The Pemmican War resulted when the Selkirk settlers attempted to take over the distribution points at Red River by passing an edict forbidding the hunting of buffalo from horseback in Selkirk territories. Miles Macdonnell, governor of the Selkirk Settlement, roused the wrath of the Nor'westers by ordering them to evacuate all their posts and confiscating hundreds of sacks of pemmican. Without an adequate supply, the Nor'westers would soon be out of business – precisely what the Hudson Bay Company hoped for.

The enraged Nor'westers incited the Indians and Métis to turn on the settlers. At several rapids along the Saskatchewan River they even had a gunboat with cannon at the ready to take on their HBC foes! But following several shootouts, the colony was demoralized and finally capitulated.

It seems incredible that men were killed over something as commonplace as beef jerky. But the distances travelled were enormous, and with little chance of finding game, men could die from starvation. A major advance in European exploration and trade was made when it was realized that pemmican could last almost indefinitely and was easily carried. More important, it could be cached for a food source on return from a trek in the wilderness. (It's remarkable how many place names in Canada use the word "cache," indicating the pivotal role played by this ubiquitous food source.)

Cumberland House, where I was heading, marked the earliest settlement in Saskatchewan. It was originally a Nor'wester fort around 1769. The Hudson's Bay Company later set up in competition, but their establishment was really nothing more than an earthen dugout, much maligned by the Indians. They refused to deal with the HBC, contemptuous of a company that treated its servants so poorly.

In 1790 Alexander Mackenzie called in at Cumberland House on his way to the annual meeting of wintering partners at Grand Portage. He was returning from explorations north of 60 to the Beaufort Sea and down the great river that now bears his name. His quest for a North West Passage met with disappointment. Interestingly, he met up with HBC mapmaker Philip Turnor at that time. Sceptical of Mackenzie's competence as a navigator, Turnor sneered, "He makes me think he is not well convinced where he has been."

Mackenzie, aware of his deficiencies as a navigator, returned to England to brush up his scientific knowledge. Turnor's scathing commentary was refuted by Franklin nearly four decades later. Using vastly superior instruments, Franklin confirmed the accuracy of Mackenzie's findings: "The survey we made on our Expedition differs very little in its outline from that of its discoverer, whose general correctness we had often occasion to admire."

The conservation officer at Cumberland House gave me permission to set up camp behind his office. It was great to be able to stroll on the lawn without disappearing into a muddy hole. Later, at the nursing station I met the charge nurse, a pleasant woman named Maryanne. She invited me for tea and allowed me to use the shower. Finally I was able to scrub off all the Saskatchewan River mud. Over a pot of tea she told me about the clinic she runs.

We spent some time talking about research on Parkinson's disease. She was especially interested in some of the studies we had done at the University of Montreal, particularly on the association between the environmental effects of manganese and Parkinsonism. Like most researchers, I can talk the hind leg off a donkey about my speciality, but it had been a hard day. After a little while I headed for bed.

In the morning I had breakfast at Stella's Café on the main street. Conversation was bantered about the room through a heavy pall of cigarette smoke. It was difficult to see who was speaking even a couple of tables away. Despite the fog that stung my eyes, it was a great way of catching up on local gossip, most of it related to who had the worst hangover. I struck up a conversation with RCMP constable Blaine Landry, who offered me a tour of the community. He told me how Squaw Rapids Dam upstream had created enormous environmental and social problems for the community. It was a recurring story everywhere I travelled.

Later, as I strolled down the main street, a little girl about five years old came up to me and asked if she could take my hand. "Sure," I said. "What's your name?"

"Cindy," she replied.

At first I thought that she wanted me to help her across the road. But after we had crossed, she continued holding my hand. "Where's your mom?" I asked her.

"She's at bingo and won't be back until late." Then she added plaintively, "Daddy's drunk again. I'm afraid to go home."

I had heard from one of the Mounties how bingo addiction is a major problem with the women of the community. Despite the $25 admission charge, the place is packed day and night. With the men's heavy drinking and the women's gambling, children are left to their own resources. In many cases this leads to glue or gasoline sniffing. The entire family becomes caught in the tyranny of dependency.

I went back for lunch to Stella's Café. It was as smoky as ever, but it was the only place in town. As I waited for my order, my attention was taken by a couple of men at an adjacent table. The older man in his fifties and a young man in his twenties were talking animatedly. Their conversation related to water diversion and the mineral content of water. Because of my own research in metal neurotoxicity, I was interested. After listening for a bit, I posed a few questions concerning their work.

They seemed taken aback. Because of my appearance and mud-stained clothes, they probably figured I was some old lag. As my probing became more searching, they said they were conducting a study of the waterways in Northern Canada, including Lake Athabasca and the Churchill, Mackenzie, and Saskatchewan River systems.

When I asked what purposes their research was being used for, they became evasive. Reluctantly, it seemed to me, they told me they were working at the University of Chicago. The man was a professor and the younger man his doctoral student. I explained that I had recently returned from Australia's Northern Territories after conducting a study on manganese toxicity among aboriginals. As I elaborated, they looked thoroughly alarmed and even more reticent. Finally, somewhat flustered, they left the café. It was evident my queries had upset them.

I was puzzled and curious about their behaviour. Whether this incident had anything to do with American aspirations on our water system I don't really know. But current events make one wonder. For example, the press reported that when Prime Minister Jean Chrétien and President Bill Clinton first met in Windsor, Ontario, Chrétien stated unequivocally, "There was nothing in NAFTA that says Canada's water is for sale. It is not at all about water."

President Clinton stepped forward to the podium to respond. His brief riposte, "You'd better believe it's all about water!" said it all. Chrétien tried to put a brave face on the humiliating experience. Later, spin doctors struggled to discount the incident as a "misunderstanding."

It's common knowledge that the United States is desperate to obtain diversion from the Great Lakes for water-hungry states like Arizona and California. In *Caesars of the Wilderness*, Peter Newman observes, "Water is very special to Canadians. No politician jealous of his mandate has ever advocated the export of a drop of the stuff."

While that may once have been the case, with the implementation of Chapter 11 of the NAFTA agreement, the gloves are off. As the global water consortium Water Inc. wait patiently in the wings, Canada's water is now up for grabs.

When I called home later that evening, Ishbel told me that all kinds of people were trying to get hold of me. "The phone's been ringing off the hook. First, ABC News in New York want an interview. They even wanted to send a news team to Northern Canada. Then CBC and CTV called several times. Joe Warmington from the *Toronto Sun* also wanted to talk to you."

Apparently the media were fired up about a story on the toxic effects of a gasoline additive, MMT, used for years in Canada as a replacement for lead. Research I was involved in had found that manganese, a major component of the additive released from tailpipe emissions into the atmosphere when gas is burned, was a risk factor for Parkinsonism. The Environmental Protection Agency (EPA) wanted me as a witness at a hearing in Washington examining the MMT threat to public health. They had sent an airline ticket for me to fly down for the hearing.

I was delighted that my efforts to highlight the potential risk to Canadians of using manganese in gas were finally receiving some attention. But how to get there from the wilds of northern Saskatchewan? Fortunately, the boys in blue came to my rescue. Blaine Landry from the RCMP detachment was leaving for Prince Albert by car and said he would take me along.

Endless fields of ripe canola created a stunning backdrop of brilliant yellow against an azure sky as we sped along in a new pickup, my canoe anchored firmly in the back. Small towns with gleaming white houses whizzed past. Occasionally I glimpsed the remnants of weather-beaten log cabins through a distant thicket. These decaying ruins in prosperous farm country caused me to reflect on the courage of the early homesteaders who had toughed out a bleak livelihood in North Saskatchewan River country. Hugh MacLennan in *Seven Rivers of Canada* considers the incredible hardships of the voyageurs as nothing compared to those faced by early settlers in this province. A hole dug in the ground and roofed with sods was all many could provide for their families. But endurance was a hallmark of the pioneers who scratched a living from a hard land.

While it is recognized that agriculture opened up the prairie provinces, paradoxically, in land-locked Saskatchewan, it was furs, not farming, that brought explorers north in the 1800s. Although it seems strange today, the prairies were originally known as the Northwest Territory. The river that later gave the province its name was the maritime hub of a corporate fur trade for 200 years. Providing a superhighway for canoes, it played a pivotal role in opening up the West.

In contrast to the quiet pace of rural Saskatchewan, the frenetic atmosphere of downtown Washington was jarring. After spending so long in a tent in the Canadian wilderness, I was unable to sleep in the hotel. The bed was too comfortable. The air conditioner made an enormous noise.

The EPA hearings gave me some insight into the murky political dynamics of big business and environmental groups. Inevitably truth was the first casualty as they battled each other in a conflict where no quarter was given. Senators stepped forward, earnestly fixing their gaze on the audience, blandly claiming that the oil industry was being painted as a villain when it was only aiding the country's prosperity. The hearing was pure theatre. A spokesperson for the Environmental Defense Fund created a stir by producing a copy of a 1925 *New York Times* in which the chairman of Ethyl Corporation was quoted that the introduction of lead into American gasoline was "God's gift to the American people." Never mind the legacy of social devastation that accrued from lead in gasoline and resulted in serious health damage and mental retardation in thousands of children. It was strange logic that Ethyl Corporation should now want to replace lead with manganese, a powerful neurotoxin implicated as a causative agent in chronic neurological disease.

My testimony took about an hour. I reviewed the effects of manganese from the first reports of neurotoxicity in 1837 to the present.

spirit and strengthened his determination to make Canadians aware of this country's extraordinary rich history, and the vulnerability of this great natural wonder.

A Canoe Quest in the Wake of Canada's "Prince of Explorers" is the story of one man's incredible journey – one day at a time.

$23 paper   ARTFUL CODGER PRESS   ISBN 0-9736161-8-0

Available at Novel Idea Books, 156 Princess Street, Kingston, K7L 1B1   613- 546-9799.

Or contact the author at westieboy@kos.net

Born in Glasgow, Scotland, John Donaldson came to Canada in 1955. He went on to gain a BSc in chemistry, an MSc in microbiology, and a doctorate in experimental medicine at McGill University. He became a neurological biochemist, a head of molecular biology in the pharmaceutical industry, and a professor of pharmacology at the University of Manitoba and the Université de Montréal. He is a former Garfield Weston Scholar in medical research and the recipient of several awards from the American Parkinson's foundation. Now a lay oblate of the Benedictine Order, he lives with his wife, Ishbel, in Kingston, Ontario.

A Canoe Quest
in the Wake of Canada's
"Prince of Explorers"

by JOHN DONALDSON

A Canoe Quest in
the Wake of Canada's
"Prince of Explorers"

ONE DAY AT A TIME

JOHN DONALDSON

Two hundred years after the Scottish-born explorer Alexander Mackenzie first crossed Canada to the Arctic and Pacific oceans by canoe, John Donaldson fulfilled a personal dream by making the same voyages. At the age of 60 he began retracing the voyages of his boyhood hero, armed with a little recreational canoeing experience, a wood and canvas canoe, and a grand sense of adventure.

His travels took him more than 12,000 kilometres from Mackenzie's starting point at Montreal to the Pacific and then the Arctic Ocean. He encountered cranky bears and rabid coyotes, impenetrable fogs and raging rapids. He nearly capsized in the wake of a Lake Superior freighter and was marooned on dismal Lake Winnipeg without a paddle. A trigger-happy madman nearly ended his journey at Buffalo Narrows. But five summers in the

I gave a wrap-up of my own research, published in reputable peer-reviewed journals, indicating that young children were preferentially susceptible to manganese's insidious effects because of the vulnerability of their immature nervous systems.

Observing the implacable expressions on the faces of the senior executives from the oil industry in the front row, I realized there was little I could do to convince them their new gasoline additive presented a serious health problem. Thus I began by addressing the business leaders from the podium: "Gentlemen, how are you going to explain to your grandchildren why you chose to market an agent with the capability of causing brain damage in children?

I dearly love the United States. Many of my relatives are Americans, as four of my aunts settled there. My cousins served in the U.S. army and navy in the Second World War. Some of them visited us in Scotland when they were drafted overseas for the invasion of France. One of them, Tommy Croall, was decorated with the Navy Cross at Boston City Hall alongside John F. Kennedy. But after only two days in Washington, I was enormously eager to get away from the Disneyland unreality of the Great Republic. I longed to be back in the vast, remote lands of northern Canada, grateful to live in a country where it was still possible to paddle off into the wilderness.

My relief on arriving back in Prince Albert was profound. I actually hummed a few bars of "This Land Is My Land." After checking into a motel I made my way downtown, pausing at a delightful park overlooking the Saskatchewan River. Gazing down at the swirling stream, I mused over tough times travelling the mucky waters of this great river. While it was exhausting paddling against a fierce current, accompanied by an array of winged tormentors, I wouldn't swap one kilometre of its muddy torrent for the entire city of Washington!

I enjoyed breakfast at the Prince Albert Inn, then strolled the main street, basking in the July sun. At the hardware store I checked for Coleman stove parts. While it seemed they sold everything, they had nothing for a backpack stove. At Fresh Air Experience, a large sports store, my quest was again fruitless. Talking over my trip with the manager, I explained I was anxious to get back onto the Churchill River. He said he had just spoken to a customer who was driving north.

"That chap over there," he said indicating a young fellow in his twenties looking over some hiking boots. I strolled over and introduced myself. Bruce Scott said he was from Oshawa and was heading north to the Churchill River.

"You're welcome to tag along," he said. "I'll be leaving early tomorrow morning." We chatted a while and arranged a pick-up for next day.

Passing the local branch of the Canadian Legion, I decided to stop in and make some phone calls. Placing an order for a coffee, I went to the phone to call my mother. An old Scot, at 92 she lives in a senior's complex in Kingston. A little hard of hearing, but highly independent, she takes care of herself in her apartment.

"When are you coming home?" Mom asked. She always gets right to the point. About ten minutes later, my head reeling from a barrage of advice, I rang off.

When I returned to my table, Jim the bartender nodded. "Couldn't help overhearing. So you're originally from Glasgow? I was overseas in the war and visited my relatives in the city near Queen's Park. Just my luck to arrive there when they had a big air raid. One of the last of the war. Boy, did my buddies kid me about that! They bombed the church that night."

I was taken aback that he knew my home and had been there when our local church had been bombed. We spent some time talking.

Scott called on me early next morning and we made our way to the RCMP building to pick up my canoe. The Mounties had been keeping an eye on it. Once or twice along the road it went spinning around on top of the car in the prairie winds, scaring the hell out of us both. After securing it, we continued on our way. Scott was good company and very keen to get into wilderness canoeing. One of his plans was to rent a canoe and paddle the Clearwater River. Since he had no experience, I tried to steer him towards a tour with one of the many wilderness-touring trips available for amateur canoeists. He let me off along the Churchill River and gave me a hand loading the canoe. Then he bid me adieu, carrying on towards his own wilderness adventure.

After the bleak, muddy, and mosquito-infested Saskatchewan, the pastoral scenery along the Churchill was a pleasant change. The river takes its name from the Hudson Bay fort at its mouth. To the Indians it was Missinipi, or "great river." It was just my luck that only a couple of hours after setting off, a violent storm came up. Waves were soon leaping over the bow, forcing me to pull in.

After I hauled the canoe up the beach, I walked along the shore to stretch my legs. About a kilometre along I found a large log cabin. The door was unlocked and it looked like it had been occupied recently. While it would have been a comfortable place to spend the night, I chose the beach.

The storm continued unabated into the wee small hours. The tent felt as if it was going to blow away. To my relief it remained anchored. However, the noise of branches slapping back and forth made sleep impossible. I began wishing I had moved into the cabin. My mind returned to thoughts of Jim the bartender at the Prince Albert legion. Meeting him had been such an odd coincidence. During the war there were many Canadian servicemen in Scotland looking for relatives, but I found it a bit of a jolt when he referred to the bombing of our local church. Our conversation had made me realize that childhood memories of that sombre night of the fires in wartime Glasgow still flickered in the back of my mind.

Chronic anxiety marked those troubled times. It manifested itself in a heaviness, an aura of gloom around our parents and teachers. Nowadays we would term it depression; then it was referred to as "war nerves," a cumbersome piece of emotional baggage carried through grey life in our beleaguered island. It was the time of Hitler's blitzkrieg as Nazi bombers carried out a campaign of terror bombing.

In my tent on this remote stretch of a northern river, I recalled vividly the daily ritual as our mothers gathered in the street on their way to sparsely stocked grocery stores. Clutching string bags of the family's meagre rations, wan faces set, they joined in little hushed groups. They exchanged recipes for cooking fare such as dehydrated eggs, Spam, or bread baked with synthetic flour that imparted an unappetizing seedy-brown colour. On other occasions, the topic was more sombre. They would draw closer, gaining comfort from shared adversity. Someone would ask in faltering tones, "Did you hear who got it last night?" Eyes averted, they tensed, awaiting an answer, silently praying it would not be a district where relatives lived.

Memories flooded me of the particular raid that Jim had talked about, one among many nights when the sirens shrieked like banshees over the city. My gut would clench as we frantically gathered things together and raced for the concrete air-raid shelter in the street. Incredibly, there was a time when we actually used to sleep through air raids! That changed after the bombing of the dockyards at Clydebank. My dad, a railwayman on duty at the marshalling yards, returned home one evening with a haunted expression. After that he made certain we went to the shelter. Later I heard from my brother that the bomb blast had killed dozens in the tenements surrounding the docks where naval ships were anchored. Many people had stayed home thinking the raid would pass them by. The bombs rained down, razing buildings. Next day scores of bodies floated in the river.

The oil tanks were still burning six months later, choking acrid fumes spreading a funereal pall of soot over the city. At night the flames were beacons for enemy aircraft. The thunderous combination of blasts from high-explosive blockbusters, mingling with the fierce phosphorescence of firebombs, left immolated and flattened corpses ingrained like shadows into the stone of buildings or sidewalks, preserved for posterity like macabre pictographs.

Those dreadful events took place in distant parts of our city. But that situation changed one evening towards the end of the war. The night they bombed the church near our home was a beautiful moonlight evening – a "bomber's moon," they used to call it. Early in the evening, shortly after the sirens had sounded, the roar of truck-mounted anti-aircraft batteries, their blazing guns pumping rapid-fire shells, erupted around us. Because of their proximity to the buildings, the guns gave off an ear-splitting *wooomf, woooomf, woooomf* intermingling with the tinkling of spent shells on the ground. Fiery tracers criss-crossed the path of an incoming enemy aircraft. The screaming of unsynchronized engines rose to a crescendo as the bomber roared down the street, barely clearing the roofs of the red sandstone tenement where we lived. Like canyon walls, buildings on either side magnified the uproar a hundredfold, while windows bent and flapped like sails in a storm. The bomber zigzagged wildly, trapped in the glare of searchlights as its pilot sought to escape into anonymous darkness.

Bathed in eerie luminescence, black and white crosses gleamed along the fuselage as it passed overheard. I watched in horror as the bomb doors opened and projectiles started to fall. Their bronzed tail fins glinted as they landed with parade-like precision smack down the centre of our street. Some struck the movie theatre with a vivid display of sparks, while a cluster fell on the roof of our beautiful Greek Orthodox Church. I threw myself down on the road, my arms over my head.

No explosion came. Instead, the street was bathed in the incandescent glow of molten phosphorus from hundreds of incendiary bombs. They emitted a hypnotic, ghostly white, pyrotechnic display like St Elmo's fire.

The clanging of fire trucks as they converged on the church, scene of the major fire, blended with the crackling flames and shouts of firemen. Miles of hose coiled from the hydrants in adjacent streets towards the inferno. Their grim faces caked with dust and sweat, the firemen slipped in the pools of water, struggling to control the gyrations of the pressurized hoses. Masonry and debris fell as walls caved in. The dying remnants of a once magnificent church, an architectural jewel among the city's historically treasured buildings, tumbled around our feet. It created a great fireball that lit the city.

Gasps rose from hundreds of throats. Our gazes fixed on the crimson sky, we saw the cupola tremble, sway from side to side, totter, then lean grotesquely askew. We watched anguished, yet spellbound.

The enormous dome was embroidered with gold leaf and topped by an angel with folded wings. Bronzed eagles lay at her feet and a gold-tinted orb and sceptre were clutched in her hand. It was the ultimate adornment in a crowning showpiece of faith. Towering above the holocaust, it had miraculously remained intact, seemingly aloof from the carnage. Suddenly, the surviving supports gave way. The massive dome shuddered, then toppled slowly into the epicentre of the fiery cauldron. This was the final consummation, the ultimate indignity wrought on this proud symbol. Borne to its funeral pyre like some ancient Viking sarcophagus, the statue fell to the ground. It shattered into a thousand pieces.

As though temporarily sated, the relentless roaring of the flames abated. A hush settled over the crowd. A few old ladies near the barricades fingered their beads, murmuring prayers. As if having witnessed a profound sacrilege, the crowd was already dispersing. All that remained of the towering symbol of an ancient Christian faith was a gaunt skeleton, a charnel house where flickering small fires cast grotesque shadows on nearby buildings. Smoke, soot, and an acrid stench met our nostrils. Exhausted, the firemen picked their way through the fallen masonry. They rolled up their hoses with despondent finality. I turned from the dismal scene and headed home.

Rising early after a night punctuated by vivid memories of my wartime experience, I peered through the tent at the muddy embankments of the Saskatchewan. When I set about preparing breakfast, to my dismay the stove refused to light. My trusty friend over many rough trails had finally succumbed, done in by the Saskatchewan River. It had taken a mountain of punishment over very difficult terrain and survived. But dunking in the muddy Saskatchewan had proven too much.

I found enough dry kindling to start up a fire and get the coffee brewing. There were few occasions when it was possible to use a fire to cook because of brisk norwesterly winds, not to mention a scarcity of kindling. A stove with minimal fuel requirements made life a lot easier. I could have a piping hot meal in five minutes even under atrocious conditions. The stove also heated the tent, and during early morning tea breaks could thaw out chilled fingers. But particularly after an exhausting day on the water, its cheery glow as I prepared supper was a great boost to morale. The last thing I wanted to do after a day's paddling was gather kindling. Now I would have to tough it out until I could pick up spare parts, or get the stove fixed.

Passing close to the village of Ile-a-la Crosse, I paddled about two kilometres on and camped at a small island. I preferred staying outside of town, since on several occasions my campsite served as a drawing card for town drunks or vandals.

Ile-a-la Crosse is a Métis community of some 1,500 residents. Memories of the original traders still live on in the names of the families living there. Surnames like Belanger, Durocher, Laliberte, McCallum, Roy, and Gardiner predominate. Twenty-one-year-old Alexander

Mackenzie arrived here in 1785 after becoming a partner in the Montreal fur-trading firm of Gregory, McLeod, making Ile-a-la Crosse his base of operations.

Au facon du nord, he took a "country wife" here, a pretty woman known as "The Catt." These relationships by fur traders could sometimes be brutal, but Mackenzie's treatment of his wilderness wife seems to have been fair. When he left Canada he gave instructions for an allowance of up to a thousand pounds to be made available to "Kitty" indefinitely. It was an extraordinarily generous sum, the equivalent of some $80,000 today. There is some indication that Mackenzie may have fathered a child, Andrew, with Kitty. Andrew became a well-known fur trader and died at Fort Vermilion in 1809.

That was the year of a devastating famine among residents of the Athabasca territory, caused by failure of the caribou and buffalo herds. Many people died. Daniel Harmon, the Vermont trader who spent two decades in the northwest, recorded the gruesome effects of starvation on the Indians. One man resorted to cannibalism and ate his wife and children, while a woman in Fort Chipeweyan was reported to have eaten fourteen individuals in the community!

A major part of Mackenzie's job was to block Indian trading with the rival HBC, much as his predecessor Joseph Frobisher had done. It was a lucky break and a great career boost for young Mack when he met the celebrated Indian named English Chief during his tenure at Ile-a-la Crosse. The chief gained the soubriquet "English" when, as head of the Chipewyan tribe, he made the hazardous overland trek to the English HBC post at Fort Churchill. English Chief was renowned for his phenomenal skill in guiding explorers through the northwest. He assisted Mackenzie in navigating the Mackenzie River in 1789 during his quest for the western ocean.

After setting up camp, I took the canoe across to a small cove and hauled up on the beach. It was raining. Later I headed towards town on the off-chance of finding some parts for my stove. As I walked briskly along the dusty dirt track, a pick-up belching smoke drew alongside, enveloping me in a great cloud of dust. "Want a ride into town?" Startled, I looked up to see a Métis man grinning down at me from the open window.

"George Raymond," the driver said affably. "These gals are my two daughters. We're on our way to a funeral." He waved his arm to indicate two pretty girls, one about 12, the other slightly older, perhaps 15, sitting alongside him. Gladly I accepted the offer and made myself comfortable in the back seat. A long-haul transport driver out of Saskatoon, George made his home in Buffalo Narrows, a small community about 20 kilometres away. "I'll drop you off at the local café," he said.

Since he had to gas up at the service station across the road from the café, I popped inside, persuading the attendant to search his storeroom for spares for my stove. He was most obliging, even to the extent of opening up new packages to see if they would match, but to no avail. As usually happens in a small community, several customers stopped by to offer advice. One man invited me to his home to "see what I can do." Bill Favel took me down to his basement and spent some time constructing a fuel valve. To my delight, it worked, and soon my little stove was hissing away merrily on the workbench. Bill's wife invited me to stay for lunch. As I was about to leave, Gerry, a local taxi driver and a friend of Bill's, called in. Gerry told me he would drive me back to my campsite and take Bill along for the ride. When we were leaving, George Raymond drew up in the driveway, honked his horn, and said he would follow us.

As our entourage drove out of town, along the side of the road I saw numerous tiny crèches containing statues, many covered with flowers. At some of these, people knelt in prayer. Noting my surprise, Bill said, "People here have great devotion to Our Blessed Lady. Every First Friday they do the Stations of the Cross. Then, he added: "I do them also, since she helped me quit drinking twelve years ago." Even during my short stay among the community it was quite evident that many people carried a heavy burden of drug and alcohol abuse.

As my two-car escort rolled into camp, I was shocked to find my canoe, which I had hauled well out of the water, now bobbing around in shallow water some 100 metres from where I had left it. In another half-hour it would have been swept out into the lake. I had figured it wasn't necessary to tie up, but a quirky wind had propelled it in circles, causing it to "walk" down the beach.

"Even if it's out of the water, tie it up," Gerry told me. "The winds here are phenomenal. They'll move a loaded aluminum fishing boat, never mind a canoe." I cringed in embarrassment. However, when I waded out and pulled the canoe back to the sandy beach, my bruised ego was mollified as they gathered around to admire it.

"My God, what a beautiful canoe," they exclaimed in unison as they enthused over my craft, patting and probing it. They were impressed with my Seaforth Highlander and Spirit of Mackenzie decals. George, a Korean veteran in the Princess Pats, was delighted by my military connection. When I recounted my adventures on the trail, they insisted that the "entrapped spirit" within my canoe when it was crafted by Cree Indians had helped me to survive my close encounters.

Suddenly, the cab radio blared into action, splurting out a report of a major fire. Since all three were experienced forest firefighters, they quickly headed back to town to pick up their gear. Before he left, Bill, who was appalled to hear that I didn't carry any weapons, insisted on presenting me with a hunting knife. Touched at his concern, I accepted it with thanks. He also invited me to stop over at his cabin down the trail. Although he made his living driving a cab, Gerry refused to take any payment.

Overwhelmed by all the generosity, I decided to dedicate my trip and my book to fostering greater understanding of First Nations people. Reflecting later on the hospitality of the people of Ile-a-la Crosse, I was moved by what seemed to be a normal occurrence in remote areas of the country. A remarkable spirit of compassion moves the community to rally around to help a stranger. Would that we could carry that same spirit into southern towns and cities. Among aboriginal people I was invariably welcomed warmly and often overwhelmed by their hospitality. I think my solitary travels kindled an especial resonance among them, perhaps a reminder of their ancient bush-craft legacy, sadly now only a memory.

Bill's cabin turned out to be close to 25 kilometres down the lake, but I sailed all the way with a southerly breeze pushing me along. Like most cabins in the north, it was unlocked. Bill stated emphatically that travellers "can help themselves to anything inside. Just so long as they don't take away my goddamned livelihood ... my tools." I made myself some soup, then closed my eyes for an hour before heading out.

Shortly after, the weather broke into a drizzle, changing to pounding rain that lasted the rest of the day and night. After a mere two hours on the lake I decided to call it a day. The weather was just like the Scottish highlands, wet, drab and miserable. To make matters worse, my stove quit again. Since the heavy rain made it pointless looking for dry kindling, a hot supper seemed out.

Then I had an idea. Rummaging around in my pack I retrieved a bundle of candles. Tying six together, I set them inside a mug to concentrate the heat and placed a beaker of water on top. I had used this method once before when I was stranded on Lake Winnipeg's swampy morass. It worked fine. My porridge tasted great, chasing the damp away and boosting my morale.

10

Bushwhacked

Along the Aubichon Arm the lake narrowed dramatically until it formed the straits of McBeth Channel. Next day as I cruised the shoreline near Buffalo Narrows, I came upon a fox washing himself with such attention to detail that he didn't notice my approach. When he finally saw me only a few feet away, he got such a shock he lost his balance, rolled backwards on the sand, and tumbled down a sandy slope. He then picked himself up and loped off, looking foolish.

There was a lot of activity on the waterfront at Buffalo Narrows, with Beaver and Cessna aircraft and occasionally a huge Canso water bomber taking off and landing almost continuously. My first stop was the Northern Store, in hopes of replacing my backpack stove. Unfortunately I had to make do with a large camping stove. As I lugged it down the street, I told myself that at least it would cook my grub.

Passing a sign for Buffalo Narrows Airways, I stopped in and met the owners, Dennis and Karen O'Brien. Karen made coffee and we sat around chatting. Dennis had a remarkable facility for choice language that had me splitting my sides. Karen just shrugged – she had given up trying to reform his language. She wore many hats in the business, monitoring the radio, sending planes on various charters, pumping gas, doing minor servicing, keeping the accounts, and selling soft drinks. Tourist guide and general dogsbody, she took it all in her stride. "If you think this is busy, it's absolutely chaotic when there's a big fire," she said. "Then you have all the fire-fighting aircraft calling in for directions, gas, and heavens knows what."

At one time she even flew the Cessna 180 seaplane. However, she told me, as she attempted to land one day under gusty conditions, the wind caught the wing and flipped it. The plane started to sink beneath the waves, the cockpit filling with water. She struggled free and swam to the surface where she was picked up by a rescue boat. "But that was the last time I flew. Never again!" she declared.

She was interested in hearing about my trip but expressed concern for my safety. "There's a lot of violence around La Loche. You don't want to spend much time there," she warned. Imploring me to be careful, she said she'd pray for my safe return. As I bid adieu she called after me, "Watch it!"

In keeping with the unsavoury character it was named for, Peter Pond Lake looked foreboding under an ominous sky. A Connecticut Yankee fur trader, Pond joined Amherst's army to fight in the French and Indian wars. Rumour was he was wanted at the time for murder. Despite being on the wrong side of the law, he earned a reputation for courage in that bloody conflict.

After the war he joined the Nor'westers, setting up a trading post near Fort Chipeweyan. He is renowned today in Alberta as builder of the province's first house. Oddly, he got his start in Canada from university founder James McGill, who gave him his first canoe. Pond revolutionized the fur trade by introducing pemmican supply depots at strategic points along the trail. It became a staple of the company's food supply, increasing profits and giving the "pork eaters" a competitive edge over their HBC rivals.

Pond had great influence on Mackenzie's career, teaching him bush skills and giving him invaluable access to maps of the northern territories. Pond had a close affinity with the Indians and spoke several dialects. Through his friendship with various tribes, he gained an intimate knowledge of the geography of the North. He had dreams that this knowledge could help make him a rich man. He even cooked up a deal with the Russians, at one time offering to sell Catherine, Empress of Russia, his map of the Northwest, which he claimed would aid Russia's territorial ambitions. Nevertheless, he died penniless, considered by many a murderer and a scoundrel.

After only a few hours on the lake, I was driven ashore by the rising wind. I made the best of it by setting up my new stove for morning tea. Drinking tea is my ritual while contemplating a difficult or hazardous crossing or when puzzling over which route to take. I have spent hours gazing across the vastness of the land, sipping reflectively.

The black sky erupted into violent thunderstorms as a menacing squall line built on the horizon. The clouds' spindly wispiness and top hats reminded me of a coven of Macbeth's witches. Fortunately I was well sheltered in thick pine. I figured the storm would last the day and passed the time planning supper: I had picked up more provisions, including fresh bread, at Buffalo Narrows. Towards evening the wind abated somewhat, so that I could set up my stove at the door of the tent, sheltered from the elements.

Eating well on the trail is great therapy. The evening's gastronomic delights included beef noodle soup, Irish stew with two fried eggs and Breton crackers, followed by chocolate pudding with evaporated milk. This was topped off with digestive biscuits, lavishly spread with Billy Bee honey, and copious mugs of tea. To digest this huge feed, I took a walk along the shore, planning the next phase of my trip. Thankfully, the rain had cleared. Strolling close to the pines, I filled my lungs with sweet-smelling air. I thanked the Great Spirit for the good times, the challenging times, even the frightening experiences on the trail thus far. I thought how most sensible guys my age would be sitting on the patio with a drink, reading the paper, walking the dog, or shooting a few balls on the green. Not me – I'm romping around the harsh wilderness in a flimsy canoe! No wonder some people figured I was crazy. Maybe so, but I'd never felt healthier, mentally or physically. I was filled with intense gratitude to my creator to be able to experience this remarkable adventure. Part of our personal journey, indeed an integral component of life, is to endure.

The following day a strong northeasterly and formidable waves again forced me off the lake. Since the water along the shore was shallow, I tied a line to the bow and towed the canoe through the water behind me. I covered 10 kilometres like this before the wind dropped.

Paddling further down the lake, I was surprised to see another boat coming towards me. "Hi there, guy," a voice hailed me. Two native men drew alongside in a battered fibreglass canoe – the first natives I had met travelling by canoe since I left Montreal. One clutched a Lee Enfield 303 rifle across his chest. They told me they were after moose but so far had no luck. They also said they'd come across a dead black bear near the La Loche River. I watched them paddle off towards Buffalo Narrows.

Shortly after, I was startled by the roar of aircraft engines across the lake. A large amphibious aircraft was skimming the water about three kilometres away. It descended swiftly, scooped up water, then climbed and continued north. About an hour later it returned. It was a CL 215 water bomber, a twin-engined Canadian-built aircraft that can take on about 5,000 litres of water in 10 seconds.

Newer versions of these versatile planes, like the CL 415 made by Bombardier Aerospace, are in great demand around the world. Originally known as Catalina flying boats, during World War II they were great submarine killers. In a tenacious battle near the end of the war, Flight Lieutenant David Hornell sunk a Nazi U-boat in the Gulf of St Lawrence. In its final moments, however, the submarine fired a lucky shot that brought down the aircraft. While the rest of the crew survived, Hornell died in the crash. He was posthumously awarded the Victoria Cross for outstanding bravery.

The water bomber made another run, skimming the surface close to me. When it appeared again, it came even closer. A canoe is difficult to spot from the air, and as the huge aircraft closed in, I was convinced he was going to suck me up in his water scoop. I scrambled to get out of the way, paddling furiously for the nearest beach. As I hauled the canoe out of the water, the plane roared over my head.

It made a second circuit, not picking up any water but pointing straight for me on the shore. I saw both pilots distinctly, waving while they blinked their navigation lights. Waggling its wings in salute, the huge machine created a downdraft that bent the trees like bows and blasted my hat away on the water. It pulled up, just clearing the trees. If the pilots wanted to scare the hell out of me, they succeeded big time! Later, Karen told me she asked them to look out for me.

Although I scanned the shoreline ahead carefully, there was no sign of the La Loche River. One problem with a canoe is that its closeness to the water makes it a poor vantagepoint. The river was an important junction, a key link in my route to the village of La Loche. From there I faced a marathon 20-kilometre portage over wild country to the Clearwater and Athabasca Rivers and Fort McMurray. I headed out onto the lake to get a better look at the shoreline. About five kilometres from shore the wind came up, and despite my best efforts I was pushed steadily across to the other side. Exhausted, I camped on the beach near a small Indian community.

Early next morning, the sun shining brilliantly, I paddled towards what the map indicated was Michel Village. I figured a prominent hill nearby would be good spot to get my bearings. Pulling the canoe onto the bank, I headed up the steep incline. From the top there was a clear view across the lake, but I still couldn't see the La Loche River.

Across the road a man sat on the porch of a large duplex. Strolling over to exchange pleasantries, I stopped in my tracks. Plainly he was drunk and belligerent. I did an about-face towards the centre of the village. Then I passed a man on a ladder painting his house. "Good morning," I called up. "Can you point out the La Loche River to me? I can't seem to find it."

He laughed heartily. "At this time of the year you'll be lucky if you ever see it. Water levels are way low. There's probably only about two inches in that river now." He pointed across the lake.

I walked back towards the shore, kicking myself for not realizing that water levels would be low this late in the summer. Fishermen in Buffalo Narrows had been complaining about low water. I picked my way down the steep path. It flattened out and continued to the water with thick clumps of bushes on either side.

I was startled from my reverie by a sharp blow in my lower back. A harsh voice demanded, "Gimme yer money!"

I turned and found myself looking at a young Indian fellow. The eyes that stared at me from a badly scarred face were glazed and unfocused. He thrust a rifle into my chest. "I told you – give – me – your – fucking – money, man!

To emphasize his demand, he poked me in the chest repeatedly with his rifle. I stared at him in shocked bewilderment. I couldn't believe that in a remote northern backwoods, this guy was actually holding me up!

Gingerly I pushed the barrel of the rifle away. "You must be joking. Why the hell would I have money, paddling in no man's land in a canoe?" He was crazy. I couldn't even remember where my wallet was – likely in one of my packs in the canoe.

He raised the rifle to point directly at my forehead. I stared mesmerized into the barrel, so close to my face that I could see tiny grains of sand sticking to the inside.

He meant what he said. He would kill me without compunction. Waiting for him to press the trigger, I quietly intoned a prayer. He blinked in surprise as I made the sign of the cross. This was deadly serious. Horror-struck, I watched his hand squeeze the trigger. This was my last moment. There was a loud click.

Rage filled me. The canoe was a few metres away. I dived headlong through the bushes. Heaving the canoe into the water, I made a mad leap aboard. The force propelled it out into the lake. I shoved the paddle deep into the water. Maybe I was going to make it.

I heard another click. My belly turned ice cold. The sound of a rifle bolt clearing the magazine carried across the stretch separating us. Expecting the crack of a rifle at any moment, my muscles tensed for the thud of bullet in my back. I bent low over the canoe, not daring to risk a glance behind. Again I heard the shifting of the rifle bolt and the fumbling noise of a cartridge in the magazine.

I paddled like a bat from hell, keeping as close to the shore as I could. I'd be a sitting duck if I headed directly across the lake. Hours later, totally exhausted, I pulled under an overhanging branch close to shore, my heart pounding.

After a brief rest I headed out again into the lake, but the sudden snarl of an outboard motor sent me back towards the trees. The crazy asshole could be intent on running me down.

Several kilometres further, I pulled into a small bay and waited for sundown. When it grew dark, I headed silently across the lake. A partial moon made the crossing relatively trouble free. I passed up the comfortable beach area where I would be easily spotted, setting up camp instead in the bush. A precautionary walk down the shore assured me it was unlikely my presence would be observed. Although I wasn't hungry, I decided to make some soup and tea.

The tea helped restore my frazzled nerves. That crazy bastard was likely spaced out on drugs and booze. Now I knew what it was to experience emotional rape. I had never been closer to death. Why he hadn't shot me in the back as I paddled away, I'll never know. The clicks and fumbling with cartridges suggest that the rifle or the rounds may have been faulty. The sand in the barrel could support this explanation. He was also stoned out of his mind.

I hardly slept, rising early and heading back towards Buffalo Narrows. Every time I heard an outboard, I sped towards shore, dragging the canoe behind bushes. Just along the lakeshore from where I had camped two nights before, I passed a deeply furrowed area where at one time water had flowed swiftly as it met Peter Pond Lake. Now there was not a trace of water anywhere. This was the "missing" La Loche River. The two men I had spoken to in the canoe must have been pulling my leg. There was no way they could have come downriver from La Loche.

Anxiety drove my paddles, and I made speedy progress. Late in the afternoon I pulled up at Buffalo Narrows landing and made straight for the RCMP station. Somewhat incoherently I spoke to the constable on duty, blurting out the story of my encounter.

"How come you're only reporting this now!" he exclaimed. "Where the hell have you been the last three days?" He found it hard to grasp that I was travelling by canoe. "My God, it's like something you read about in the tales of the old Northwest!"

Finally convinced that my story of being bushwhacked was authentic, he led me through to the next room. "This is the rogues' gallery," he said, handing me a thick photo album. "See if you can find him there."

When I opened the album, the very first picture I saw was the gunman himself, a first-class likeness! The constable was floored. "You're sure this is him?"

I hadn't a shred of doubt. He headed off to the back of the building, where I could hear him speaking animatedly to someone.

A few minutes later a sergeant came to the counter. "Are you absolutely sure this is the man who held you up?" Again I went over my story.

The sergeant was convinced my encounter at Michel Village rang true. "This guy you tangled with is a real bad hombre. He's wanted for a lot of serious stuff and on the lam after escaping from custody." He looked straight at me. "I know this is a lot to ask, but do you think you could show us where you saw him? It would help us a great deal. We have a half-track vehicle, and there's a lumber road going in most of the way, so we should make it okay."

What the hell, I thought, taking part in an armed posse would be something to tell the grandkids. In about half an hour or so, four Mounties in bulletproof vests piled into the half-track laden with sub-machine guns, smoke bombs, pistols, and rifles. Plainly they didn't underestimate who they were up against. We roared overland through wild bush country, occasionally crashing through scrub pine along the rough lumber road. As we approached Michel Village, the tension increased. The men checked their equipment with impressive thoroughness. Dealing with an unstable individual high on drugs, they knew anything could happen.

In the village I pointed out the house where the partying had been going on. "Whatever happens, you stay in the back of the truck," the sergeant warned. He didn't need to tell me twice. No way I was going to get in the middle of a gunfight!

Three of the men took positions near the front door, guns trained on it. One officer, his pistol out of sight, knocked on the door. The tension rose as we waited to see who would open it. To everyone's surprise, it was an old lady. She appeared unperturbed at the sight of heavily armed police on her lawn. After questioning by the Mountie, she said that her son had gone off to La Loche. Everyone relaxed. Guns slung over their shoulder, the Mounties headed back to the truck.

At the RCMP post in Buffalo Narrows, the sergeant told me they were putting out an all-points bulletin for my assailant. I assured him I would testify against him in court when they caught him. Just as I was leaving, the sergeant looked sharply at me. "This guy's a real bad bastard, John. Make no mistake, he would have killed you. You're going to have to watch it till we get him behind bars. Since you can identify him, you're a marked man. It might be a good idea to move out of this area as quick as possible."

Those sombre words still ringing in my ears, I looked furtively over my shoulder as I headed down the street. Finding myself outside Buffalo Airways, I called in to speak to Karen. She had heard about my traumatic experience and was relieved to know I was all right.

When I told her the former La Loche River was now a dried-up gulch cutting off my route to La Loche, she picked up the phone. In a moment she had solved my predicament by arranging transport on a hydro truck, leaving in twenty minutes.

Karen's husband, Dennis, told me "You'd better get in touch with Craig Schnell of La Roche Airways about making a fast exit out of the territory. I'll let him know about you."

A few minutes later Don Wilson of Saskatchewan Hydro pulled up at the front door, and we headed to the waterfront to pick up my canoe and gear. On the trip to La Loche, I listened with growing unease as the hydro guys exchanged horror stories about crime around the region. The RCMP had also been pretty negative in their comments. Someone at the rear of the truck called out, "La Loche holds the record per capita for murders in Canada." I didn't doubt it was one tough town.

Don dropped me off near the Northern Store in La Loche. Thanks to the bush telegraph, the manager already knew about my recent troubles and was happy to keep an eye on my canoe. As I walked across to the RCMP station across the road, I noticed that many store windows along the main drag had been boarded up, and paint was peeling off doors. Drunks were everywhere. I fought off an aggressive panhandler with a hard-luck tale. The place reminded me of shootout scenes from old cowboy movies with sagebrush blowing along mud-choked streets.

At the RCMP station I enquired whether they'd any luck in catching my assailant. "Not as yet," a constable told me. He warned me to be careful in La Loche, particularly after dark. "Until we find this guy, it might be a good idea if you made yourself scarce. He has friends here who are into drugs in a big way."

It was time for evasive action. Along the lakefront I'd seen a large sign advertising La Loche Airways. A Cessna 185 floatplane was tied up at the dock, its engine cover open. A man was slouched over the cowling, his head deep inside. As I approached he stepped back onto the dock. "What can I do for you?" he asked cheerfully.

Craig Schnell did a lot of work flying canoeists and fishermen into the Clearwater River. He had read about me in the newspaper and was impressed with my ambition to follow the trail of Mackenzie. "I understand from Dennis at Buffalo Narrows Airways that you've become persona non grata around here."

I agreed that among certain criminal elements I wasn't popular. After we spent some time chatting, Craig said, " I'm going to take you down to the Whitewater to get you on your way."

I stammered my thanks. After packing my gear into the back of Craig's truck, we picked up *Spirit of Mackenzie*, still under the watchful eye of the manager of the Northern Store, and I loaded my provisions. Back at the dock, Craig secured the canoe to the left float of the Cessna. It was strange seeing it there instead of on the water.

Bypassing the famous Methye Portage left me feeling sad. This 19-kilometre marathon trek to the Clearwater River was one of the great challenges on the entire historic cross-Canada canoe route. However, the aerial portage was marvellous, a ringside seat on the spectacular scenery of the Clearwater Valley. And as the town receded behind me, I was filled with a sense of freedom. I realized how deep my anxiety had been that the bandit might have popped up anywhere around La Loche.

Below us, tightly packed pines stretched to the horizon. A downed aircraft in these parts would be swallowed up. More to the point for me, canoeing in such terrain was going to require all my skills. A short ways ahead, the serpentine loops of the river – our destination – came into view. Less than ten minutes from takeoff, we were heading for a landing.

Craig cut the throttle, and we glided down between the trees. Despite my strong protestations, he refused payment of any kind. "Take care, John, and good luck," he called as he swung the Cessna out onto the river and took off.

I watched the plane until it was a speck on the horizon. The silence was profound. I was touched at the bush pilot's generosity, as well as that of Kathy and Dennis. They had all gone out of their way to help me. Watching the plane disappear left me with a pang of loneliness. The feeling soon dissipated, though, as I hustled around making preparations to set up camp on the sandbank.

With a strong downstream current, I made swift progress the next day. It felt good to run several challenging rapids after the nervous tensions of the past days. When I pulled out of the river and onto a convenient sandbank for tea, I was heady with elation. Once again it felt good to be alive.

Despite its name, the Clearwater River is actually brown-tinted. It flows westwards to meet the great Athabasca River at the oil-sands city of Fort McMurray. The portages on the Clearwater are laborious, and combined with navigating the very fast water and tricky rapids, they quickly depleted my energy. I was reading Eric Morse's *Freshwater Saga*, and took his advice to go slower than the flow to allow more time to work my way around frequent unexpected obstacles. In fast white-water, this involved frequent back paddling, and soon my arms were stiff and sore.

The weather, however, was excellent. After a couple of days the river widened, and the frequent sandbanks provided good camping as well as rest stops. At Fort McMurray I hauled out near the seaplane base on a sheltered cove known as the Snye. Stiff and creaky, caked in mud and desperate for a shower and clean clothes, I walked towards the town centre. After my bushwhacking experience, I found myself much more tired than usual.

The Peter Pond Hotel was a short two blocks from the river. Once I'd checked in and showered, I made my way to the dining room for lunch. I was glancing over the menu when a well-dressed man stopped at my table and stuck out his hand. "Jack Fix. I'm the manager of the hotel. So you're the intrepid canoeist that's following the great Mackenzie."

He smiled at my surprise. "We know everyone who comes into town. Heard on the radio about your adventures on Peter Pond Lake," he added. My fellow diners stopped eating to listen.

"I just hope I don't have a similar experience in the Peter Pond Hotel!"

He laughed. "No way. We also have a school, a shopping mall, and a street named after him, just so you won't forget one of Alberta's first citizens when you tour our fair city. Of course, you're a guest of the hotel. Enjoy your stay – it's on the house."

The smiles and muted applause from the other tables indicated approval of his generous offer. It also made me feel a little sensitive about my reference to their province's hero, Peter Pond, as a crook!

Fort McMurray is a friendly town with population of some 35,000, many of them expatriate Newfoundlanders drawn by the lure of jobs with the Alberta tar sands project. When I strolled downtown, my sourdough-like appearance attracted the usual share of odd looks. On my second day in the city I received a call from the local newspaper. The reporter asked if she could interview me at the hotel. I suggested a time after lunch.

When I made my way into the dining room, a young woman rose to greet me, clutching a notebook. "I'm Laurie. You're obviously the Montreal canoeist."

We got down to the reasons for my trip and adventures en route. But as the interview progressed, it seemed to me our roles were reversing and I was interviewing her. When I asked if she had done any canoeing, she looked flustered. She said she had been down the Athabasca River.

"It's a very dangerous river, Lake Athabasca even more so. It's extremely treacherous. Be very careful," she pleaded. Suddenly her eyes brimmed with tears. She told me that a friend who had accompanied her in his own canoe was missing when they reached Fort Chipeweyan. A search revealed his overturned craft, and eventually his body was recovered. She was still clearly grieving from her harrowing experience. Although she took detailed notes, the story of my canoe trip never appeared. I believe it was too painful for her to write a story that rekindled memories of her friend's death.

Not wishing to overstay my welcome at the hotel, I decided after four days in Fort McMurray it was time to move on. One of the guests gave me a ride down to the floatplane base to my canoe. As I shoved off from the Snye, the current took me swiftly downstream en route to Fort Chipeweyan.

Passing alongside the enormous Syncrude Athabasca Sands plant, I smelled the distinctive odour of melting tar. I had reached the precise spot where, 200 years before, Mackenzie had stopped to record this phenomenon. His astute observation signalled to later geologists the presence of large deposits of bituminous oil material:

At about 24 miles from the fork [of the Athabasca and Clearwater rivers] are some bituminous fountains into which a pole of 20 feet long may be inserted without the least resistance. The bitumen is in a fluid state and when mixed with gum, the resinous substance collected from the spruce fir, it serves to gum the Indians canoes. In its heated state, it emits a smell like that of sea coal.

Nearly ten years earlier in 1778, Peter Pond had also come across the bitumen and used it for caulking canoes. Even earlier, in 1719, a Cree trader took samples to the Hudson Bay Company.

The discovery of an economically viable process to extract oil from sand led to the development of the Syncrude tar sands, a bonanza for Alberta. The Athabasca region near Fort McMurray has an oil reserve spanning an area of some 26,000 kilometres. It is estimated to contain more than one trillion barrels of bitumen.

Downstream from the plant the river widened and the current increased dramatically. With the wind at my back I raised sail and was soon bowling along at a breathtaking pace. Although I could see great camping spots on islands with hard-sand beaches, in some places there was a gooey scum of oil. The bush was lush and the pine trees were tall and healthy, but there was little evidence of wildlife in the river or along the banks. No fish jumped, and birds were noticeably few and failed to sing. Late in the afternoon, an incredible 50 kilometres into my journey, I stopped on a large sandbank and set up camp.

The sun rose next morning on another beautiful cloudless sky. About 40 kilometres downriver I came to a log cabin on the bank surrounded by several dilapidated buildings and a variety of pipes and funnels rusting on the ground. It seemed like a good spot for a breather, so I pulled in quickly – too quickly! The current caught me unawares and spun me around. After a bout of furious paddling I regained control with no damage other than to my ego.

Hauling the canoe out, I climbed up a rock-strewn path towards a cabin high on the bank. Reaching the top, I encountered a woman weeding the garden. "You sure gave me a surprise!" She wiped her hands on her smock as she rose to greet me. "We don't get many callers out here in the boondocks."

Maureen Duseault told me that she and her husband looked after the old tar-sand recovery plant. "It's part of a 1923 heritage site marking early pioneering attempts to extract oil from the tar sands. We're trying to get it into some kind of shape to make a decent attraction for tourists. But come on in. I've just baked some bread."

I polished off slice after slice at the kitchen table, washed down with copious cups of coffee. During the winter, Maureen said, she worked as a cook in a lumber camp. Her husband was building them a bigger log house about eight kilometres downstream, trying to get as much done as possible before winter.

She filled me in on the history of the tar sands plant. She also told me there'd been a major oil spill from Syncrude a few weeks before, which explained why the wildlife was so sparse along the riverbanks. The catastrophe had been hushed up by a government renowned for its sensitivity to environmental criticism.

When it was time for me to head out, Maureen handed me a fresh loaf. She couldn't have given me a better gift. But fresh bread without butter isn't a treat, and greed won over polite restraint. Placing my spoils carefully in the canoe, I paddled on my way, feeling mighty pleased with myself.

On my fourth day on the river, the weather broke. Thunder, darting lightning, and torrential rain turned the ground into a quagmire. I camped on the bank close to the site of Peter Pond's crude log cabin, the first house in Alberta, built when he entered Athabasca country in 1778. Designed as a trading post, it was 65 kilometres south of Lake Athabasca. Next morning I crossed into Wood Buffalo National Park near the Northwest Territories–Alberta border. At an incredible 56,000 square kilometres, it is one of the largest parks of its kind in the world.

Embarrass Portage, a small hamlet on the river, was a short distance from my next destination, Fort Chipeweyan. In the post office there I met Kathy McGinnis, the assistant curator at the Fort Chipeweyan museum. She told me that one of their acquisitions for the museum was a canoe used by an Ottawa man who followed the voyageur route from Montreal. She and husband, Larry, have an ambitious project underway: having recently bought property nearby, they plan to operate a marina and museum. We spent a pleasant couple of hours chatting about local politics and catching up on national events. Promising to take a look at the museum, I continued on downriver.

Next day I paddled sedately down the Embarrass River and Fletcher Channel, enthused that this was my final leg to Fort Chip, as the locals called it. The fine weather made for an easy paddle. Crossing Lake Athabasca with the sun setting, a large British flag flapping over the fort, I stopped to take in the scene. It was little changed since Mackenzie arrived there in 1788 as a 24-year-old greenhorn to take up a new job with the notorious Pond.

I pulled the canoe out of the water near the Queen of Angels church. The Oblate father gave me permission to camp on the lawn. The sun was well up next morning when I struggled out of bed. I felt great. The view from the Fort Chip Lodge dining room window was remarkable, and I exulted in the luxury of a meal I didn't have to fix myself.

Later I called in to the museum. An interesting exhibit described the history of the fort, which had served as the most northerly depot for the Nor'westers, some 2,600 kilometres north of Lake Superior. Fort Chipeweyan was second only to Grand Portage on Lake Superior as a key post to explore the interior. One of the staff asked if the museum could have my canoe when I completed my trip, but I politely declined.

Peter Pond wintered at the fort in 1781-82, where he met up with Jean-Etienne Waden, who had served in Wolfe's army at Quebec. Waden's daughter, Veronique, married the Reverend John Bethune, a Presbyterian minister in Montreal and later at St Andrew's Church in Glengarry County, Ontario. The Bethunes had a son, Angus, who joined the Nor'westers. Angus Bethune was the great-grandfather of one of Canada's remarkable figures, Dr Norman Bethune.

Waden and Pond quarrelled, and Waden was killed. Pond took off for the south, but five years later he was back in Athabasca country. The trader John Ross died in the course of another quarrel, but this time the slippery Pond managed to avoid being charged. Pond, thoroughly tainted with a violent reputation, was also believed to be responsible for killing an Indian on the Saskatchewan River. However, he again managed to escape retribution. An aboriginal research website claims that Pond was responsible for distributing smallpox-infected blankets in the Athabasca country and along the Saskatchewan. He left Athabasca in 1788 and died in Milton, Connecticut, an embittered man.

Pond spent his last winter at Fort Chip working on the map he figured would provide a route to the opulent markets of the East. It was this map he hoped to sell to Catherine II of Russia, who had a particular interest in expanding her country's territory. Mackenzie accepted his northern assignment with enthusiasm, undeterred by Pond's dark reputation. No doubt his diplomatic skills and intuitive ability to get the most out of people helped. Certainly his tenure paid off, since he had access to Pond's map. But while following Pond's advice led him down the "River of Disappointment" to the Beaufort Sea, it ultimately paved the way to the Pacific, bringing him a knighthood and a healthy bank balance – not bad for a 24-year-old impoverished newcomer to Canada!

When I returned to camp, the church door opened and an elderly nun came out to greet me. "I'm Sister Martha. You sure look like you could use some supper. What about joining us? We're having buffalo steaks. We have a house just along the road a piece on your left – can't miss it. Say, half an hour?"

I quickly accepted. "Sounds great, Sister!"

She was right – no way I could miss the house, a large green frame two storey on a pristine lawn with a crèche and a statue of the Virgin. In the kitchen she introduced me to Jean, a Chipeweyan native band elder, a remarkable lady and an authority on the history of the Chipewyans.

The buffalo steaks were first class. Surfeited, we sat talking around the table. In soft lilting speech Jean told me that Lake Athabasca was probably the most dangerous waterway in Canada. "Almost every member of our tribe has lost a relative at one time or another in that lake." As she got up to pour coffee, she added quietly. "As for myself, I lost five sons." I sat reeling at her grim disclosure, not knowing how to respond.

Eventually, sipping her coffee, she sighed reflectively. "Our life changed drastically in the community after they built the Bennett Dam." Following construction of the huge dam on the Peace River some 1,200 kilometres west of the lake, water levels had fluctuated wildly. This effectively drowned muskrat, beaver, and other small animals, destroying ancient trapping and hunting areas, along with sacred burial sites. The social devastation from this misguided project was widespread, resulting in increased alcoholism and abuse.

Everywhere I travelled, I heard a similar story. A law unto themselves, driven by grandiose dreams, government planners rarely consulted aboriginal communities. Although I listened to similar melancholic tales across the country, they never failed to enrage me. Politicians like "Wacky" Bennett indulged enormous egos, enshrining their names on monstrous pieces of concrete while disrupting the social fabric of a nation. No amount of land-claim settlement money will ever make up for the crimes perpetrated on First Nations people.

As we moved outside to the patio, Jean told another story. "I remember one remarkable day long ago, in the 1920s, I think it was. Late in the afternoon, when the men were getting back from the fishing, we heard this loud noise. The whole settlement turned out, pointing towards the sky. We looked up in amazement to see this great bird zooming over the lake. It was the first time any of us had seen an airplane. A lot of us were scared and ran away. It circled around, then landed, and we saw a white man walk from it towards us. Figuring it was likely okay, we came closer to stare at it."

What Jean was describing was the epic 1929 flight by Canada's most famous bush pilot, W.R. "Wop" May. His pioneering flight from Edmonton in an open cockpit plane to the high North under hideous conditions of -50° Celsius remains one of the most outstanding achievements in aviation history.

Walking along the lake before making my way back to camp, I decided to head out the next morning. The comments Jean had made and those of the distraught reporter in Fort McMurray had unsettled me. The quicker I was off this dangerous lake the better.

In my sleeping bag I thought over Jean's story of her first encounter with an aeroplane. Wop May's pioneering flight ushered in a new era for the Territories as aircraft opened up the North. When I was a kid in Scotland in the air cadets, one of our most popular officers, Joe Wood – "old Joe," as we affectionately named him – entertained us with thrilling stories about the Canadian aces he knew in the First World War. We were enthralled by his tales of his days over the trenches with Wop May, Billy Bishop, Roy Brown, and Punch Dickens. As an observer, Joe sported on his tunic a winged brevy with a large O in the centre – "the flying asshole," it was termed irreverently by those who wore it.

Wop May was representative of many of Canada's intrepid bush pilots who honed their skills over the trenches in the Great War. Sadly, most are forgotten today. Who remembers Grant McConnachie of *Bush Pilot with a Briefcase* fame, who became founder of Canadian Pacific Airlines? Or Punch Dickens, another World War I ace? Or Roy Brown from Carleton Place, Ontario, credited with downing the famous German Baron von Richthofen, the Red Baron, following a stupendous dog fight over the trenches? Joe's tales infused me with the desire to become a pilot. In the meantime I made do by playing hooky from school and puttering Walter Mitty-like in the cockpit of an old Bristol Bulldog biplane in the squadron yard.

Next morning, the lake was calm and placid. Heading down Chenal de Quatre Fourches or Catfish Channel, I was pushed along by the current at a steady clip. Since all trips through Wood Buffalo National Park require registration, I pulled in at the ranger station. Filling in the paper work, the ranger warned me to be sure to report when I left the park: "Otherwise we'll have to dispatch an aircraft to search for you."

After the construction of the Bennett Dam, unstable water levels resulted in enormous changes in the delta, a highly enriched food source for waterfowl. Huge areas of wetlands have dried out, and there has been irreversible damage to the entire aquatic ecosystem. In the prestigious on-line journal *International Rivers Network*, researchers have summarized the results of numerous studies of the environmental consequences of dams like the Bennett: "Large dams and river diversions have proven to be primary destroyers of aquatic habitat, contributing substantially to the destruction of fisheries, the extinction of species, and the overall loss of the ecosystem services on which the human economy depends. Their social and economic costs have also risen markedly over the past two decades." Just as at First Nations people told the government in the first place, there is a serious problem.

But despite all the studies indicating the disastrous consequences of such large dams, a third dam is being considered for power generation in Peace River country. From my own experience dealing with labyrinthine government bureaucracy, I have concluded that despite the weight of hard scientific data by competent researchers, the political will to resist a powerful industrial lobby is sadly lacking

Hemmed in by muddy bush and accompanied by clouds of mosquitoes, I paddled down the narrow channel. Only through sheer luck did I find a dry spot to camp. The insects made setting up my tent a real misery. It was just about 20 kilometres to the junction of the Peace and the Slave rivers. This was the same spot where Mackenzie took the wrong turn and went on to discover the Mackenzie River – the "River of Disappointment," as he supposedly termed it.

Next day I swung into the south channel of the Peace River, feeling excited about the hundreds of kilometres that now lay behind me. The next province was British Columbia – and the end of the trail next year, if all went well.

But after my freewheeling paddle downriver on the Athabasca, the Peace was a profound shock. Only with great difficulty could I make the slightest headway against the powerful current. It didn't help when the weather, which had been idyllic for the past several days, turned savage. As the wind rose alarmingly, the temperature plunged from a balmy 25 degrees to around 8. With the wind gusting close to 100 kilometres, I was soon chilled to the bone.

I heard a loud splash about five metres in front of the bow, and the canoe rocked dangerously. To my horror, a large tree had simply slid into the river from the eroded bank. Many more trees along the bank looked to be on the verge of following suit.

I manoeuvred frantically towards the right bank, managing to pull up onto a sandbar. There was no question of erecting a tent or even leaving the canoe. I slid under the spray covers, grateful to have some shelter. Later, when I got out to stretch my legs, a huge burst of wind got under the canvas. For a moment I thought the canoe was going to take to the air, but it just rolled along the sand as I chased frantically behind. There was nowhere to tie a line to secure it, so I piled in sand as ballast. The sandbar provided no shelter from the wind, but there was really no place else. On either side of the river trees were still falling into the water. The only way I was going to make any headway upstream would be to take advantage of swift back-eddies close to shore. However, that meant I might get clobbered by a falling tree.

It was a serious dilemma. An unremitting line of squalls stretched limitlessly to the horizon. God only knew when the weather would break.

After hours in the cramped confines of the canoe, wearing two pairs of pants, three shirts and two sweaters as well as my windbreaker, I decided to bring the tent out, though I knew there was no way I could set it up. This was not only because there was nowhere to anchor it but also because of its height. I'd bought it thinking this was a great feature since it allowed me to stand upright. But in the strong winds of Alberta, this feature was an impediment. I decided instead to simply "wear" the tent. I pushed my sleeping bag inside, then followed. I could stretch out comfortably even though the fabric tickled my nose. After several hours I turned the tent around with the door on the bottom. Using my paddle as a pole, I raised the fabric enough to provide some space. Mercifully, I was now able to have a brew-up. Later, I even cooked supper. But with the weather still vile, I settled myself with a book for a long wait

It was a bitter night with the wind shrieking as furiously as ever. This was the worst storm I had encountered so far. And here I was on a shifting sandbank in the middle of a river with gale-force winds and chilling temperatures! After a night of little sleep, I was glad when morning finally arrived. I took advantage of a let-up in the wind to set out for Carlsson Landing. Launching into a stiff current, I felt my heart sink as the wind rose again. Trees once more began falling into the river. Hurtling by me, they stretched like massive nets to trap the canoe. I managed to avoid their clutches, but I was soon exhausted, cold and demoralized.

What the hell, I thought. Who needs this? I was really pressing my luck. My gloomy reverie was interrupted by a loud honking. Just below the storm-tossed clouds a huge chevron of Canada geese was making its way south. That did it.

It was only early September, but winter was making an appearance in the north. I turned the canoe around. Travelling speedily downstream on course for Fort Smith, in no time I reached the Slave River, then a couple of small rapids, Primose and Demi Charge, before I finally hit the portage point, Fort Fitzgerald. Dead Man's Rapids downstream at Fort Smith are impassable.

As I was wondering how I was going to manage the portage, a car pulled up along the shore. A couple of young native lads told me they had seen me coming. Did I want a lift to Fort Smith. Did I!

As we passed the headquarters for Buffalo National Park at Fort Smith, I called in to inform them I was out of their territory. When I explained ruefully to the ranger that I hadn't been able to get through the current on the Peace River, he laughed. "A lot of people haven't been able to make it through. Last week we had the crack British SAS doing canoe training here. They were exhausted. They tried for two days to get up the Peace and couldn't make it. So you shouldn't feel too bad!"

I struck it lucky in the local restaurant, a real small-town coffee house with smoke billowing in your face but good-natured repartee going on all around. It was evident from the conversation that everyone knew all about me.

It had definitely been the right move coming to Forth Smith instead of trying to buck the fierce current and weather on the Peace. It was a base to prepare for next year and would be a good taking-off spot to get back east.

One of the diners questioning me about my trip turned out to be retired RCMP Superintendent Jack McCullough. He was leaving next day for Regina to take part in the ceremonies at the RCMP training depot in that city and offered me a ride south. Jack also found me a place to store my canoe over the winter. Northern hospitality is fabulous.

I was sorry to be finishing up earlier than I would have liked, but there was no question that I didn't have the same zip as when I set out in the spring. If you're not in tip-top shape, fast and tricky waters are no place to be.

PART 4

THE FOURTH YEAR 1993

FROM FORT SMITH

TO BELLA COOLA

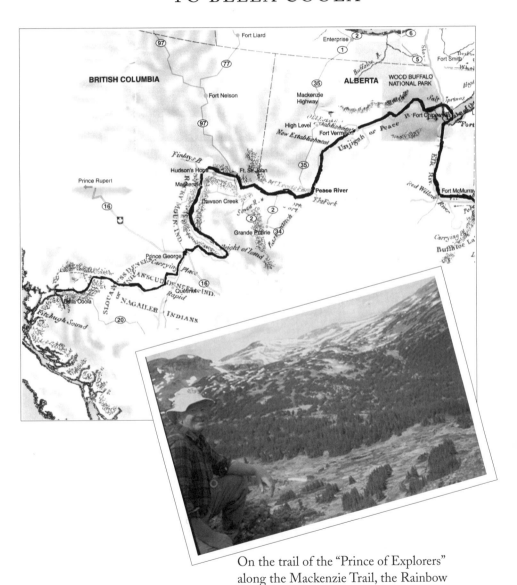

On the trail of the "Prince of Explorers"
along the Mackenzie Trail, the Rainbow
Mountains provide a stunning panorama.

Ed and Sharon Linfitt, a couple who epitomize truly the warm hospitality of wilderness folks everywhere, outside their property on Lake Williston, near Hudson Hope, Northern British Columbia.

The noble westie, Angus, protecting his master from marauding seagulls on Bella Coola Sound.

The end of the trail at Mackenzie's Island, Dean Channel, British Columbia.

HMCS *Mackenzie* provides a pleasant change from paddling as Angus and I enjoy a luxury ride back to Bella Coola and home.

11

Twelve Foot Davis

In March the telephone rang and a cultivated female voice asked, "Would I be speaking to John Donaldson?"

When I said she was, she went on. "I'm calling from the office of the Speaker of the House of Commons. The Honourable John Fraser would like to know if you could have lunch with him at his office sometime next week."

Stunned, I mumbled assent. When I asked several times for an explanation of this request, she was unable to offer one. We arranged a time and date the following week, and I replaced the receiver. What in heaven's name could the Speaker of the Canadian Parliament want with me?

I have little patience anytime, but the wait to learn the reason for the invitation was interminable. At last I headed for Ottawa. At the entrance to the House of Commons I spoke to a smartly uniformed commissionaire, chest bedecked with campaign medals. He pointed me to the Speaker's chambers, where a secretary directed me to a seat.

As I waited, government ministers came and went. Several looked at me quizzically. One of them, Don Boudria, seemed consumed with curiosity, perhaps piqued that a lesser mortal had precedence. A short time later I was admitted to the inner sanctum.

A stocky man wearing the Speaker's robes crossed the room, hand outstretched. "John Fraser. Glad you could come along." He motioned me to a chair. A valet appeared and handed me a menu. "What about a drink, John? I can recommend our single malt."

Before I could reply, the secretary entered with an apology. "The Prime Minister is on line two, sir."

While I waited for the conversation to finish, I took in the chambers. They were palatial, apparently larger than those of the Prime Minister. The Speaker has a personal valet and a chef who prepares his meals, since he dines in his chamber. The menu was better than a five-star restaurant.

Finishing his conversation, Mr Fraser gave me a history lesson. "Being a former serviceman, John, you may be familiar with Winston Churchill's famous speech when he visited our House of Commons during the war – the one where he quoted that Hitler had said he would 'wring England's neck like a chicken.'"

I was. In his famous quip, Churchill had retorted, "Some chicken." Pausing theatrically, the master of rhetoric then added, "Some neck."

John Fraser went on. "Mr Churchill wrote that speech in this office before addressing the Canadian House of Commons." Reaching into a desk drawer, he handed me the original quotation in the great man's hand, written in the dark war years of 1941. I was thrilled at seeing this unique piece of history.

As we relaxed over lunch, Fraser finally shed some light on the reason for the summons. "There was a story about your canoe trip in one of the papers – the *Victoria Times Colonist*, I think. I was intrigued when I read about your desire to repeat the voyages of Mackenzie by canoe. Now tell me why your canoe carries the Seaforth Highlanders crest."

I explained that my father, along with several other family members, had been a Seaforth. Fraser told me that he had served in the Seaforth Highlanders of Canada himself. He had also visited Mackenzie's gravesite in Avoch, Scotland, and had long been a fan of the great explorer.

After a couple of hours during which he shared personal anecdotes of his family history, which traces its roots to Scotland, it was time for me to leave. As we shook hands, Fraser said that he would be on Mackenzie's Rock for the bicentennial celebrations and looked forward especially to greeting me when I landed there. "I've no doubt you'll make it, John," he said warmly.

In April I began preparing for my last lap across the continent. I drove south to Maine to the giant department store, LL Bean, considered by Americans the mecca for wilderness equipment. However, most of the merchandise on display was fashionable outdoorswear, with only cursory attention given to equipment and the nuts and bolts of wilderness gear. Despite this, I managed to pick up a first-class dome tent. It would be useful in Alberta's fierce winds, and could be assembled in under five minutes – a decided advantage when the area is alive with winged demons! As well, I picked up a flexible plastic pad that could be placed on the netted canoe seat, a terrific aid to comfort on long paddles. When conditions were tricky, I paddled while kneeling, and it could serve then as a knee pad. It would also make a great pillow when I wanted to grab forty winks on the beach or under a tree.

I'd intended to replace my defective backpack stoves, but the Coleman company repaired both of them free of charge. They were now as good as new. Alas, Magic Pantry's "Boil 'n a Bag" meals were unobtainable. In 1993 Swift withdrew them from the market. Despite my enquiries, no one was able to provide a satisfactory explanation for terminating a great product.

Also new this year was a cassette player and tapes including Kenneth McKellar's unsurpassed rendition of Robert Burns melodies. This was the first time I had taken music with me on the trek. I intended to use it only when camping, not in the canoe. Wearing earphones in the wilderness diminishes the appreciation of the natural world. It's easy to lose touch with what's going on around you. The wind blowing through the trees or glancing off high terrain tells a lot. It can be a vital clue of weather change.

This was to be the final leg of my four-year transcontinental journey. On 22 July 1993 I intended to be at Mackenzie's Rock in Dean Channel taking part in celebrations for the 200th anniversary of Mackenzie's landing on the Pacific coast. My plan was to continue my journey of the previous year on the Peace River. This would lead me to the Fraser River and the final hurdle by land.

For the first time I would be leaving my beloved canoe for quite a while. After four years of hard slogging, I was looking forward immensely to trekking across the beautiful coastal mountains to a grand finale at Mackenzie's Island. Turning in my canoe for hiking boots and a hefty 60-litre backpack, I would tackle the 250-kilometre hike to Bella Coola. My route would be the one used by the Nuxalk Carrier Indians for thousands of years when they traded their rendered fish grease with the Plains Indians. Known as the Grease Trail, the route was used by Mackenzie and his men in 1793.

But there was a series of formidable challenges before I would reach that trail. The thought of going down the mighty Fraser with its whirlpools and strange hydraulics was causing me some concern. My experience the previous year on the Peace was kindergarten compared to the fierce current and white-water conditions along the Fraser. I was relatively inexperienced in white-water canoeing. It's one thing playing in an empty canoe in turbulent conditions, but when it's heavily loaded, the hydrodynamics can cause drastic changes in performance.

On a fine spring day in May 1993 I picked up my canoe at Fort Smith where I had left it in the care of a helpful aboriginal couple. Tightly wrapped in a tarpaulin, it had survived the winter in good condition. By a stroke of luck, some trappers heading down the gravel road to Peace Point gave me a lift, piling my canoe and gear into the back of their '60s-something van.

While I was always nervous setting out for the first time in the spring, I found it hard to contain my excitement. To my relief the current was not as formidable as it had been the previous fall, allowing me to make reasonable progress by working the eddies along the bank. The weather was also great. Although the mornings could be glacial, the sky had an aquamarine clarity, and the sun soon took the chill off.

Since it was my first day on the water, when I spotted a good camping area in early afternoon, I decided to pull in. I was delighted with my new tent. It was everything that the salesman had claimed. The water was soon boiling on my reconditioned backpack stove. Hugging my brew, I savoured the comforts of my new abode. From experience I knew Alberta's winds could blow mighty cold.

Setting off next morning, I found the current stiff. Fortunately, as the river got wider, an assortment of sandbanks provided convenient breaks from paddling. The weather stayed fine, and my traverse along the river proceeded smoothly. However, near Vermilion Rapids I received a rude awakening. A fisherman in an aluminum boat shouted to me across the river that there had been a serious accident. Police were searching for the body of a German canoeist, apparently on a trip down the river to Fort Smith. His canoe was found upside-down, caught in aspen branches. Likely he had overturned in the rapids. I hollered back that I would keep a lookout. I had heard similar stories of missing and drowned canoeists more times than I could recall. It made me uneasy, particularly in cases where the canoeist was highly experienced.

The banks on either side of the Peace are similar to those of the Saskatchewan River, so steep they effectively cut off much of the scenery. This makes for long, boring stretches. However, unlike the muddy Saskatchewan, there were good camping sites on the riverside. Sometimes I climbed the banks to find green pastures at the top.

A remarkable feature of Peace River Country is that it is composed of some 165,000 square kilometres of arable land. This is a real geological anomaly since northern Alberta is predominantly boreal forest. The drainage runoff from some 15 million acres of farmland explains the muddiness of the river. I had to filter the water or carry bottled supplies.

At the town of Peace River I pulled my canoe up on a high grassy bank and headed downtown. The single coffee shop on the main street was easily spotted. Over the years I've developed a knack for zeroing in on the local gossip shop. Such places provide the lone long-distance canoeist with a convenient place to touch base with fellow humans. They not only provide a running commentary on the history of the community but can be a source of help when portaging canoe and gear.

The momentary lull in conversation indicated I was the focus of scrutiny. After four years on the trail, I was used to inquisitive stares. Wisecracks from the resident joker flew around the room: "Maybe he's a long-lost gold prospector from the trail of '98!"

The room erupted with laughter. In small towns, any fresh source of amusement is grasped like a starving hound seizing a bone. I smiled, and the friendly banter continued around. As I waited for my coffee, some seniors at the next table engaged me in conversation. "Just passing through, are you?" a lanky guy enquired.

This was my cue to set them on their heels and launch into an account of Mackenzie and my "retirement project." However, one of the guys at the table, a man named Fred, was a historical society member and well-versed on Mackenzie's voyages.

"One of the great Nor'westers is buried up the big hill here," he told me. "Name of Twelve Foot Davis. There's a statue of him up the hill you've got to see."

It was plain Fred wasn't going to give me time to think over his offer. I was still finishing my coffee as he propelled me firmly towards the door. "I'll bring you back again," he promised.

As we drove up Judah Hill on the valley slope south of town, he continued expounding on local history. The Sagitawa Lookout at the top of the hill was named by the Beaver Indians, he said. "It's the place where you can see the meeting of the waters that forms the junction of Peace and Smoky Rivers. It's also the burial place of Henry Fuller Davis, a Vermont Yankee who came to the Caribou in the late 1850s gold rush."

At Williams Creek, Davis had astutely noticed that a 12-foot strip of land between the area's two most productive claims had not been staked. He quickly headed for the mining office and made a claim. His tiny plot of land yielded the crafty pioneer gold dust worth more than $100,000 in today's dollars, earning him his nickname and a legendary place in Peace River Country folklore. After the gold bonanza went bust, he became a trader for the Nor'westers and earned a reputation for fair dealing. He came to despise the Hudson's Bay Company for their skinflint sharp practices with native trappers. He never forgot a debt and always kept his door open and stocked with provisions for weary travellers.

One story records that when a trapper died before collecting the money due him for his pelts, Davis spent 10 years tracking down the man's son to pay him. When Davis died, his friend Colonel Jim Cornwall erected his tombstone with the epitaph: *He was every man's friend and never locked his cabin door.* Davis's last wish was to be buried at a spot overlooking the beautiful Peace River crossing. Nowadays there is a large statue of him there with a commanding view over the town.

I didn't let on that I was already familiar with the legend of Twelve Foot Davis. Nor did I mention that I particularly favoured the version recorded by Peter Newman in *Caesars of the Wilderness.* Newman notes that the real reason Davis wanted to be buried in this location was not because it had a panoramic view but because it overlooked the Hudson's Bay Post on the river below. According to local folklore, confirmed by Colonel Cornwall, he had made a last request to "bury me with my feet pointing downhill so I can piss on the Hudson's Bay Company!"

Fred drove me back to my canoe and enticed me to linger in town with numerous historical vignettes about the area. However, I was eager to press on. The weather was fabulous, and I wanted to make headway while it lasted. The current was often strong, and I looked back with nostalgia to the Athabasca River where it was possible to lie back, even reading a book, while bowling speedily downriver. The Peace was work all the way.

At Fort Fork, a short 15 kilometres upstream from the town of Peace River, I dragged my canoe up the bank, conscious that Mackenzie had performed the same task at this spot 200 years before. I scanned the terrain before me with a lump in my throat. The great explorer had set off from here on the final stage of his quest for the Pacific. He had arrived from Fort Chipeweyan on 1 November 1792 and immediately set about constructing winter quarters. But the cold was already intense, causing the axes to become as brittle as glass and slowing progress considerably.

The task of running such an isolated post in the middle of nowhere and hundreds of kilometres from any kind of help dictated that those manning it should be made of stern stuff. Historian J.N. Wallace notes:

> Courage and tact of no ordinary degree were needed to take charge of so isolated a post. The task of a winterer was not to command a military garrison in a strong fort, but to carry on a trade which was entirely dependent on avoiding conflict with superior numbers who, nonetheless, had to be kept under control. The Indians could, at almost any time, destroy the whole party ... Those from the Highlands of Scotland who had been leaders in their own country were well fitted for such a task. Self-dependent, inured to Spartan conditions, accustomed to scattered communities, their character was suited to their new surroundings, and the clan system, whatever its faults, certainly produced men who knew how to rule in their own small circle.

Also, as one wag noted, Scotsmen with a Bible in one hand and a bottle of whiskey in the other seemed ubiquitous in the Canadian wilds

A tremendous burst of gunfire on the first day of January startled Mackenzie awake. He soon realized what the noise was all about. Christmas in the Northwest Company, run exclusively by highland Scots, was essentially a working day, though their competitors, the English Hudson's Bay Company, had a holiday. But the Nor'westers celebrated the Celtic solstice festival of Hogmanay on New Year's Day in true highland style. Thus their canoemen and traders also celebrated the day as a holiday. Mackenzie took the broad hint and dished out rum, wine, and flour for cakes.

During that winter a young Indian boy had his arm badly mangled in an encounter with a bear. Mackenzie attended his wound daily, saving it from amputation. He had earlier gained stature among the Indians when he cured a young woman with a painful abscess of the breast. He had a good knowledge of pharmacy, and whenever he went into an encampment, his first question was to ask if anyone required medical attention. His exceptional abilities eventually gained him the exalted title of Great Spirit.

He acquired his medical knowledge on the job, but on a visit to Scotland following his gruelling voyage to the Beaufort Sea in 1789, he beefed up his expertise when he stayed with his brother, recently graduated from the University of Edinburgh as a surgeon. During his time in Scotland Mackenzie improved his navigational skills as well. In the Outer Hebrides he had been familiar with Gaelic as well as English, and naturally he also possessed a good knowledge of French to communicate with his voyageurs. He was now fluent in Cree and several other Indian dialects, an asset that served him well in bartering with the Indians.

Mackenzie launched the final stage of his search for the North West Passage from Fort Fork on 9 May 1793. Ostensibly seeking new beaver sources, he was at the same time promoting the grand imperial vision to bring British dominion and trade to the Pacific. It was a dream doubtless fuelled also by rumblings of a "manifest destiny" from the great republic to the south. Twelve years later this set in motion the transcontinental expedition of the American explorers Lewis and Clark. As the *Caribou Observer* stated of Mackenzie, "His voyage epitomized the tenacity, vision and Spirit of Canada's early pioneers. His was a voyage of courage, leadership, strength and empathy ... yet most Canadians know very little about this man and his role in shaping this very unique country."

Mackenzie's incredible journey to the "stinking lake," as natives termed the Pacific, was fraught with danger at every turn. Compared by many to the Argonauts' quest for the golden fleece, the feat ranked Mackenzie among an illustrious elite, gaining him the title of Prince of Explorers. W. Kaye Lamb, former dominion archivist, wrote in a preface to the explorer's journal:

> Mackenzie may be hard put to it to overcome a few yards of rapid current, at another he is thinking of trans-Pacific commerce with Canton. He may be standing waist deep in a rushing river, holding onto a wrecked canoe, but this battered craft is still the needle drawing

behind it a thread which knotted with those drawn across the world's greatest oceans by Cook and Vancouver, will form the basis of a network on which Canada still depends for economic survival. Mackenzie may have been from the military point of view almost unarmed, yet the permanent effects of his penetration of territory were at least comparable to Marlborough's [the Duke of Wellington] leading an army to Blenheim.

Accompanying him on his quest into an unknown and savage land were six French-Canadian voyageurs, his assistant Alexander McKay, two Indians, and a large friendly dog. As they shoved their seven-metre (25-foot) canoe into the river on that bright May morning, a volley of shots filled the air as those remaining behind gave the adventurers a rousing farewell. Mackenzie waved his hat and paddled out into the river, turning westwards. Striking an unusually sombre note, he records:

> Those who were left to look after the fort until the party returned expressed misgivings, fearing greatly for our safety and shed tears at the thought of the dangers which our expedition might encounter. They offered up their prayers that we might return in safety from it.

During the 1920s Fort Fork was the launching site for another dramatic adventure, not by Nor'wester canoe but by air. The discovery at that time of a great oil bonanza at Norman Wells on the Mackenzie River traces its origins to Fork Fork. The strike set off a stampede as people flocked north to stake claims in scenes reminiscent of the old sourdough days on the Klondike. It crossed my mind that it was in fact Mackenzie's observations in 1789 that had led directly to the discovery of oil on the Mackenzie River. But the vast fields of black gold were only developed following the introduction of aircraft into the North. They too were piloted by intrepid voyageurs, departing from the Fort Fork launching pad used by Mackenzie nearly two centuries before.

One famous aerial voyageur, Wop May, hit the headlines in 1931 when he was hired by Imperial Oil to fly an executive to the North Country. They used two Junkers aircraft with several men and a huge pile of freight, taking off from an improvised grass runway on the original site of Mackenzie's dwellings at Fort Fork. The oil man didn't take any chances, insisting on bringing along two dozen homing pigeons, "just in case."

After a dicey landing on the ice at Fort Simpson, Wop's aircraft smashed its prop nosing into an ice bank. An ingenious helper at the trading post used glue prepared by boiling moose hides and hooves in water to laminate wooden sleigh runners to improvise a prop. It worked, and they were able to continue downriver to Norman Wells, the site of the black gold bonanza. This remarkable ability to improvise typified many legendary events in bush flying.

A short piece upriver, a low-flying aircraft zoomed overheard, its snarling engines abruptly ending my reverie. It crossed over the trees heading for a landing. Along the fuselage was the insignia of Little Red Airways. I recognized the name, recalling a story about the company I had recently read in an aviation magazine. Launched by the Little Red River Cree Nation in 1986 with one aircraft, it had expanded to over a dozen planes. Refusing government subsidies, it retained complete ownership of the company, a terrific aboriginal success story. Little Red Air proved to be an economic booster for small towns in the high Peace River Country, linking communities. The service also provided an ambulance plane to transport critically ill patients to hospital in Edmonton.

Much of Western Canada's early economic growth can be attributed to aviation pioneers, usually ace pilots from the First World War who settled in Peace River Country and set up air services, often flying under very difficult conditions. It was the brilliant airmanship by hard-nosed aviation roughnecks that propelled aviation from flimsy open-cockpit biplane aircraft to scheduled service in commercial airliners linking isolated communities and accelerating economic growth.

Little Red River was formerly a Hudson's Bay post. The small town on the Mikkwa River became the centre of international attention in the mid-1920s when Wop May made an epic flight to Peace River to pick up medicine for a desperately ill HBC employee. The illness was diphtheria, greatly feared by the Indians because of its ability to spread rapidly and wipe out whole tribes.

Since Little Red River was 12 days by dog team from the hospital in the town of Peace River, the only hope was to deliver diphtheria antitoxin by air. Wop had just bought an open cockpit Avro Aviant biplane. Following an appeal by the local health officer, he offered to make the flight even though the temperature was 32 below. Flying just above the river in near-zero visibility, he landed at Peace River on a landing strip marked out by branches laid on the ice-bound river.

After fuelling up, he took off again into a blinding snowstorm. He couldn't get the plane to pull up over the railway bridge and at the last minute slipped underneath it. Radio bulletins were broadcast on his progress through Peace River Country and picked up by U.S. and European press services. Wop's mercy mission got prominent coverage worldwide. Listeners across Canada waited for word until Wop and his mechanic, Vic Horner, landed at Vermilion, literally frozen stiff in the minus 50 temperature. Wop's hands were stuck to the control column and had to be pried off finger by finger. Vic Horner, stiff as an ice sculpture, was lifted out bodily by two policemen. A dog sled stood by to take the serum the remaining 80 kilometres to Little Red River.

For his heroism Wop was awarded the prestigious Order of the British Empire. Later he gained further international attention and fame using a plane to track down Albert Johnson, the "Mad Trapper" who shot three policeman. Thanks to Wop, the Mounties cornered Johnson in his hideout along the Mackenzie near Fort MacPherson.

Pioneering flying in the harsh northern wilderness was definitely a man's game. It was taken for granted that it was best carried out by tough wartime fliers. But the male bastion of bush flying in Western Canada was broken by a 20-year-old slip of a girl. Katherine Stinson wiped the patronizing smirks from the faces of crack aviators when she performed breathtaking simulations of aerial dogfights over the Calgary fairground in 1916.

City matrons in long dresses and tight corsets gasped in dismay as she stepped from her plane. Her leather jacket, helmet, goggles, and pants provoked disapproving looks and murmurs of "hussy." The remarks were tinged with envy for a woman who had plainly discarded the shackles of Victorian society. The young, pretty face radiated confidence and determination to succeed.

Katherine Stinson eschewed the refinements that the culture dictated for women, but she could hold her own when it came to making an impression at celebrity functions. A protégé of aviation pioneer Amelia Earhart, she opened a flying school in Texas. Although an American, she was selected to make the inaugural airmail flight between Calgary and Edmonton. She went on to become America's first woman aeronautical engineer.

As I made my way on a lovely June morning towards Fort Dunvegan, my next port of call, the water levels fluctuated wildly. The dramatic changes in levels accounted for the large number of newly exposed sandbanks in the river. Such unpredictable changes were major cause for concern among the Chipeweyan people at Lake Athabasca. Now I realized first hand what they had been talking about.

Fort Dunvegan was a former Northwest Company post. After pulling onshore and stretching my legs, I called Ishbel to let her know that all was well. She told me that Angus, my wee Westie, was pining for me, refusing to take direction and being more stubborn than ever. "When I want to go one way, he wants to go another," she said in exasperation.

Suddenly I had an idea. Mackenzie had taken along a "large friendly dog" on his journey. Why shouldn't I do the same? I asked Ishbel to look into flying Angus out to travel with me on the last part of my journey from Bella Coola down the Dean Channel.

After ringing off, I telephoned a young fellow I'd met in Peace River, John McGillivray, who lives near Hudson's Hope. He had promised to drive down in his pickup truck and help me portage my canoe and gear around the dams when I reached his neck of the woods. He was waiting as promised near Hudson's Hope, the site of the huge Bennett Dam. Together we loaded my gear into his pickup. When he dropped me off, we arranged to meet later for lunch. Meanwhile I wandered across the road for my morning caffeine fix. When I opened the door the coffee shop was buzzing with good-natured conversation, punctuated by an occasional loud guffaw. The noisy talk quieted momentarily while the patrons sized me up. They seemed to be mainly BC Hydro guys. Great, I thought, maybe I can learn something about water problems in B.C.

After I ordered, a man at the next table leaned towards me, shouting above the hubbub. "Are you part of the Mackenzie celebrations?"

I told him I was celebrating Mackenzie's bicentenary all right but not quite in the way he meant. After explaining, I asked him why the water levels were so low. Suddenly the room fell silent, all eyes focused on me. It was like I'd asked why the emperor was wearing his birthday suit.

After a minute or two conversation resumed, though it was more muted than before. Like most folks in a one-industry town, they were reluctant to criticize their employer, especially to a stranger. A couple of men from an adjacent table volunteered, somewhat hesitantly, that the low water resulted from stepped-up power requirements and a massive holdback to increase levels at the Williston Lake reservoir. Then, sensing that some guy in a canoe wasn't likely a threat, all around the café people began shouting comments back and forth.

"Ah, bullshit!" cried a young man the others called Bob. "The real reason for low levels is because Hydro has iron-clad contracts with California that demand maximum power. We're bound by law to export power to the States, John, whether we like it or not. This means BC Hydro is killing fish, including some rare species in the Peace River. We're damaging fish habitat by hampering spawning, because the periods when Hydro needs to release substantial amounts of water to produce power don't coincide with the seasonal needs of fish."

Figuring I didn't understand, he explained patiently. "Too little water in the spring period can strand fish. Too much in the fall and winter can wash away spawning beds. Hydro is actually violating the Federal Fisheries Act. Anyway, I'm quitting. How the hell do you explain to your kids or grandkids that your job means robbing them of their heritage by destroying an entire ecosystem?"

Murmurs around the room indicated that most agreed with him. I was impressed that he was willing to quit a well-paid job because of the effects the dam was having on the environment. It's easy enough to spout off about the environment but it takes guts and real commitment to give up a good livelihood for a cause, especially in a time when jobs are hard to come by.

Leaving the café, I made my way down the street towards a log-cabin structure I had noticed earlier on the riverbank. The building looked more like a large doll's house. In fact it turned out to be a church, quaint and quite delightful. From the number of pews, it would seat about 50. Literature on a table in the foyer indicated it was St Peter's Church, built in 1938 with volunteer labour and funds provided by the congregation of St Peter's in Montreal. While I lived in that city, I had visited St Peter's many times. This church was tiny, but it had character and blended nicely with its natural environment. I found it typical of many uniquely designed Anglican churches I visited in remote hamlets around the world.

As I was going out, I met an attractive lady coming in. "I'm Sharon Linfitt," she said. "You like our church, huh?" She looked pleased when I said I found it charming.

She told me she and her husband, Pat, lived in a log house on Williston Lake. "You can't miss it. It's near Clearwater Creek, about 40 kilometres from the town. Make sure you drop in." She gave me directions and also urged me to take in the museum next door. "There's some great stuff on dinosaurs."

It was an excellent suggestion. The museum, in a former Hudson's Bay post, featured numerous legends and tall tales of the trappers and canoe men who once traded at the post. The collection of dinosaur prints is unsurpassed. Some 1,700 dinosaur prints have been identified around the area of Hudson's Hope. Also on display is a 12,000-year-old mammoth tusk uncovered when the Bennett Dam was being constructed.

The museum depicts Mackenzie's discovery of coal seams along the riverbank when he passed through Hudson's Hope in June 1793. He recorded numerous sightings of bitumen during his voyages of 1789 to the Beaufort Sea and to the Pacific in 1793. Canadians have him to thank for the discovery of vast reserves of petroleum, coal and gas deposits in the Northwest. Some of the fascinating uses of the versatile bitumen are listed by James. K. Smith in his book *The Mackenzie River*:

> Bitumen was a very well known substance in his [Mackenzie's] day, commonly being used as caulking in canoes and sailing ships. Remarkably, according to the Old Testament, the ark that Noah built was coated with "pitch within and without," which was likely bitumen, also known more commonly as asphalt. The walls of Jericho were bonded

with bitumen, and the streets of Babylon paved with it. As a medicine, it effectively checked bleeding, aided the healing of wounds, reduced leprous sores, cured chronic coughs and some forms of diarrhoea. In Mexico it was used as a toothpaste and chewing gum. In South America it waterproofed the homes of the living and embalmed the bodies of the dead.

I had a pleasant walk along streets lined with attractive homes and neat lawns. At the Sportsman's Hotel where I was meeting John McGillivray for lunch, the manager filled me in on local news. The big event coming up was the hatchet-throwing competition.

He knew I was canoeing across Canada, and warned me that the lake was hazardous. "Just last year we had two young guys heading down Williston Lake to Mackenzie. They stayed here overnight. Sounded like experienced canoeists, like they knew what they were doing. Three days later somebody in a power boat found their upturned canoe. One body washed up on the lakeshore a month later."

He continued to regale me with harrowing stories of canoeing mishaps. A couple of weeks before, an exploratory geologist setting out on a project had a narrow escape. "He had $50,000 worth of seismic gear in his canoe. About 10 kilometres down the lake he hit a deadhead. The canoe tipped, dumping all his expensive gear. Fortunately, he had the presence of mind to swim with the canoe to shore. That lake can be a killer. There's thousand of deadheads floating around. They lie just beneath the surface like crocodiles. They're a real menace to any kind of boat ... so watch it!"

Over lunch, John McGillivray told me how he too gave up his job at Hydro and now did casual work around town. "It just didn't sit right with all this talk about the environment. The bloody fish are all screwed up. A lot of guys have quit because of it." Later he drove me to his home about eight kilometres north of town. It was a huge five-bedroom log house on several acres. A well-groomed horse was grazing in the stockade.

When I asked how he could afford this spread, he said land prices were reasonable and obtaining logs for the house building was easy. "But since I've been on pogey for a while, things are getting tight. Particularly since my wife split with the two kids. But if I put this place up for sale, I'll be lucky to get $40,000."

I was incredulous. Further south, John's home alone would fetch easily ten times that amount.

John had to leave to do a plumbing job at the local school, but on the way he took me and my gear past the Bennett Dam. The yacht club seemed a good place to launch, and we hauled the canoe off the pickup, setting it down near one of the finger docks. John took me to the clubhouse to meet the caretaker, Pat Carson, then wished me bon voyage.

A tall spare man with thinning hair, Pat was preparing supper and told me to pull up a chair and join him for steak and eggs, my favourite meal. I could spend the night at the club if I wished. This was great, giving me an early start next morning.

Although Pat suffered from Menuieres' disease, he had held some responsible positions prior to developing the disorder. He now had difficulty maintaining his balance, but despite this handicap, he was a serene and spiritual person. We recognized each other as loners but enjoyed sitting up into the wee small hours solving the world's problems and downing mugs of tea. Pat gave up his own bed and kipped on the chesterfield.

I fell asleep almost immediately, and was wakened in the morning by the aroma of bacon and eggs. After a hearty breakfast, I loaded my canoe. Pat wasn't happy about my venture and tried to dissuade me. "Most of the boats you see here rarely go out very far on the lake. They're scared of deadheads. I wish you'd think it over."

His words made an impact, particularly when he said he would pray for a safe voyage. When experienced outdoorsmen like Pat warned me about risks ahead, I took their advice seriously. At the same time I balanced their counsel with my own experience. It's normal to be anxious when setting out in new country. Nonetheless, with the best of intentions, well-meaning folks can sabotage morale. After a handshake, I headed out.

12

Aquatic Obscenity

Paddling away from the dock at Fort Dunvegan with the mammoth Bennett Dam at my back, I felt jittery, fearful of getting caught in the current and plunging into the whirling blades of the enormous generators. Anytime I ventured in close proximity to a dam, my fertile imagination took off.

But I was fortunate that I wasn't facing what Mackenzie and his men faced at this spot 200 years previously. In 1793 they fought the rapids on the Peace for three exhausting days, an ordeal that shattered the men's morale. Although they had faced enormous difficulties through the Northwest, they had never come across a mountain river in flood. Many of them expressed grave doubts about continuing with the expedition. They were mutinous. Even Mackenzie admitted it was "one white sheet of foaming water." However, at the strategic moment he called for a dram of whisky all round, and his highland charm worked wonders on the terror-stricken crew.

Now the roar of that vast cataract had been silenced by dams, and the foaming water was long gone. Driftwood and water-sodden logs were everywhere. Like Cedar Lake in Manitoba, the stumps and twisted trees on the gravelly shore reminded me of a 1920s movie set, the images of a scenic panorama painfully contrived, a painted fake. The weather, however, was beautiful, and azure sky above the hills on either side of the lake lifted my spirits.

Weary from scanning the water and dodging deadheads, I pulled into shore early, deciding to call it a day. There wasn't a lot of choice: the beaches were covered with a motley assortment of brush and dead trees, like the tangled beaches along Lake Winnipeg. Fortunately I spotted what seemed a likely spot on the riverbank. The sand made a nice soft undercover for my groundsheet. Slipping into bed, I wondered at it being so still. Even the birds had ceased their chatter although it was early twilight. I drifted off to sleep.

It seemed but a moment before I awoke. Something had disturbed me, yet all seemed quiet. Just as I was about to pull up the covers again, I heard scratching outside. Then came a low menacing growl: *Grrrrr...rrr ... grrr ... rrrrrr.*

Suddenly a demonic howling filled the tent. I sat bolt upright, my heart pounding furiously. A moment later I heard an animal running along the beach howling and moaning like a mad thing. Then it was immediately outside again, snapping and growling. The tent fabric shook violently, as if it was being punched.

Like a demented soul in Dante's inferno, the thing continued to circle the tent, wailing. The sound was somewhere between a nerve-wracking howl and a plaintive whimper, as if whatever was out there was in great pain. The noise receded as it ran off, but just as I began to hope it had gone, the gruesome cacophony resumed close by.

I flailed around for a weapon. My flashlight! Hunting frantically in the tent pocket I found it. As I shone the light directly towards where I thought the animal's eyes would be, the screaming stopped.

What kind of animal was this? No way I was going to open the zip to peer out. It was either a wolf or coyote, but its behaviour was baffling. Obviously it had no fear of humans. It made no sense for any animal to behave in such a fashion. It had to be crazy.

Then it hit me: It *was* crazy. Jesus Christ, it must have rabies! The thought of a rabid animal biting its way through the fabric, dripping infectious saliva, sent a chill through me. I rolled around the tent hauling on my pants and shirt. I'd never felt so scared. Despite bear encounters, treacherous white-water situations, wolves and moose sauntering outside my tent, this was a totally different experience. My fear was intensified by being shocked out of sleep.

The rest of the night I stayed on guard, praying the crazed beast wouldn't lunge through the tent wall. Someone said that faith is the bird that sings when the dawn is still dark. Finally, a glimmer of light appeared through the mesh, and my fear lessened. I felt sure the Great Spirit had heard my prayer.

I packed up hurriedly, casting nervous glances around in case the animal should return. I examined the tent but couldn't find any tears. There were scuffled tracks on the sand, but it was impossible to say what they were. I didn't stick around to find out. As soon as the canoe was loaded, I shoved off. The sheer physical effort in plunging my paddle deep into the water, thrusting the canoe swiftly forward, was a tonic. I don't know how far I went at maximum speed, but finally I slumped against the seat. My frazzled nerves slowly began to recover.

About 10 kilometres down the lake I spotted an impressive log home perched on a promontory. I figured this had to be Clearwater Creek where Sharon Linfitt, whom I met at the log church in Hudson's Hope, lived with her husband. I headed across the lake and pulled into a shallow bay. Securing the canoe to the dock, I looked around for steps running up the steep embankment. Instead, a long rope dangled. Grabbing it, I pulled myself up, slipping and sliding on the rocky incline.

Sharon was waiting at the top. "Hello, John! Come on in," she greeted me. The pleasant aroma of pine was heavy in the air. "Ed is round the back. Step out and introduce yourself. I'll get coffee going."

At the rear of the house I found Ed, wrench in hand, tinkering with an outboard motor. He straightened up. "You must be John. Heard all about you from Sharon. Great stuff – time somebody gave a shit about our history." This affable greeting came from a fiftyish, well-built man with a mischievous smile.

We headed back to the house. "You're taking a big chance in this country," he said on the way. "This lake's dangerous for any craft, even a canoe. But right now the bears are very aggressive, likely because the berries are scarce."

When I told him that it wasn't bears that had been bothering me but a crazy coyote or wolf, his expression showed concern. "There's a rabid coyote that's been running around. It's terrified all the animals. That's probably the one you ran into. I've tried to put a bullet in it, but it's too damned smart. Has absolutely no fear. You're lucky – even the bears run from a crazed coyote."

As we sat around the kitchen table enjoying our coffee, Ed recounted a cautionary bear tale. "I was fishing for steelhead down the lake last week when I heard a big splash and saw this grizzly come swimming towards me. I couldn't believe it. I was anchored about two kilometres offshore. But no question, he was coming after my catch! I can tell you I started the motor in a hurry. But not quite fast enough. He got his huge paw on the side of the boat and nearly tipped me over. I got the hell out. Jesus – even when I was speeding down the lake, he was still swimming after me!"

Sharon, a former nurse, told me that she and Ed were on their second marriage and had recently become grandparents. When I bragged that I was a grandfather of triplets, they were clearly impressed.

Ed had worked in the logging industry for years, but the job finally got to him. "One day I couldn't face myself in the mirror any more. I lost my stomach at destroying magnificent 200-year-old trees and clear-cutting prime areas of forest."

Like many of the conscience-stricken Hydro workers I'd talked to, he'd walked away from a well-paid job. When he met Sharon, they recognized each other as free spirits and worked side by side to build their dream home in the wilderness.

"We don' t have much money, but we sure love our life," Sharon said. "I wouldn't swap it for all the jacuzzis and BMWs in Edmonton. Where else could you look from your house and see a procession of animals – deer, lynx, fox, bears, elk, wolves, coyotes - passing by your window."

She had become nurse to a variety of injured animals Ed brought home. Remarkably, some had even come to the door. "They seem to sense that this is a safe haven." She told of a young elk which had its hindquarters frozen. "We brought it into the living room. It would place its head in my lap and look at me with soft brown eyes that just melted me away. Unfortunately, it didn't respond to treatment, and Ed had to shoot it," she said with a sigh.

"One winter there were several deer just below our house, trapped on the ice. Their hooves gave them no traction and they kept falling down. A pack of wolves had craftily herded them towards the clear ice in the bay. The deer would try to escape by climbing up the bank, but they couldn't walk on the ice and rolled back down. It was terrible to watch them just being picked off one by one. Nature can be so cruel." The story brought a lump to my throat.

As she bustled about preparing supper, Ed and I sat in the living room in front of the huge stone fireplace. Ed told me that he was originally from prairie farm country in Saskatchewan. His dad was drafted into the army when Ed was too young to remember him. "He was captured in the Dieppe fiasco and served three long years in a POW camp. One day I was sitting outside on the porch and saw this lone figure in the distance, some five kilometres away. That's how long our driveway was." Ed grinned.

"The dog started barking furiously. As the man drew nearer, it started whining and hollering all over the place." Suddenly it leaped, biting the man's pant leg. Ed's mother came running, wondering what was going on.

"Christ, what a welcome!" the man cried. "Even my goddamned dog doesn't know me!" Ed's mother gave a shriek and threw her arms around him.

From Ed's softly spoken words, it was easy to imagine the loneliness of the prairies and the vastness of Saskatchewan. The poignant scene he described had been repeated throughout the prairies as the heroes from the South Saskatchewan Regiment, including two VC winners, who had survived the bloodshed of Green Beach at Dieppe, returned almost as strangers to their families.

"You might as well stay the night, John," Sharon said. "We got lots of room." Delighted, I accepted the invitation to bed down in the loft. In the morning, pancakes and eggs were on the menu. After listening carefully to Ed's navigational advice, I assured him and Sharon that I would stay in touch. Sharon gave me a hug and pressed a package in my hand. "Just some pancakes and fruit for your lunch." How fortunate I was in four years of travel to meet so many people with giant-size hearts. In a world that appears to have gone berserk, such encounters keep the zest in life.

While the lake was placid, it was too quiet, with not even the sound of an occasional outboard. Weirdly shaped stumps were everywhere, the beaches stacked with waterlogged lumber and brush. When the light was fading, all that debris produced uncanny optical illusions of snakes, ducks, fish, and sometimes crocodiles. Especially as dusk fell, it gave me the creeps.

Remarkably, there were no mosquitoes or blackflies – scant insect life of any description, for that matter. No birds sang. It was like a graveyard. The air of melancholy again reminded me of Cedar Lake. Further along the lake, a lone tree, defying all known laws of gravity and apparently still rooted, rose about ten metres above the water.

The artificial lake was like a cover placed over a once-vibrant ecosystem. Now degenerated into another drowned forest, it occasionally spewed warped remnants of once proud and towering trees. It was something else to see this lone survivor reaching up. In an act of defiance, a bespoiled nature was raising a one-finger gesture at human folly. Remarkably, the tree had a large nest with several young birds peering down at me. Just then two eagles flew over. One had a small rabbit in its talons and landed on the nest, while the other remained circling. What an incredible place to choose for a nest – a forlorn tree rising in an aquatic desert like a rose blooming in a war-torn land.

To my surprise I came across a small patch of unspoiled beach and made camp. After a comfortable night with no animal visitors, I set off the next morning past a shore lined with scrubby trees. Through the thick brush, I glimpsed an animal in a small clearing. Oddly, it was crouching on the ground. Paddling closer and barely dipping my paddle to muffle my approach, I could see it was an elk in a kind of half-prone position. Its forelegs were on the ground, its rear end hunched. Filled with curiosity, I pulled in almost onshore. The animal made no attempt to run off.

The reason for its peculiar position soon became clear: it was delivering a calf! I quietly retreated. When I looked back from out on the lake, a newborn calf was trying to stand, gangly legs flailing in all directions as the mother looked on.

Because the weather was exquisite and the lake serene, I plunged the paddle deep, making good speed. Suddenly the canoe came to a dead stop, catapulting me forward on top of the spray cover. The bow reared like a spooked horse, almost tipping me in the water. About a third of the canoe was teetering precariously on top of a huge log.

Grabbing the gunwales on either side, I crawled cautiously forward. Then, lowering my leg onto the massive deadhead, I grabbed the side of the canoe, easing it alongside, then gingerly crawled back in. Greatly relieved at getting off so lightly, I paddled off cursing the numerous man-made hazards on this lake. While Mackenzie faced grave perils 200 years ago, at least the challenges he braved arose from a natural environment.

After nearly a week on Williston Lake I had yet to see a single boat. Pat was right: the many deadheads were a major hazard for small recreational boats. In addition to the fluctuating water levels, ferocious winds off the nearby mountains could turn the lake into a sea of foaming whitecaps

The Rocky Mountain Trench is actually a great gouge in the mountains separating the Rockies from the coastal mountain range. Lake Williston meets this trench at the westerly end. At one time the Finlay River thrust along its length in a surging cascade, joining the Parsnip River to form the mighty Peace. Now the entire trench is filled with water from the Lake Williston reservoir.

When the haze that had covered the lake all morning finally fell away, my jaw dropped. Straight over the bow the majestic Rocky Mountains appeared. Also, dazzlingly revealed by their snowy white tops in the distance were the Omineca and coastal mountains. My emotions soared. At precisely at this spot in June 1793 Mackenzie had gazed across at these same mountains "running south and north as far as the eye could reach." But while the mountains inspired him, he was filled with dismay that his long and arduous quest to the Pacific was now threatened by this enormous impasse. His dream of discovering a viable route to the Pacific, a North West Passage, appeared dashed.

In my voyage, however, this was a major milestone. Elated to have actually made it this far, I raised my paddle high in the air and ripped off a few choruses of the scandalous "Ball of Kirriemuir" and other student songs not on any university curriculum.

I had no illusions there was still a lot to face, particularly the Fraser River. Simon Fraser's account of his journey down that mighty waterway had revealed to me the enormous power of the river. How he and his men survived it defied logic. Just thinking about paddling down that chancy cataract made me cringe. But I put that problem on the back burner. Experience had taught me that difficult times can be manageable one day at a time

The soaring mountain ranges around me crystallized just how far I had come, not just in miles travelled but in my personal journey as well.

The first stage, four years before, had taken me from Lachine outside Montreal to Dorval on tranquil Lake St Louis, a mere 14 kilometres. But it's not the actual distance that matters. It's really about overcoming negativity, ignoring seductive voices in your ear: *You ain't going to make it, play it safe.* But the hardest step, that vital first one, is getting your foot outside the door. Memory of that short trip will always remain with me. Launching my canoe at the very spot where the Nor'westers set off for the northern wilderness was an inspiring beginning.

Following in the wake of Mackenzie had taught me a lot. There were times when I would have been astonished to think I would one day find myself contemplating the magnificent mountain barrier beyond which lies the Pacific Ocean and Mackenzie's Rock. I was not the same person who timidly set out four years ago.

No doubt the romantic in me had led me take up this challenge. My hope had been to draw attention to the deplorable lack of awareness of our Canadian heritage by giving public exposure to a great, albeit forgotten, Canadian hero. Perhaps in a small way my trip might help bring Canadians to a deeper appreciation of that remarkable legacy.

It was now a short 10 kilometres down the lake to the town of Mackenzie, my next port of call. I was looking forward to arriving. From what I'd heard, Mackenzie's name was associated not only with the town but a school, shopping mall, and even a new dock.

Once I arrived, I was confronted outside the tourist bureau by a large "Welcome to Mackenzie" billboard boosting the town's image. It indicated several accomplishments, but it was the grandiose claim of ownership of "The World's Biggest Tree Crusher," that really caught my eye. In a superb demonstration of dubious taste, the grotesque machine was actually on display like some treasured relic of precious historical significance. Never mind that this monster had defoliated a forest, ripping out and drowning magnificent old-growth trees and permanently sullying a once majestic setting. Enthusiastic technocrats consider that the monster tree crusher's effectiveness in helping to create the Williston Lake reservoir was its state-of-the-art efficiency. In my book it was merely a mechanical version of Agent Orange. I found it hard to digest the tourist hype that possessing the world's biggest tree-crushing machine somehow confers status on the community.

At the doughnut shop in Alexander Mackenzie Mall, I was sipping coffee when a tall man in his early fifties sat down nearby. "You sure don't look like a tourist," he remarked. Pat McGee, a former military man, introduced himself. Soon he was filling me in on the local gossip and quizzing me on my trip. Like most people living in a one-industry town, he was non-committal when I questioned him about the pulp mills.

Pat offered to give me a tour of the town in his pickup. As we drove around, I was impressed by the pretty homes, most with an expensive RV and boat in the driveway. "We have 90 per cent employment, the highest in Canada," he said proudly.

"That's great," I agreed, "But there's a price tag that goes with it, isn't there?"

When I told him I hadn't met a craft of any kind in the entire 200-kilometre trek down the lake, he nodded sadly. "People are afraid to go on the lake. They use the one around the other side of town." He waved his hand to indicate a small lake, more like a pond. "Over there."

I was dumbfounded. So much for the B.C. tourist promo boosting wilderness locales and the "biggest man-made lake in the province." Despite the enormous lake at their doorstep and all their sophisticated boats and fishing gear, townspeople were compelled to use a tiny back lake. What price jobs at any cost, I thought, remembering the conscience-stricken workers at Hudson's Hope. Sickened at the environmental vandalism of their employer, BC Hydro, many of them had walked away from high-paid secure jobs.

Pat let me off in the centre of town, inviting me to "Come on over for supper later." At the newspaper office, I picked up a copy of the local *Times.* Just as I was about to leave a staffer asked if I was "the canoe guy heading for Mackenzie's Rock." When I nodded, she asked to interview me. Pleased at any chance to boost Mackenzie, I readily agreed.

After she had finished with her questions, I asked her about the state of the big lake. She told me that most of the fish caught in it are deformed. This didn't surprise me, but it provided a sombre indication of the extent of the pollution.

Deciding some vigorous exercise was called for, I headed briskly out of town along the main road. Repair work was underway and traffic was held up by a gal with a stop sign. She was glad for an opportunity to chat.

"No, believe me, John, I don't get bored," she retorted when I put the question to her. "There's bears galore around here. Those big guys keep me on my toes. This morning alone I counted 18 of them crossing over right there." She pointed at a spot a few metres up the road. "I get the hell out when they get too close. Keep my car door open too, just in case one of them gets too familiar. No way I'd want to share the back seat with them." She laughed.

Later that evening, when I was having supper with Pat and his wife, Janet, the tourist office called asking if I would be willing to donate my canoe to their museum. The thought of having *Spirit of Mackenzie* displayed alongside their giant tree crusher almost brought me to tears. I politely declined their invitation.

Pat and his wife asked me to stay overnight. Being really beat, I accepted with alacrity. In the morning Pat drove me to the dock where my canoe was parked. It was another splendid day, and I was looking forward to getting out on the water and pushing on towards my goal, which suddenly didn't seem that far distant. Leaving the dock, recently renamed Alexander Mackenzie Landing, I had to admit I found the town a bit of an enigma. While there was an air of prosperity, there was also sensitivity, perhaps embarrassment, at the pathetic state of their waterway.

All along Williston Lake I had been dismayed at the extent of massive clear cutting. This had left gaping wounds in mountainous forests as well as a jaded lakefront. The extent that timber companies will go to secure prime lumber was revealed on my way down the Pack River. Startled by a loud roaring, I looked up to see a gigantic helicopter hovering close to a thickly treed mountain slope. The trees were growing at such a steep angle it seemed impossible for anyone to stand upright, never mind get heavy equipment up there. Unfortunately, even inaccessible terrain no longer ensures escape from clear cutting, thanks to modern technology. The huge helicopter was plucking out trees of an enormous size, tucking them beneath its underbelly and making off with them.

On these waters in June 1793, Mackenzie found the current brutal and the portages backbreaking as his crew made their way along the Parsnip River. He was moved to comment on "the inexpressible toil these people had endured, as well as the dangers they had encountered ... the canoe has been reduced to little better than a wreck. I therefore thought it prudent to comfort each of them with a consolatory dram."

He would have been just about where I was now paddling, the south arm of the lake, where the river, its wildness irrevocably tamed, now lies deep beneath a befouled and perilous lake, in company with old-growth forest. I couldn't held wondering what *he* would have thought of this environmental debauchery. Certainly for me, the wounds inflicted on my beautiful adopted land sickened me. The poisoned chalice of Wilderness Inc. is hard to swallow.

It was a relief to head into the narrow channels of the swiftly flowing Pack River. Here at least there were no debris-covered beaches or deadheads. The banks were verdant with spring freshness, the water clean. I felt great paddling upstream into this environment. The current, while very fast, was shallow, forcing me to jump over the gunwales at times and pull the canoe with a tether. It reminded me of the wild fast-water stretches on the Ottawa River.

On the shoreline at MacLeod Lake I spotted a large group of young people, most of them sprawled on the beach or lounging in the grass. Figuring it was time for a brew and a chat, I hauled up on the beach. They were very friendly, mainly students from eastern universities. They told me they were planting trees on areas that had undergone massive clear cutting. Sunburnt, clothes stained with mud, faces filthy, most were in high spirits and brimming with health. Some of them, though, were clearly bushed. They related horror stories of heat, blackflies, mosquitoes, and exhaustion. Their plaintive cries, ringing all around me, would have melted a stone: "Oh, man, those mosquitoes were the size of sparrows!" … "The blackflies are man-eaters … just tore my flesh out!"

They seemed to think I was an old coot out for a Sunday trip on the placid lake waters. They were obviously taking pains to impress me with their litany of hardship. I strung them along, insinuating sympathetic "ahs" and "ohs" into the conversation at appropriate intervals. A group gathered around *Spirit of Mackenzie*. With the paint scratched and muddy, the odd dent in the bow from encounters with deadheads, it looked pretty beat up. Eyeing it sceptically, they clearly considered my canoe could never pass muster.

Finally, one tall lanky-haired guy asked, "So where did you put in?" After a suitable pause, I replied, "Oh, Montreal."

There was a stunned silence. "Holy shit, did you hear what the old guy said? He's travelled here from Quebec in that beat-up canoe," one of them exclaimed.

Eventually, convinced that I was the genuine article, they warmed up. The next hour or so was spent in high-octane discussion as I recounted my adventures along the Fur Trade route. They plied me with questions about wildlife and "Don't you get scared being all alone?" The favourite was "Where's your GPS?" They were astonished to hear that I didn't possess one.

"So, how do you find your way around, then?" someone asked. When I told them that I used the old-fashioned system of dead reckoning with map and compass, they looked at me like I was a Neanderthal. However, when I asked how they would find their way around if their batteries ran out or they lost their GPS, they got the message.

Shared interests between generations, especially those relating to the environment, inevitably set in motion a warm commonality. With a captive audience, it seemed to me a golden opportunity to deliver some commercials. I put on my lecturer's hat and proceeded to talk history, explaining that the first Nor'wester trading post in B.C. was set up by Simon Fraser on this very lake. Originally called Fort McLeod, after Simon Fraser's close friend Norman McLeod, it was a major transhipment point and one of the company's furthest posts. In fact, it was part of a long thread connecting posts all the way back across the country, stretching to the Montreal HQ some 7,000 kilometres away. Even our trans-Canada highway today runs alongside the old voyageur routes.

I told the students the best way to understand our history was to break out their backpacks and retrace the voyageur heritage trails across our land. In this way they could connect and create a link with the past. The same paths carved by our ancestors when they pioneered our vast nation. A sort of on-the-job History 101.

"Great stuff, John. We should get you to teach the course," someone shouted.

It was becoming less of a surprise to discover that many college students haven't a clue regarding Canadian history. Coming from a country like Britain, where history was merely a boring compendium of royal dates, I found this lack of interest about a heritage packed with adventure, derring-do and romance hard to understand. Eventually the tree planters set off down the lake towards their camp, while I headed across the lake to find my own spot for the night.

Next morning as I made my way down the Crooked River it became clear why Mackenzie had chosen this name. The convoluted waterway snakes its way across the country like a dog chasing its tail. Occasionally it stretches out to form a number of pretty lakes. Most mornings began with drizzly mist, which developed into intermittent showers by the afternoon. Sometimes a thunderstorm or downpour broke up the routine. In many ways the meandering stream reminded me of the Mattawa River in Ontario. Both had a similar profusion of debris piled high at beaver dams. The water was also extremely cold, which, at the present altitude of nearly 800 metres, was hardly surprising.

At a convenient clearing among the trees on Summit Lake, I decided to make camp. An important milestone for river travellers, the lake's position represents the continental divide. Aptly, it is also known as Arctic Lake and Pacific Lake, names reflecting its unique geography. One end of the lake drains waters north, the other drains rivers west.

Hauling up on a fine gravelly beach, I dragged the canoe well out of the water and up into a cluster of trees. My legs were really cramped and thinking a walk would help, I set off briskly along the lakeshore. A few kilometres along I came to a roadhouse built from logs. The place was alive with conversation, mainly from a throng of young tree planters. They looked like they were enjoying a break from their demanding job. After placing my order at the counter, I sat down at a roughly hewn bench and pine table.

The door was suddenly flung open as a man poked his head inside and hollered, "Time to head back to the salt mines, guys." Amidst groans, the room emptied. The horde of young workers, clutching half-eaten sandwiches and coffees, made for a bus outside.

Only one other person was left. A young woman sipping coffee at a nearby table was writing assiduously in a notebook. As she caught my eye she smiled. "Thank God I'm not planting trees this summer." At my quizzical look, she continued, "I was a planter last summer. But it's really back-breaking work, usually in the middle of nowhere. The blackflies are voracious and you're always filthy, with nowhere to wash your clothes. Ugh." She wrinkled her nose in disgust. "Also, the money sucks."

"So where are you working now?" I asked.

"BC Hydro. Actually, I'm on contract to them. But in the winter I'm studying biochemistry at UBC."

That was my field, I told her. We embarked on a long discussion about science and the environment. However, when I asked if her summer job would help in her chosen profession, she laughed heartily. "Absolutely no way. In fact I have a hard time convincing people what I do. I could have made a packet on that old TV show, *What's My Line*. You may not believe this ... in fact some people think I'm from the loony bin when I tell them I'm a shepherdess."

I was gobstruck. "But I thought you worked for BC Hydro. What's the connection?"

"Well, a major problem for hydro is servicing the transmission towers, especially in remote areas of northern BC . The bush grows fast around the base of the towers. It creeps everywhere and is difficult to control. This can make it impossible for the helicopters to land to do servicing. They employ pilots to fly overhead checking for breaks in the cables as well as the state of the towers, but when the bush becomes too thick they can't spot these faults from the air. The terrain is impossible for trucks to get in.

"But sheep chew greenery up at a fantastic rate. I meander along the trails behind a herd of hungry grass-cutters, enjoying the ambience. Just like Little Bo Peep! It's fun, really, and I get a lot of studying time in so I don't get bored. It sure beats breaking your back planting trees."

Back at camp, I began to prepare supper, a procedure that increasingly made me nostalgic for my Magic Pantry meals. But the Irish stew was delicious and I scoffed the entire can. It was a fine evening with just a hint of coolness and lots of light. I sprawled outside the tent browsing through a book. I hadn't had much chance to catch up on any reading. Bruce Hutchison's *Fraser River*, a masterpiece on the history of the great river, was an excellent read packed with information. This was the waterway that caused Mackenzie so much trouble. He knew it then as the Great West River. Convinced it had to drain into the Pacific, he searched desperately to locate it. The river turned out to be the most challenging of his experience. In the upper canyon near Fort George, his canoe was wrecked and his crew almost drowned.

I had first heard about the Fraser from an uncle who had emigrated to B.C. He told gripping tales of the hardships faced by naive homesteaders, prospectors burning with gold fever, and crazed adventurers on crudely made rafts – all driven with an obsession bordering on a death wish, to conquer the awesome cataract. Many ended in a watery grave. Listening to these stories as a youngster, I was fascinated, but fearful too of this formidable waterway. The river, only short kilometres away and next on my agenda, was the fiercest dragon I would face. For some time now I'd had qualms about running it.

Hutchison summed up the Fraser River simply as a nightmare, "the savagest of all the major rivers of North America and probably the savagest in the world." Nonetheless, it is this river which practically created British Columbia – it played as large a role in Western Canada as the St Lawrence did in the east.

It staggers the imagination to learn that some floods on the Fraser have recorded velocities at 600,000 cubic feet per second with speeds of more than 30 kilometres an hour! Fraser navigated the river in 1805 in what has been described as "the most terrible and wonderful inland voyage in the history of North America." Hugh MacLennan provides an apt description of the perils Fraser and his crew endured:

> Tiny in their birch-bark canoes, the voyageurs stared up thousands of feet at the walls of that canyon. The river roared so loud they could not hear each other speak, it twisted so fast they could not prepare themselves for what was around the next bend. When they watched the walls of the canyon flashing past, they must have realized that not even a canoe, for that matter no ship hitherto built, had ever travelled for such a length of time at such a speed and survived. They were spun like tops in the whirlpools, and when backwashes swept them ashore, they portaged over cliffs thousands of feet high, for they could not survive if they stayed still – their food was running out – and they did not believe it possible to return. Finally they reached Hell's Gate.

Their return journey was worse than the passage down. The Indians turned against them and bombarded them with rocks from the cliffs above, while lower down they were greeted with a shower of arrows. Their supplies nearly gone, their clothes in rags, their morale was at a low ebb.

At this point, Fraser, an unusually taciturn man with the highlander's distaste for emotional scenes, turned to his Scottish and Canadien voyageurs, and made them join hands to swear an oath: "I solemnly swear before Almighty God that I shall sooner perish than forsake any of our crew during the present voyage."

Later, he recorded in his notes:

> I have been for a long period in the Rocky Mountains, but have never seen anything like this country. It is so wild that I cannot find words to describe our situation at times. We had to pass where no human beings should venture ... having found it very strong and full of tremendous whirlpools, were greatly at loss how to act ... the canoes having been in continual danger of sinking or of being broken to pieces; it was a desperate undertaking!

I closed the book and tried to sleep, but what I'd read had done nothing for my peace of mind. The night was punctuated by vivid dreams in which fanged monsters frolicked among whirlpools and dreadful rapids. I awoke in the morning hung over and feeling like I hadn't been to bed. I felt ready to throw in the towel. But after a decent breakfast of porridge, brown bread, marmalade, and copious quantities of Tetley, the blues vanished, at least for the moment.

My charts indicated I was entering a relatively trouble-free area. In this stretch of the upper Fraser the current, although fast, was manageable, with wide-open water and only one set of rapids. Despite my fear of tangling with sweepers – underwater branches or trees just under the surface that could create an instant upset – paddling was straightforward.

I had just picked out a choice landing spot for lunch, when I was taken by surprise: the current increased markedly. Despite my attempts to brake, I continued at a fast clip downstream. Cursing my ineptitude, I thrust my paddle deep to slow down, but only succeeded in careening dangerously towards the riverbank. Fortunately, I was able to recover, setting the canoe clumsily on a strip of mud. I was furious at my slipshod paddling but grateful that I hadn't come a-cropper. Obviously paddling this river was extremely tricky. And this was the easy stretch! I was unlikely to find forgiveness during the next phase through the treacherous Fort George Canyon.

I'd never experienced anything like the swiftness of this river. Since the canoe was heavily laden, balance at high speed was critical, and I thought it prudent to remain on my knees. You can also pray better in that position! Further downriver, buildings appeared high up on the riverbank. This had to be Prince George. Pulling into a park-like area, I hauled the canoe onto the grass. It was a great relief to step out and stretch.

Figuring a reward was in order, I decided to splurge on a room. I was desperate to get the muck off my body and clothes. The thought of luxuriating in a hot bath followed by good night's sleep in a nice soft bed sounded like heaven. An obliging motel manager said he would look after my canoe and briefed me on some of the local sights.

Prince George possesses a natural ambience not only because of its position astride the historic Fraser River. A bustling commerce reinforces its claim as the capital of Northern B.C. On my walkabout through the town, a sign boosting a lunch special of bangers and mash at the Legion hit my eye. There were only a few patrons inside the freshly decorated dining room. After placing my order, I passed the time chatting to Brian the barman. Desultory conversation about the weather soon turned into a game of history trivia. Brian was a history junkie. He told me that the name of their new educational centre was New Caledonia College, the name reflecting the town's pride in its heritage. New Caledonia was the name given to the entire Pacific western territory by Simon Fraser, because it was thought to remind him of the wild beauty of Scotland.

Ironically, Fraser had never seen Scotland. Brian was taken aback when I told him that their town hero was actually born in Bennington, Vermont. Fraser's enchantment with Scotland, I explained, came from his widowed highland mother, who talked nostalgically of "auld Scotia" when he was growing up.

Fraser founded the town at the mouth of the Nechako River in 1807 originally as Fort George when he built the Nor'westers' most westerly post there. Fort George was a staggering 7,500 kilometres by canoe from the company base in Montreal. Much later it was to become a key airbase in the development of Alaska. The town was eventually relocated about 20 kilometres further north where it became known as Prince George.

Brian set me on my heels when he told me the town actually derives its name from the Duke of Kent. I had assumed it was King George. The choice of name itself is a bizarre piece of wartime lore. The Duke of Kent was killed in 1942 in an aircraft crash in the Scottish Highlands, not far from my home at that time. The cause of the accident still remains a mystery. Rumours abounded that he had been part of a peace movement, along with the Duke of Windsor, the former King of England, who was banished to the Bahamas under a cloud. Apparently their aim was to make a special arrangement with Hitler that would give Britain an honourable out from the war. Britain would then look the other way while the Nazis took on Russia. However, the plan turned sour when British intelligence got wind of it. One rumour even suggested that the Duke of Kent was taken care of by the cloak and dagger spooks in MI6. The full extent of the iniquitous appeasement efforts of some Royals towards the Nazi regime has yet to be revealed. Despite numerous attempts of historians for access to pertinent World War II files, they have been locked away until 2017.

13

In Search of the Stinking Sea

On the banks of the Fraser River I turned in for an early night right after supper, clutching my book. I was intrigued by Fraser's diary, which reveals his extreme jealousy of Mackenzie. Fraser was handpicked by the upper echelon of the Northwest Company to succeed Mackenzie, who was 12 years his senior. Interestingly, both men's fathers were highlanders who served with the rank of captain in Burgoyne's army during the Revolutionary War; both died in American POW camps.

In 1805, Fraser closely followed Mackenzie's route across the prairies and up into Peace Country. Fraser's expedition received considerable support from an alarmed British government, acting on information that Lewis and Clark, with over 50 men, were determined to secure the entire Pacific coast for the young American republic. Fraser's run to the sea turned out to be a race of territorial ambitions. In any event, Canada lost heavily in the big land-grab, but Fraser's formidable achievement ensured at least that British Columbia would remain in Canada.

Fraser went to great pains to point out several errors Mackenzie had made, ridiculing certain portages and channels the master explorer had stated to be impassable but Fraser found to be only trivial inconveniences. With sarcasm bordering on the vindictive, he notes some landmark that "does not appear to have been noticed by Sir A.M.K as he used to indulge himself in a little sleep. Likely he did not see it and I can account for many other omissions in no other manner than his being asleep at the time he pretends to have been very exact; but was I qualified to make observation and inclined to find fault with him, I could prove he seldom or ever paid the attention he pretends to have done, and that many of his remarks were not made by himself but communicated by his men."

Twisting the knife, Fraser continues: "Sir A.M.K. appears to have been very inaccurate in the courses or there must have been a vast difference in the compass he made use of and the one we had which is perhaps not very good."

Much of this sniping emanates from the jealousies common between explorers. But it also illuminates the human side of two courageous individuals who drew the map of Canada. In fairness, Fraser had the benefit of hindsight, as well as access to Mackenzie's travel notes, when he navigated across the same terrain 12 years later. Nonetheless, for some unaccountable reason, Mackenzie did miss the huge tributary of the Nechako River. This would have led him via several lakes west to the Pacific, thus avoiding the dangerous canyons on the Fraser and an arduous portage of 300 kilometres across the coastal mountains to Bella Coola. Mackenzie thought he was travelling down the Columbia River and was determined to proceed to its mouth. Ironically, Fraser made the same mistake, but after reaching Vancouver realized he had blazed a trail to the Pacific that was completely impractical as a trade route.

The night before leaving Prince George, I carefully checked the stowage of my gear to ensure it was balanced, with a bias towards the stern allowing the bow to ride high in the rapids. The following day dawned pleasant and sunny, and I skipped breakfast and got underway at once. After a quick prayer to the Great Spirit for my safety, I pushed off from a mud flat. As I adjusted my legs comfortably onto kneepads, the flow caught the canoe, pulling me into the mainstream.

Passing a large house overlooking the river, I saw a man standing on the veranda smoking a cigarette. "That's a beauty of a canoe. Where are you going?" he yelled across at me.

"Quesnel," I yelled back.

"Jesus! Watch it at the canyon, it's real fierce. Where did you come from?"

"Montreal," I bellowed as the current pulled me on.

"F a n...t a s...tic! Take care!" Despite the distance, the exhilaration in his voice was unmistakable. The warmth of his approval and concern thrilled me. It felt great to have an audience, even of one, cheering me on.

White water surged around me, pulling me on at breathtaking speed. Buoyed with euphoria, I was psyched up by the knowledge my journey's end was near. The thought of following the river where Fraser and Mackenzie had passed 200 years before gave me the shivers. Here was I, a romantic Scottish-Canadian, for most of my life never closer to big water than sailing a toy boat in a pond, now fulfilling a lifelong dream. I chuckled to myself at the irony of someone with allegiance to the Donald Clan, implacable foes of the Mackenzies, boosting a rival. Adrenalin rocketed through me. Raising my paddle high, I roared out an old clan taunt: "Here's tae us ... wha's like us ... damn the yin ... and those that are, are all dead!"

My progress downstream was swift but fraught with anxiety. I searched the turbulence for signs of unseen trailing branches that could instantly flip the canoe. There were about 10 kilometres before the canyon's steep walls would emerge across the bow. The previous night I had carefully read up on water conditions in my guidebook. There would be no second chances once I entered the rocky bottleneck.

I repeated the mantra: "On entering the canyon it's essential to keep to the left of the first large rocky island. At the next rocky island, also remain left. Then move quickly to the right of the third island." This last move was essential, as remaining on the left side of this island would sweep me directly towards a very large, powerful whirlpool.

The Prince George Canyon compresses the mighty Fraser into a narrow constriction accelerating the flow in a tremendous thrust of savage energy. I had intended hauling off the river just prior to the canyon to size things up. Unfortunately I was now totally committed. No way could I make it out of the midstream current that held me in its ferocious grip.

In a remarkable display of indifference to the dangerous rapids awaiting them, Mackenzie and his men stopped at the canyon and pulled onto shore to gather wild onions, "which, when mixed with our pemmican was a great improvement on it, they produced a physical effect on our appetites which was rather inconvenient to the state of our provisions." Mackenzie's main concern was that the men demanded seconds, threatening their rationing system!

Because of the current, my paddling now consisted of timid dips into the water to maintain direction. I was tearing along at high speed, as if 10,000 elephants were pushing me. A large rock rushed at me. Was this the first island, or was it just an ordinary boulder? Why the hell hadn't I confirmed the directions through the canyon when I was in Prince George?

Should I count that large boulder or not? On this simple but desperately important enumeration everything depended. Was it the island referred to? For Chrissake! Why the hell didn't the sonofabitch who wrote the guide clarify such critically important information? How I wished he were here with me in the canoe – I'd know where to stuff his goddamn book!

Almost immediately a large rocky island came in view. Was this really number one – or was it number two? I anguished. But whizzing in front of the bow was another large rock. Was it number two or three? If it was the third island and I continued on course, I was about to run into a monstrous whirlpool. Never had I been in such a farcical predicament with such momentous consequences.

What to do? I'll have to turn ... but what if that first rock is ... Holy shit!
Fierce whirlpools and huge boils of foaming water mixed with powerful
eddy currents swirled around me. The canoe's stern twisted from side to
side as if gripped in the jaws of some huge animal. I berated myself for
tackling the canyon when it was at maximum water level. Icy tentacles
in my chest took my breath away. I prayed fervently that Alexander
Mackenzie's spirit, as well as any other interested deity, would come to
Spirit of Mackenzie's aid.

I plunged the paddle into the foam and turned towards the right of
the island. At first all seemed okay. I was heading towards the canyon
wall on the opposite side, but more important, my speed seemed to have
dropped. But as I glanced down at the water, my morale plummeted.
The canoe was travelling at high speed in both directions! Caught in a
giant eddy that was pulling me forward, I was also being hauled by the
main current 90 degrees to the left. With my attention focused on the
canyon wall directly ahead, I had missed seeing the rapids. I was moving
sideways at high speed towards the main rapids. Their roar now rose to
a crescendo. I was trapped in a situation that is every canoeist's nightmare:
broaching in heavy water.

The canoe was now broadside to the current, being driven towards
two large rocks about six metres apart. Like the jaws of a prehistoric
monster, they appeared poised to crunch my canoe like a twig. A massive
white-capped cataract spilled between them. Horror-struck, I rose from
my kneeling position to a half crouch and thrust the paddle down as far
as my arms could take it. Again and again I plunged deeply, trying
desperately to straighten the bow and turn the canoe. I was almost upon
the twin rocky sentinels when slowly ... agonizingly slowly ... the bow
slewed around. In a flash I was swept through the gap. My white knuckles
clutched both sides of the canoe and I arched backwards in a desperate
bid to maintain balance. Swept along on a Valkyrie ride, I tumbled over
the edge of the rapids.

It was likely only about a five-metre drop but it felt like thirty.
Momentarily suspended in time, the canoe plunged. There was no way
my heavily laden craft could defy gravity and stay upright. Either that
or the acute angle it entered the water combined with the weight would
ensure its plunge straight to the bottom. The bow hit, dipped underwater
briefly. Then slowly it reared, a wall of water spilling over the sides.
Bouncing and rolling from side to side, I clung to the gunwales, gyrating
my body to maintain balance as my craft bucked and reared its way out
of the souse-hole that has been a graveyard to boats of all descriptions.

Despite being surrounded by haystacks of spuming white water, I
was beginning to breathe a little easier. But after careening about 50
metres downstream, I was suddenly jerked to one side. The canoe was

now caught in the outer vortex of a large whirlpool. This time I half stood and thrust the paddle as deeply as I could to break free of the water's stubborn hold and get back into the main current. It was a close thing.

About 10 kilometres downriver I spotted a tiny sandbar and pulled in to rest and gather my wits. I jumped around stretching my cramped limbs. I'd had a hell of a scare, but I was wildly exhilarated – I'd run the treacherous rapids at Prince George Canyon and come out alive. The very idea had haunted me for a long time. Hard to believe it was now over!

My prayer to Mackenzie's spirit to guide my canoe through the rapids had worked! The monkey was finally off my back! It was time for one of Mackenzie's celebratory drams. Never had Tetley tasted so good. I spent about an hour tossing back copious quantities of tea and knocked off several digestive biscuits with honey. Exuberantly, I packed up to continue my journey.

It was near this point on the river that Mackenzie became alarmed as he realized his Great West River was now heading southwards, away from the sea. Spotting a group of Indians onshore, he hailed them. In return he received a shower of arrows and boulders dropped from the canyon wall. Throwing his pistols along with some gifts on the ground in a gesture of goodwill, he walked unarmed towards them, making signs of friendship. At this they finally relented. (Mackenzie, no fool, had hedged his bets, delegating one of his men as a sharpshooter to hide in a nearby tree.)

The people were of the Takulli nation but were generally called the Carriers because of the peculiar custom for the widows of warriors to carry their husbands' ashes in a box around their neck for three years.

Drawing a map on the sand, Mackenzie made it known he was seeking the "stinking sea" to the west. The natives made it plain that to proceed further on the river was hopeless because of impassable rapids.

Stunned, he struggled to hide his disappointment from his dispirited crew. He could no longer believe that the river they were travelling could lead to the Pacific. He was now convinced that a feasible North West passage was impossible. The only way to the Pacific was by land, across the mountains. However, convincing the crew to continue overland was unlikely. Already badly demoralized by several brushes with death, they were clearly mutinous.

As the rag-tail collection of weary voyageurs gathered around the campfire, he praised them for their incredible courage and fortitude. Then, he told them their quest to the sea was taking a drastic turn. "At all events," he wrote in his journal, "I declared in the most solemn manner that I would not abandon my design of reaching the sea, if I made the attempt alone, and that I did not despair of returning in safety to my friends."

There was no doubt that the young Scot, now 29 years old, was determined to take on the hazardous trek overland through mountains and dense wilderness. It is also easy to understand why his chosen motto was "Perseverance."

Once again his charisma worked. His crew agreed they would follow him, come what might. After reaching this critical decision, they unanimously agreed to name their camp spot "Alexandria."

There was a huge sandbar in the middle of the river ahead and I decided to make it my campground for the night. I wasn't especially tired, but the river gradient had dropped significantly, causing an increase in current. While it was exciting zooming along at breakneck speed, it was tiring having to keep a constant lookout for deadheads and debris. I needed to be fresh to handle it. I estimated my speed would be around some 20 kilometres at the high spots – quite astonishing.

It was drizzling early next morning and visibility was poor. I decided to sleep late. As I would be hitting the rapids in Cottonwood Canyon likely sometime during the day, it was vital to be able to spot them in enough time to plan my approach. The scenery of hills abounding with pine and fir was awesome as I swept past the riverbank at high speed.

The rapids came up faster than I expected. Fortunately, it was easy to spot the massive haystacks dancing in front of the bow about two kilometres ahead. I decided to go with the flow and run straight down the middle. This turned out to be a good move, as the eddy currents on either side of the river were very powerful. Pushed and pummelled by the haystacks, the canoe bucked repeatedly, making it impossible for me to hold a straight course. In some stretches I felt like I was riding a Brahma bull at the Calgary Stampede. Still, these rapids were a piece of cake compared to those at Prince George Canyon.

Coming out of the white water, my speed increased markedly. I would have loved to pull into a sandbank, but picking a landing spot on this river was as tricky as landing a jet in a farmer's back forty.

In any event, it wasn't long before a bridge appeared ahead. This would be Quesnel. I could hardly take it in. I had run the 160 kilometres from Prince George in less than two days and hardly lifted my paddle!

The gauntlet of cement forms that made up the bridge supports were reaching out of the river, looming nearer every time I glanced towards them. They appeared increasingly menacing. I had underestimated my speed, leaving it almost too late for corrective action. This was definitely not how my entrance to Quesnel was supposed to happen. I had figured on spending the last kilometres enjoying the tranquillity and scenery while listening to the river speak. Now I had to paddle like hell broadside to the flow to fight a strong undertow determined to sweep me onto the pylons. It was also essential that I reach the shore before the confluence of the Quesnel and the Fraser rivers synergized to further complicate the hydraulics.

Intensive paddle work through the powerful crosscurrent finally won the day. Totally exhausted, I pulled up onto a convenient strip of sand at a park. I spent my remaining energy unloading gear and, groaning with fatigue, hauled the canoe onto the grass and sprawled beside it.

An hour or so later, greatly rejuvenated, I walked through the park towards the Quesnel River. As it joined the Fraser, there was a tremendous roaring. The current and white water were absolutely fierce. I was awestruck. How wonderful it felt to be on dry land! A sedentary stroll to view from a safe spot the miniature Niagara Falls cascading into the Fraser was fine with me. I had my fill of white-knuckling it.

I was at a point of land called Ceal Tingley Park, and it turned out to be a superb camping spot. I set up camp on trimmed green grass close to a picnic table – luxury indeed, with no mosquitoes or a single rabid coyote romping around.

As I was preparing supper, a man stopped to chat. He said his name was Jim Thompson, and he evidently knew a great deal about canoeing. Examining *Spirit of Mackenzie* thoroughly, he quizzed me about my trip down the Fraser. "Wood canvas, isn't it? Jeez, you were lucky. I don't know how you made it past the canyon at Prince George."

It was evident he didn't think much of my canoe or its workmanship. He stared in astonishment when I told him it weighed about 85 pounds. "You would really need four different types of canoes for the water conditions you'd face in fast white water – as well as the enormous lakes and rivers – to come all the way from Montreal."

His last remark was accompanied by much head shaking. Too polite to call me a liar, he plainly thought I was pulling his leg. He went on to say he spent a lot of time "shooting the rapids" in a specially designed kayak and had developed all sorts of deft manoeuvres for running white water. He told me I should have stuck to the left all the way through the Prince George Canyon. He was right on that score.

Jim gave me his business card, which described him as a "canoe consultant." So much for "experts," I mused. He clearly had little notion of travelling long distances in a heavily laden canoe. I couldn't help wondering what these self-styled "experts" would do in the frigid waters, clammy fog, and high rollers of Superior. For long-distance travel, give me an aboriginal craft anytime. My canoe had covered a lot of territory and taken terrific punishment, but it had bounced back each time. Despite some desperate situations, it had never tipped me.

Next morning after a leisurely breakfast of porridge, eggs, and toast, I headed towards town and called Ishbel. After I told her I was now off the water and getting my hiking boots ready, she laughed. "Hope you've got lots of foot powder for the long march. Anyway, you're going to have company. Your beloved Westie will be with you soon."

Ishbel had purchased a travel kennel and had arrangements well in hand for sending Angus to Vancouver on Air Canada. I was delighted that I would be able to take him with me for the final 100-kilometre run to Mackenzie's Rock from Bella Coola. Making my way down the street, I thought how nice it would be to see Angus. More important, how was he going to react to roughing it on a wilderness trek after leisurely romps through parks?

The Caribou's first gold strike was made at Quesnel. At one time it was the northern terminus for steamboats, their decks packed with gold-rush hopefuls making for Quesnel Lake. Downtown I spotted a Tim Horton's, and despite a London fog of smoke, managed to penetrate its murk towards a table. The talk buzzing around me was mainly local gossip. Then it turned to the town's forthcoming Mackenzie celebrations on Canada Day.

I nearly fell off my chair when an old timer drawled out, "There's talk about the Indians closing down the Mackenzie Trail. I don't know what the hell it's all about. Seems they're really upset over these young fellows re-enacting Mackenzie. Heard they're pulling the signposts down along the trail and blockading entry points. Jeez, sounds like they're really on the warpath this time."

Someone at the far end of the room, a farmer by appearance, chimed in. "Yeah, but it's the young guys high on booze and running around with rifles that cause all the trouble. The elders can't talk sense into them. They're out for blood. There's gonna be trouble, you can bet on it!" He shook his head morosely.

My mind was in turmoil at this unexpected revelation. If the natives decided to close the trail, that slammed the door on my plans to make the overland hike to Bella Coola. No question, I would have to rethink this phase of my trek. But first I had to confirm just what the heck was going on. There had been talk about something in the paper.

I left hurriedly, making for a newsagent down the street to pick up a copy of the *Caribou Observer*. If even half of what had been said was true, I was going to have to change my plans drastically.

The Blackwater River where it flows into the Fraser is just north of Quesnel and marks the start of the 340-kilometre Alexander Mackenzie Voyageur Route. The entry point to the trail is where Mackenzie and his crew left the Fraser on their overland trek across the mountains. A designated heritage site, the trail is derived from the ancient Grease

Trail, taking its name from the eulichan, or candle fish. The eulichan spawn in huge schools along the Pacific Coast rivers in spring. They are very oily and can be dried out and burned as candles. Rendered and mixed with berries and cedar, they were used as a staple for trade between the coastal and interior Indians.

Preparing for this important task was a joint effort. The Nuxalk, residents of the Bella Coola Valley, picked berries at spawning time, a task they were aided in by the Ulkatcho, who made their home on the 1,400-metre Chilcotin plateau to the east. The fish are still rendered for cooking oil by the local Nuxalk today.

In recent years the trail was designated as the Alexander Mackenzie Voyageur Route. However, there is a strong push by the Ulkatcho and Nuxalk elders for changing the name to the Nuxalk-Carrier Grease Trail. First Nations bands stress that ancestors of the Ulkatcho, Kluskus, Red Bluff, and Nuxalk developed this trail system thousands of years before Mackenzie.

I sat on a park bench to scan the newspaper and quickly found a reference on the editorial page. Sure enough, the article mentioned the determination of the Carrier chiefs to block the trail. Quoting Chief Frank Bouche of Red Bluff, the report said that Carrier people would establish blockades beginning at the mouth of the Blackwater River where it meets the Fraser.

"Blockades will continue along the Trail wherever it intersects with a Reserve," the article said. Ominously, the chief said also that "allies" – bands supporting the Carrier stand – would be coming to the Caribou-Chilcotin to join the blockades.

"Indians have been trying since 1974 to secure ecological heritage and archaeological rights over the entire Grease Trail system," Chief Bouche said. He described as "inadequate" a ban on logging within 200 metres of either side of the trail, noting evidence that some logging companies were already cutting within the 200 metre limits: "Indians want a five mile ban on logging and mining on both sides of the trail," he stressed.

When asked if the blockades could get confrontational, the chief replied that if it did happen, "it won't be initiated by Indians." But he went on, "There is a lot of frustration on the part of our young people. They are anxious to do something to right some of the historic wrongs."

I couldn't help but agree with such sentiments. They seemed a good enough reason for using a name that accurately reflects the traditional life of Canada's First People, who have lived and hunted along its route for two millennia. But I felt saddened at such a lack of understanding of Mackenzie. The story was tinged with a menace that left me uneasy.

After chewing over the dilemma that had been suddenly thrust upon me, I reached a conclusion. Having travelled some 7,500 kilometres, there was no way I was going to pack up and go home with my goal in sight. I could be just as bloody-minded as the next guy. Besides, my ancestors had their beginnings in the same part of the world as Mackenzie – a country whose imprimatur is a prickly nettle and where a common adversity has drilled "Perseverance!" into its very gene pool.

Following a few telephone calls, I set out to do some research at the library. I scrutinized a map of the Chilcotin country and coastal mountains and picked up some key points from an excellent trail guide, *In the Steps of Alexander Mackenzie* by John Woodworth and Halle Flygare. This little gem describes in detail the overland route from the Fraser to Bella Coola. As I pored through other related material, a plan began to emerge. It was important to avoid confrontation with First Nations people at barricades along the trail. This meant giving a wide berth to the reserves along the trail. One possibility was by hiking from the highway across the plateau near Anahim Lake, then crossing the Rainbow Mountains and Bella Coola Valley to the fiords at Bella Coola.

Back at camp I checked out my hiking equipment and stuffed all my gear into the new 60-litre backpack bought at Trailhead back in Kingston. I had to be extremely fastidious with every article, since I was essentially carrying my house on my back like a snail. Everything had to be contained in or attached to my pack. How much fuel for my backpack stove and the amount of food to carry were serious logistic problems. There were no stores along the way. It seemed strange to carry a large water bottle after having lived surrounded by water for the previous four summers.

Donning my new hiking boots to break them in, I headed into town for last-minute supplies. Dave Martin, a delivery truck driver I'd met over coffee at Tim Horton's, was very helpful. He had some deliveries to make in Bella Coola, and we arranged that he would take my canoe to Hagensborg at the end of the trail for me to pick up after my traverse. He could also give me a ride up the highway to the entry point near Anahim Lake, where I would begin the Mackenzie Grease Trail.

Good as his word, Dave picked me up early the next morning. After breakfast we loaded the canoe and headed towards Williams Lake. Then Dave took the gravel road across the mountains to Anahim Lake, where he dropped me off. I intended to camp there and hike overland towards the Mackenzie Trail.

Walking across the Chilcotin Plateau where Anahim Lake is located was like stepping backwards in time. I could see a variety of pine-pole fences along the road, and old homesteader log cabins were everywhere. I was intrigued to learn at the general store that cowboys still ride horses to town and hitch them outside. After setting up camp at a spot near

Eagle's Nest Lodge, I strolled down to the shoreline of Anahim Lake – actually the widest part of the upper Dean River – to watch the sun go down on a pristine setting.

I breakfasted next morning at the lodge, where one of the staff told me the area around the lake was a bird-watcher's paradise, home to many fish-eating species like eagles, ospreys, and blue herons, as well as pelicans, found in only a few lakes in British Columbia.

After an excellent breakfast and with time to kill, I strolled down the road to the small community airport to check out the planes. Really more of an airstrip, it had a good paved runway about 1,200 metres long and a number of small hangars, but no control tower. The waiting room served passengers connecting to Vancouver on Wilderness Airlines, which uses small 6-8 seater twin-engined aircraft. There was only one other person in the room, a tall man reading an airline schedule. After the requisite desultory chitchat between strangers, I asked if he was travelling far.

"You'd better believe it, mate. Auckland," he said in a tone that was unmistakably Kiwi. The previous winter I had spent some time in New Zealand, so we had a good discussion of the country and its politics.

"What brought you to the boondocks of Anahim Lake?" I asked.

"Well, I'm into fly-fishing in a big way. This year the International Fly Fishing Championship was held here. Just wound up, in fact."

I was impressed that Dean River was up to global standards. But when I asked who had won, his smile faded. He blurted out irately. "Bastard English again!" I burst out laughing. Clearly he had identified that I was a Scot.

After wishing him bon voyage, I made my way outside where several recreational aircraft were parked on the grass by the tarmac. I spent some time going down a line of interesting planes, some of them rare antique birds. I was checking out the cockpit of one old-timer when a voice boomed out, startling me.

"She's a real beauty, that one. Piper Cub." At the front of the plane, running his hands caressingly over the engine nacelle, was a guy about my age, with a fresh open face and a broad smile. "A tail dragger from the forties, but with new instruments. No question, a real cream puff. But you should have seen it two years ago. A basket case. The owner's made a nice reconstruction job." Bob Phillips, an inveterate aviation junkie like me, stuck out his hand to introduce himself. Soon we were engrossed in hangar talk. He was fascinated by my Mackenzie odyssey. He told me that he had made the trip to Mackenzie's Rock from Bella Coola by canoe.

"Watch for those god-damned westerlies. They produce strong turbulence in the afternoon and set up giant-size waves. The fiords funnel the wind into mini-squalls that can tip you over real easy. Make sure you leave very early in the morning if you want to avoid them. Even the bigger boats have a hard time. The float-plane jockeys find it tough landing there in the afternoon too." I thought to myself, this would be the last of the dragons I would encounter.

Bob suggested a coffee. Inside the hangar, several aviation types with mugs in their hands were standing around a beat-up old Cessna engine. Bob introduced me. When they learned I was planning to cross the Grease Trail, they shifted their feet uneasily.

Eventually someone said, " I heard the barricades are being put up all along the trail. Also, many of the markers along the trail have been torn down."

This was disturbing news. It's one thing reading about problems in the paper, but hearing them from hard-nosed individuals who had little time for "stories" was something else. It was clear there was genuine concern that the Mackenzie Grease Trail could set the stage for a violent confrontation between natives and the government, as it had at Oka.

Incredibly, there was even talk that some young band members had actually acquired grenade launchers and missiles to fire at the visiting warship, HMCS *Mackenzie*, which was scheduled to be at Mackenzie's Rock for the celebrations on July 22. I was stunned.

Just how safe was it going to be along the trail? More bad news: one of the men said that he had flown over the area north of Anahim Lake and found it badly flooded. "Even the ATVs can't cross when it's flooded like this." This was the overland corridor I was planning on hiking to meet up with the Mackenzie Trail.

I was relieved when Bob told me the gas truck was making a delivery later in the day and would be returning to Bella Coola. "He can drop you off near Tweedsmuir Park, at the entry point there. I'll have him pick you up outside your camp." Thanking him profusely, I headed back to camp to gather my gear.

14

The Grease Trail

The truck driver let me off near Beckman Pass after pointing out the access road to Tweedsmuir Provincial Park. I spent about twenty minutes ensuring that everything was packed securely and that my straps weren't too tight. Just as I was about to set off, my attention was taken by a notice tagged to a tree: WARNING: BEAR NOTICE.

The literature about the park already gives cautionary warnings about the grizzly. Tweedsmuir Park has the highest concentration of the bears in the country. Known as *Ursus horribilis* – even the name strikes a chill – the Great Grizzly is undisputed monarch of the glen in this part of the country. The warning notice on the tree was about particularly *aggressive* bears. Numerous reports had appeared in the local paper of bears chasing fishermen and trying to take their fish. One resourceful bear had ambushed a pickup truck containing fish, jumping in the back and smashing its way into the cab, forcing the terrified driver to abandon it. One recommended precaution in country with a high density of bears was to wear a bell around the neck, the idea being that since they are usually shy of humans, they will tend to keep out of your way should you come upon them suddenly. I had picked up a bear bell in Prince George. Attached to my parka, it tinkled with every step, making me feel kind of foolish, like a medieval court jester. But a bell would have been very handy during my frequent bear encounters on Lake Winnipeg.

I set out along the trail leading to Octopus Lake. This route would eventually take me onto the Mackenzie Grease Trail. The first few kilometres were trouble free, and my boots and gear seemed to function well. As the gradient steepened, I began to appreciate that canoeing was almost a sedentary mode of travel in comparison to hiking. Paddling develops chest and arm muscles, but the legs get no exercise. A canoe is a great vehicle for transporting huge piles of gear; carrying all your belongings on your back demands sheer muscle power.

Towards the end of the day I noticed ahead of me an enormous tree that had fallen just off the trail beside a nice flat grassy area. With a sigh of relief I eased myself out of the straps of my heavy pack. Suddenly the pack fell to the ground, almost taking me with it. It reminded me of the cumbersome parachute harness we used in the Air Force, which caught our legs and sent us sprawling.

Too tired to think of setting up camp just yet, I stretched out along the giant trunk. My feet aching, I took off my boots, exulting in this simple relief. After an hour or so, I put up the tent and threw my sleeping bag inside, climbing into it too tired to make a brew. I had hiked only a paltry five kilometres, but I drew comfort that it was at least a start. My greenhorn state along with the high altitude – presently 2,000 metres – resulted in my extreme fatigue. But hiking, like canoeing, has a steep learning curve.

I awakened after a couple of hours freezing cold. I put my parka on, pulling the parka hood over my head, and eased myself back into my sleeping bag. Soon I was warm, snug, and asleep again.

The sun was shining brightly through the fabric of the tent as I opened my eyes. I creaked out of bed, trying to work up some enthusiasm. Pulling on my boots took a real effort. However, after an invigorating icy wash in a nearby stream, I looked forward to breakfast. As the stove's cheerful glow combined with the heady aroma of porridge bubbling away, I began to feel better. Generous amounts of Tetley under my belt helped ease my aches and pains.

Everything was packed up and ready to go. Now was the moment of truth: how to get my house atop my back with minimal trauma. I winced at the weight, swearing it had got heavier since yesterday. The standard procedure was to swing it deftly upwards at just the right height, using my right arm, then swiftly thrusting my left arm through the strap while maintaining a gorilla-like half-crouch. Clutching for the other strap, I found only air. The small of my back screamed as I gyrated to prevent the pack from falling.

Taking off the pack at the end of an exhausting trek is fraught with as many booby-traps as putting it on. On many occasions I made the mistake of pulling one arm free of the strap before bracing my body for the oncoming weight, forcing me into the posture of an unbalanced teeter-totter. Finally, gravity had its way, and I would end up falling backwards, legs flailing.

After securing the pack and praying I hadn't forgotten anything, I was on the road to the Mackenzie Grease Trail. It was one of those mornings with a glacial tang in the air, but with the promise of a warming sun emerging. A short distance down the trail I encountered tracks. One set was fresh – and bigger than any I'd ever seen. Mackenzie reported his astonishment at finding grizzly tracks that were nine inches across.

Suddenly, that bell didn't seem so silly after all. I rang it furiously until I could see no more tracks.

Several shallow streams presented no real problems in crossing. I was feeling like I was on a roll when I came upon a narrow, shallow-bottomed river. Removing my boots to keep them dry was my first blunder. At first all went well as the rocks underfoot were fairly smooth, but near the middle they became sharp and started to cut into my feet. Without a firm foundation, the heavy pack on my shoulders began interfering with my balance. This situation quickly turned precarious. Soon I was staggering, with the pack pulling me in all directions.

I lost my footing and fell backwards. My head was suddenly submerged. The water was only a metre deep, but the pack pinned me down like an overturned beetle. The situation seemed more bizarre than real. The ice-cold water was quickly paralyzing my limbs. I seemed to be outside my body, observing myself. Struggling against the excessive weight, I finally managed to half roll over and rise on one knee. Gulping air, one knee wedged against a rock, I gathered the strength to raise the rest of my body from the water.

Somehow I managed to raise my other leg. After a few moments, I slipped my arm out of the strap and let the pack fall from my shoulders. I clambered to my feet, willing my body to the riverbank, hauling my pack behind me. Once on solid ground I forced myself to jump around, waving my limbs to restore circulation and warmth. When it seemed my legs would support me again, I ran in circles. Finally, warmth returned.

I rested on the riverbank badly shaken. Never again would I take my boots off to cross a stream. Digging through my pack in what I figured was a hopeless quest – a dry sweater – I was delighted to find that my clothes, tightly wrapped in plastic bags, were still dry. I set the tent up, lit the stove, and changed into dry clothes, then called off further travel for the day.

How ridiculous my plight seemed: near drowning in a tiny spit of a river, after crossing a vast and perilous continent of water unscathed! Life is fragile, frequently driven by macabre irony. I recalled as an air cadet receiving training on tiny Kirby Cadet gliders. One weekend a highly decorated Battle of Britain Spitfire pilot came to visit our squadron. For a lark he went up in our glider, towed by a winch on the ground. We were stunned when he crashed shortly after take-off and was killed.

I broke camp next morning and hiked out towards the Tweedsmuir Trail. This route goes north from Highway 20 to Bella Coola, linking up with the Mackenzie Grease Trail 15 kilometres north of Octopus Lake, where I had spent the previous night. It was a bright sunny morning, but chilly again. I felt fit despite my cold ducking and stepped out strongly, passing alpine meadows filled with delicate, brilliantly coloured wildflowers. It was easy to understand why they called this area Rainbow Country.

To my joy there were many running streams with clear spring water. Dumping out the brackish water I had been lugging with me, I refilled my container with authentic mountain dew. As I climbed above the tree-line, the interior plateau lay behind me. For the first time the peaks of the Rainbow Range came into view.

The terrain was now like the Arctic tundra. Spreading out my groundsheet on a patch of pleasant meadow, I lunched on tomato soup and Breton crackers, then chucked off my boots and rested for an hour. The weather was still looking good as I pushed off again at a brisk pace.

Gradually I became aware of a peculiar whistling sound around me. I was puzzled, until I remembered that Mackenzie had written about this: "We now perceived many ground-hogs, and heard them whistle in every direction." These "hoary marmots," similar to a groundhog, had burrows running everywhere like rabbit warrens.

After about 12 kilometres I decided to set up camp, pleased that my distances were beginning to improve. It was strenuous hauling a heavy pack up a mountain slope, but each day was making a difference, and my body was beginning to adapt to the altitude.

That night was very cold. I didn't want to waste fuel using my stove for warmth and instead pulled on my parka. When the first glimmer of light appeared, I had a quick breakfast, anxious to make progress towards the Mackenzie Grease Trail by the end of the day.

I opened the tent door on a foreboding scene. A heavy mist covered the mountaintops. After I'd walked about five kilometres, the visibility was so poor I had trouble locating the blazed trail signs, critical navigational beacons to keep me on track.

Now it started to snow. Light at first, it increased steadily, finally developing into a full-blown blizzard. Icy particles stung my face. I tightened the string around my parka hood, my eyes slitted as I scanned the trail for markers. At least my hands were warm: I'd remembered to pack gloves, although I hadn't expected ever to use them.

Peering frequently at my compass, I hoped I was still on track. It was impossible to see more than about 10 metres. It was a knee-cracking, tough, exhausting climb, but at least the intense exertion kept me warm. As the blizzard continued, I slipped and slithered along, thinking I should have brought snow shoes! Covered completely in snow, I probably looked like Scott of the Antarctic. Before long I began to wonder if the heavy physical effort was worth it. Although I didn't carry a watch, I figured it must be mid-afternoon. Time to set up camp and wait the blizzard out.

One advantage of camping in winter conditions is that the compacted snow under the tent makes a comfortable insulating pad. It was pleasant lolling about with a book on early pioneers in B.C. as I waited for the weather to moderate. Rummaging in my pack, I realized I'd lost a pair of socks. More important, my ground sheet and knife and fork were also missing. It was a nuisance, caused by poor packing technique.

The snowstorm continued unabated, making further progress today unlikely. While it's okay to hole up when the weather is lousy, the downside is that the longer you wait, the faster you use up your food, with no mileage towards your goal. The thought of running out of grub was always daunting. To hike the entire 300-kilometre trail from the Fraser River to Bella Coola, an air drop of supplies is necessary. There are no stores along the way. For this reason, rigorous planning of fuel and food supply is absolutely essential. Since patience is a quality I am meagrely endowed with, my anxiety provokes me to risk hitting the trail even though conditions are poor. But with no let-up in the snow and visibility still poor, I reluctantly accepted that it was better to stay put.

Next morning was bitterly cold. My socks near the tent door were frozen solid. Once I was outside, though, the snow looked so soft and fluffy that I filled a pot, lit the stove and melted a pile for tea. Tetley never tasted so good. But my fuel was running low, and I switched off the stove as soon as I could.

The going on the trail was hard at first. Fortunately there were patches where the wind had blown the snow aside leaving a hard-packed surface that gave good traction. After about three hours of climbing, I was able to make out Mount Mackenzie ahead. Then a small log building appeared below. My heart leaped. According to my map, this was Rainbow Cabin. I was now on the Alexander Mackenzie Heritage Trail!

The way down to the cabin was easy. The warm sun, assisted by a beneficent Chinook, had already melted the snow. Pacific air masses constantly pass through the park, and the weather is dramatically unpredictable, changing from warm sunshine one minute to snow crystals or rain or fog the next. The log cabin was set in an open grassy area amidst pine and willow trees. Inside was a huge room and an open log fireplace with pots and pans available for cooking.

When I looked through the guest book, I was agreeably surprised to read many of the hikers recording average daily distances of 15 kilometres, a figure I was now averaging. Since most of these were young experienced hikers, my ego bounced – a greenhorn senior citizen was right up there with them! A party of experienced hikers from Holland had recorded their ten-day trek along the trail the previous year. They vented their spleen against the recent installation of a small bridge across a river they had intended to ford. Previously it had been necessary to wade to the other side, floating across packs on a raft of small trees and branches. Park personnel had recently installed a wooden bridge as a convenient aid to crossing. The tough Dutchmen took a dim view of this – the bridge was just for softies and an intrusion on the environment. They had waded across the river up to their chests in freezing cold water, environmental puritans to a man!

The cabin is named after Tommy Walker, a well-known pioneer who not only built this hunting cabin but also Tweedsmuir Lodge, a handsome log building in the Bella Coola Valley. Tommy, a versatile character, also cut the old Tweedsmuir Trail east in 1937 for the visit to the park of Lord Tweedsmuir. The fifteenth governor general of Canada, Tweedsmuir was better known to Canadians as John Buchan, author of the gripping spy story and later movie, *The Thirty-Nine Steps.*

This country attracted its share of colourful pioneers. Another remarkable character I had read about was "Panhandle" Phillips. *Grass beyond the Mountains*, once a best-seller written many years ago by Pan's partner, Richmond Hobson, is still available. It tells about two Yankee cowboys who undertook an incredible cattle drive during the Depression into the northern Caribou wilderness. This was a near 100-kilometre trek through dense bush north from Anahim Lake The aim of this astounding venture was to open up Caribou country to "the biggest cattle spread north of Texas." While the dreams of these two pioneers to establish a thriving ranching community went unfulfilled, their achievement in driving cattle through the mountains is a testimony to those intrepid souls who sought to conquer an unforgiving wilderness.

Leaving the cabin, I hiked another five kilometres in fine weather through long alpine fields on which the snow was melting rapidly. The tiny tips of flowers were just showing as they struggled to raise their heads above the snowy blanket. Ascending the Caribou Pass, I forded innumerable small creeks as the trail made its way through alpine fir and white bark pine. The pass is well named: I saw many caribou tracks.

Under the shadow of Mount Mackenzie, the trail suddenly changed from a pleasant walk to a tortuous climb. The terrain changed drastically to small pieces of volcanic rock with a murderous effect on the feet. After a couple of kilometres treading over jagged splinters, my feet gave up. I set up camp on a fairly flat piece of rock, then pulled off my boots and socks and plunged my feet into the soothing icy coolness of some drifted snow.

After an hour's rest I headed out feeling much better. But about eight kilometres on, the weather changed. Thickening mist once again enshrouded the landscape. Fine particles penetrated my clothing and sent cold rivulets down my neck. Soon I was soaked to the skin. The major problem was navigating in the fog. I decided to pack it in for the day.

I lit the stove inside the tent to take away the damp chill as I prepared supper. Splurging, I used my last can of Irish stew with vegetable soup before and a dessert of chocolate pudding after, followed by Billy Bee honey on biscuits, and tea. I felt justified in making a hole in my rations. Unlike canoeing, at the end of a day's hiking, I usually found I was too tired to feel hungry. But tonight my spirits were buoyed by the fact that my progress had been pretty good. I had covered about 100 kilometres in a week, despite several lay-ups – much better than I had anticipated. If all went well, I should reach Fish Lake tomorrow, and then be ready to make the gruelling descent to Burnt Bridge Creek.

In the tent I studied the map and brochure of Tweedsmuir Park. In 1937 Lord Tweedsmuir had travelled the enormous park by floatplane and on horseback. In a booklet issued to commemorate his visit, he wrote: "I have now travelled over most of Canada and have seen many wonderful things, but I have seen nothing more beautiful and more wonderful than the great park which British Columbia has done me the honour to call by my name"

Most Canadians would probably consider the appointment of an English lord like Tweedsmuir further evidence of our colonial status – just another inept Englishman foisted on the country. Nothing could be further from the truth. John Buchan was given the title of Lord Tweedsmuir because the job of governor general required that the appointee should be a peer of the realm. But Buchan was the very antithesis of English landed gentry – he was a Scotsman.

Reading about him stirred poignant memories. As a young lad I lived in Glasgow's south side, an area Buchan knew well. Born in Perth, he went to a grammar school in Glasgow a block from where I lived in Queen's Park. My brother, an errand boy at the local grocers, used to deliver groceries by bike to Buchan's home on Queen Mary Avenue. The house still stands there and carries a heritage plaque recognizing his many achievements, as novelist, statesman, and politician.

Buchan graduated from Glasgow University, producing a brilliant anthology of Bacon's essays and winning a coveted honours degree. He went on to Oxford for graduate studies. In a display of academic arrogance, Oxford compelled him to repeat his undergraduate work; at that time they considered that no provincial university, especially one north of the border, could award a valid degree. After all, the University of Glasgow was only 500 years old. Buchan gritted his teeth and went on to take an Oxford first.

Oxford's snub did serious dishonour not only to Glasgow University but also to Scotland. Later in life Buchan's crowning literary triumphs were considered to reveal an undertone, a sense of the divided loyalty of Scots. I can readily understand his dilemma in having to touch his forelock to the English establishment. England's intransigence on Scottish affairs is rife with a multitude of similar injustices. This is illustrated by Sir Walter Scott's famous quotation, " I am a Scotsman, therefore I had to fight my way into the world." A keen outdoorsman with a gifted intellect, Buchan had the balls to take on the English establishment and emerge from the fray in one piece, rare indeed for those not to the manor born.

At the beginning of World War II while serving as GG in Canada, Buchan took on a real-life Scarlet Pimpernel role by making several secret trips to Washington to visit President Roosevelt. He was instrumental, in fact, a key player, in Canadian attempts to enlist U.S. aid in the forthcoming conflict. Several days after signing into law Canada's Declaration of War in 1940, however, he died of a brain haemorrhage.

I peered out of my tent next morning on a bleak snow-covered landscape. Reluctantly I dressed and headed out after a hasty breakfast. The sun gradually burned through the mist, melting the snow. I was saddened to see that many of the markers along the trail had indeed been torn down, evidence of native people's resentment towards the Mackenzie bicentennial celebrations. The terrain was almost impassable at places, as if a huge cattle drive had just trampled through. Whether this was an attempt to block the trail or simply due to regular horse traffic crossing, I couldn't decide. It certainly set my own resentments working overtime

I could sympathize with the native cause, but it scared me how easy it would be to become lost in this challenging terrain, perhaps starving to death or falling down a fog-shrouded ravine. The wanton damage along the trail made my already difficult trek a hike from hell. The melting snow turned the churned-up ground into a muddy quagmire. Several times I skidded and fell backwards, but my heavy pack cushioned me. I spent a fruitless half-day trying to decide on the right direction using my compass where markers had been torn down. Eventually, worn out, I set up camp in what turned out to be a swamp. Too tired to make supper, I tumbled into an exhausted sleep.

Despite my surroundings I slept well, but woke stiff and aching. I pulled on my mud-saturated clothes and stepped out along the trail. I noted a marked change in temperature as I began my descent along the Burnt Bridge Grease Trail, renowned for its "thousand and one knee-cracking switchbacks." Occasionally the series of steep switchbacks broke into a short plain for which I was very thankful.

After about two hours, I stopped and drew in my breath. Through the large pines just ahead there emerged a huge tabletop snow-capped mountain, its peak partially shrouded in cloud. Below was an incredible view of the Bella Coola Valley. I fumbled for my camera. This must be the same mountain that Mackenzie sighted in July 1793! My eyes misted as it came to me that he and his men had stood on the same spot where I was now standing. Two hundred years before, Mackenzie made an entry in his diary: "Before us appeared a stupendous mountain, whose snow-clad summit was lost in the clouds." At some 2,700 metres in height, it is now aptly named Mount Stupendous.

I had thought that going downhill would be much less strain than climbing, but I was in for a rude jolt. Descending from an altitude of about 1,700 metres to sea level over a distance of less than eight kilometres was knee-cracking, bloody murder. The back of my legs took the brunt. As if this weren't enough, parts of the trail were blocked by huge trees. At least 50 trees seemed to have been blown down by high winds. The only way around them was to clamber up on top and through the branches. Several times I tried to crawl underneath but gave this up after my pack got stuck. Trapped for what seemed eternity but likely was about an hour, I was unable to move back or forward. Finally, squirming around on my belly, I managed to loosen the straps, wiggle the pack off, and escape.

The cumbersome pack sometimes tipped me over when I tried to manoeuvre around these forest behemoths. Once I tripped on a root and, falling backwards, rolled downhill like a runaway log. Fortunately, my pack protected me from the worst of my tumble through rocks and stumps. I finally came to a halt shaken and bruised, but apart from bruises and a torn and scratched face, I was undamaged.

The alpine levels behind me, I reached the plateau near the location of the aboriginal fishing camp that Mackenzie named Friendly Village. He was impressed with the ingenious "fishing machine" the natives used for trapping fish. He was also taken with their openness and friendliness. But he was ecstatic about their ability to design and construct exquisite dugout canoes as well as admiring of their skills in handling them when they transported him and his crew down the Bella Coola River. "I had imagined that the Canadians [voyageurs] with me were the most expert canoe men in the world," he wrote, "but they are very inferior to these people, as they themselves acknowledged, in conducting those vessels."

The back of my legs began to recover from the strain of my tortuous descent. I gratefully dropped my pack and made lunch. Relaxing on a mossy patch after soup and a sandwich, I was astonished to hear a sound that could only have been a car speeding by. It finally dawned on me that Highway 20 was just a short piece away.

An hour later my feet were touching asphalt and loving every step I took on the even, flat surface. Across the road a small recreation area beckoned from the densely packed Douglas fir. I flopped down on top of a picnic table.

Figuring that the B.C. Parks might look the other way in an area that was off-limits to campers, I decided to set up my tent there for the night. In the morning as I was packing up, a car made its way into the grounds. An elderly couple who were touring the province gave me a ride to Barb's Pottery about ten kilometres further down Highway 20 where Dave, the helpful trucker, had left my canoe for me to pick up.

I was delighted to be loading all my gear into a canoe again instead of humping it on my back. Once I was launched into the nearby Bella Coola River, it was a short but thrilling seven-kilometre run in glacial, chalky waters down to the town of Bella Coola. The scenery was breathtaking, with the mountains as a backdrop and Douglas fir and pine climbing the slopes. The tangled branches from fallen trees stretched into the river, so that I had to swerve madly to avoid them on several occasions. It demanded all my concentration. But finally I was paddling through the salt water of Bella Coola Sound. Seeing the clusters of seaweed strewn along the shore gave me quite a charge after travelling for four years in fresh water.

Set picturesquely in a valley with an impressive backdrop of coastal mountains, Bella Coola has stands of magnificent western red cedars, many measuring more than five metres across. There are even some patchy spots of Douglas fir. In 1894 a group of Norwegian colonists arrived from Minnesota and settled in Hagensborg and the Bella Coola Valley. Looking across the water at the landscape with its rising fiords and snow-capped mountains, it's not hard to understand why they chose this area: it's just like Norway. One Norwegian explorer renowned for his oceanic Kon-Tiki expedition, Thor Heyerdahl, visited Bella Coola to study the remarkable petroglyphs just outside the town at Thorsen Creek. He suggested that the Easter Islanders originated here because the incised rock symbols on the canyon face greatly resemble the Polynesian stone carvings. It is intriguing that similar markings have also been found on Mackenzie's Rock.

I left the canoe on a small stretch of sand and wandered along the shore towards the town centre. Fishing is big in Bella Coola in these prime salmon grounds. The Clover Leaf Canning Company makes its home here. From some locals I heard there was a café specializing in the best spring salmon rolls in B.C. I love fresh fish and I looked forward particularly to a fresh Cohoe salmon roll.

The restaurant turned out to be directly across from the main docking area. Several fishermen sat at tables set with gleaming cutlery. But I was dismayed to hear the waitress tell a couple of patrons that the spring salmon was not available. When she came to take my order, she exclaimed. "Oh, we've heard about you. You're the guy that's canoed all the way from Montreal, Everybody's talking about it. So what can I get you?"

When I lamented that the spring salmon rolls were off the menu, she left with a cursory "Just a moment, sir," and disappeared into the kitchen. When she came back she set a covered plate in front of me, remarking loudly, "Here's your bacon and lettuce on a roll." She gave me a wink and whispered, "Our cook recognized you from your picture in the paper when you came in. We kept the last one just for you."

I removed the paper napkin and surreptitiously began to eat my contraband salmon roll, ignoring the eyes of the other diners on me. It was delicious, nectar for the gods. It reminded me of my holidays as a lad in the Scottish fishing village of Lossiemouth. For two weeks my family ate nothing but fresh fish three meals a day!

I have dined occasionally in upscale restaurants renowned for their cuisine, but nothing on the menu in those elegant places could ever approach the taste of that fresh salmon spring roll. It wasn't just the taste alone: I was deeply touched by the gesture of making a rare specialty available to a stranger. It was a spontaneous and very special welcome.

After thanking the waitress and giving a knowing wink to the cook smiling through the kitchen door, I made my way outside. As I passed a table where several fishermen were drinking coffee, they hailed me. One of them held out his hand and offered his congratulations. "Fantastic trip over some pretty rough seas, huh?" The warmth and admiration in his greeting, the tone of inclusivity, moved me. This camaraderie from men who knew the risks of sailing in dangerous waters was one of the finest compliments I have ever received.

Along the waterfront a three-person, eight-metre seagoing kayak was just tying up. I was impressed when the two kayakers told me they had made the difficult coastal trip from Washington State. They said their trickiest stretch was crossing estuaries where tidal races set up currents of some ten knots – quite an achievement. It caused me to wonder what it was going to be like making my way in a tidal waterway through the fiords to my ultimate goal, now almost in sight. In the 80 kilometre trip to Mackenzie's Rock in Dean Channel, I would slay the final dragons.

I called Ishbel and was delighted to learn that Angus, my Westie, was on his way. He would be arriving in Vancouver this evening courtesy of Air Canada and from there would travel on to the Bella Coola airport, where I would pick him up tomorrow. In the morning I telephoned Wilderness Airlines and learned that a delivery truck would be coming into town in two or three hours with Angus on board. I passed the time by taking a long walk along the shoreline. Near the river mouth I came across a bronze plaque commemorating Mackenzie's arrival in 1793 when he touched the salt waters of the Pacific.

Angus appeared in great shape despite his long stint in the baggage compartment from Ottawa and Vancouver. He was delighted to see me, making low barks while wagging his tail profusely. Jumping around in a state of great excitement, he cast an enquiring eye on the nearby trees, obviously glad to get romping around again. We set off together for a long walk around town. Tying him up outside the local market, I picked up supplies for the trip, including a large water container. It was the first time I'd had to carry fresh water in the canoe, and it seemed like carrying coals to Newcastle. But with a dog's demands for water, I made sure I had lots. This was also the first time in my four-year trek I would have company on the voyage.

Shopping around for souvenirs I came across a store that seemed to be part library as well as an arts and crafts boutique. Ainsley Manson, a writer in her early forties, ran the store. She told me that she had recently published a children's book called *A Dog Came Too*, based on the story of the dog that Mackenzie and his crew adopted on their trip to the coast. Their pooch was certainly not a pet but worked hard, tracking game for their larder and warning of imminent bear attacks. He was apparently a great favourite with the men. When he disappeared, the men became morose – until a joyous bark one day announced the big black dog's return. Ainsley laughed when I introduced Angus as the Westie "that came too." We agreed that his presence provided a touch of authenticity to my desire to recreate Mackenzie's trek to the Pacific.

I felt contented and at peace. Mackenzie's Rock was a short distance away in Dean Channel. I didn't think the reputed high winds would deter me from my goal. But Pacific dragons were an unknown and tidal changes and salt water a novel experience for me.

Just after sunup I rose and made a light breakfast of porridge and tea. It was generally an anxious time, loading gear and preparing for launching. But setting out this time was quite different, since it was only about 80 kilometres to the Rock and the last stage of my trip. I pinched myself to be sure that it wasn't all a dream. Grasping my paddle, about to shove off, a pang of nostalgia hit me as I recalled my early days on the Ottawa River. What a greenhorn I was then! Only by sheer luck had I avoided several catastrophes. I'll never forget the shock of opening the tent flap to see my canoe and gear tethered to a large log and floating off downriver!

Four years of sweat, toil, and tears later, I had defied the gloomy forecasts of many armchair explorers. I now stood on the shores of the

Pacific near the completion of my 8,000 kilometre trek across Canada. I shoved my canoe into the water and leaped aboard. Angus, sitting behind me in the stern, surveyed everything with nonchalance. He had already adapted to his new environment and was relishing his role as old sea dog.

West Highland Terriers are versatile and highly independent, with lots of guts. I remember one time when another Westie, Macgregor, was romping with our family through a field when out of nowhere a bull suddenly charged. We fled for the nearest fence and were incredulous to see our tiny Westie hadn't moved. There was the indomitable Macgregor standing his ground and staring up indignantly at this huge snorting animal, which had braked to a halt. Westies aren't lap dogs but make great hunters for small game such as rabbits, snakes, and vermin. During threshing time on the highland farms, one Westie is said to have killed 100 rats in five minutes!

I pulled on my parka against the damp, chilly air. But the sun soon burned its way through the last foggy tentacles, revealing the breathtaking panorama of great fiords and peaks of towering, snow-capped coastal mountains.

15

"From Canada by Land"

It was a fine day for crossing Bentinck Arm. Huge cliffs hovered like sentinels over the water. Waterfalls flowed from the mountains to their base and gently merged with the sea. I couldn't resist drawing up to sample the water. Cupping my hands under the clear stream, I drank deeply. It tasted heavenly. There was no longer any need to worry about how I was going to replenish my water supply.

I had covered about ten kilometres along the coast with no sign of the capricious Pacific winds. I was pleased that the sea was calm for my first day on the ocean. My search for a campsite was finally rewarded when a tiny spit of beach appeared among a pile of deadheads. Hauling the canoe ashore, I emptied out my gear and heaved it up onto an large log for security. Angus romped among beach debris, intrigued by a variety of olfactory delights.

From my dwindling supply of dehydrated food I made a nice meal of chicken supreme, chocolate pudding, and biscuits and honey with lots of Tetley tea. Angus, rejecting his pellets, fixed me with an appealing look until I relented and shared my food. After dinner I attempted a walk along the beach, but windfall trees and other jetsam made it a perilous undertaking, and I quickly abandoned it.

As the light faded I crawled into bed with Angus at my feet. It had been a good day, and we slept soundly. In the morning I skipped breakfast in favour of an early lunch. Loading the canoe was labour intensive and a pain in the neck. Carrying heavy gear across great slippery logs was a dicey udertaking, but it was necessary to prevent my canoe and supplies being carried away by the high tide. Ocean canoeing is certainly different from paddling lakes and rivers.

Heading down the coast in a light easterly breeze with the sun warming my back. I was suddenly startled by a chorus of snorting sounds. Angus responded in kind with a gruff bark. Directly ahead of the bow were four seals basking on a large rock. The sight thrilled me, proving that despite the calm waters, I was actually on an ocean. Curiously, I saw a resemblance between Angus and the seals: they had similar faces with the same forlorn eyes and bulbous noses.

Suddenly a deep-throated roar of motors filled the air as a fleet of fishing boats passed me, heading out for salmon. Their wakes rocked the canoe violently. Angus was perched precariously at the stern, and the disturbance earned his disapproval.

That evening I set up camp at Labskate Point on a small stony beach with just room for the tent – and, I hoped, enough space to keep me well away from the tide water. I fell asleep readily but in the middle of the night awoke with a sense of unease. My sleeping bag was soaking wet! As I jumped out of bed, my feet splashed in water. Angus, having chosen the highest spot in the tent, was his usual imperturbable self as he owlishly regarded my feverish gyrations.

I grabbed the flashlight from my pack. Outside a huge log was moving in front of the tent. When I'd hit the sack, it had been down near the water's edge! At least the canoe, which I had carried well back from shore, was still secure.

Hauling the tent up on top of the enormous floating log was difficult in the dark. I set Angus there too while I searched for a place that wasn't waterlogged, praying that neither he or the tent would take off into the night. At the edge of the forest I found several massive boulders, some flat on top. Stumbling back to the shore, I dismantled the tent, then dragged it and my packs up to set up camp on top of a large rock. My packs were sodden but my clothes, although damp, were wearable. Settling Angus inside the tent, I laid the sleeping bag out to dry and lay down on the hard floor with my parka as a blanket. Sleep was impossible, and I was grateful when the sun finally made its appearance. I spread my sleeping bag over the spray cover where sun and wind would dry it and pushed off.

The first few hours I paddled in calm conditions. Then the waves seemed to increase in front of my eyes. The wind also began to freshen as the day went on, until I had to battle to maintain course. When the gusts turned violent, I decided it was time to call it quits. High rollers were now pounding the shoreline. To my relief I spotted a stretch of beach with few deadheads. More important, there was a steep slope running up to an enormous rock. Up there I'd be dry, with a million-dollar view over the sea. Tying the canoe to a tree well away from the water, I carried my gear to the top.

Wind shook the tent all night. Even Angus lost his aplomb and looked anxiously at me for reassurance. We awoke to a grey morning, a furious wind, and a sea that was a mass of whitecaps. My heart sank. There was no way I could set out.

All day the winds blew hot and high. I was grateful at least for the absence of mosquitoes. Angus kept heading down to the beach to drink the salty water, and I had to put his lead on and tie him to a tree. In the late afternoon the wind abated somewhat, but my hopes of getting underway were dashed as it again increased to around 80 kilometres.

At one point the tent was caught by an enormous gust and nearly took off into the sea. I dashed to the beach and grabbed a large log, rolling it inside the tent to anchor it. For good measure I added a couple of rocks. The wind was still howling as I bedded down for the second night. I was now beginning to be concerned about being pinned down and missing the ceremonies for Mackenzie's bicentennial – only three days away.

After an unsettling sleep I rose at dawn to a scene of utter tranquillity. The sun cast a warm glow on a calm sea. I was ecstatic. Suddenly Angus ran from the tent, went into high alert, and gave a low growl. I heard an odd sound I couldn't place.

Then across the water I heard a great commotion and splashing. At first I thought it was seals sporting. I was astonished to see in the water below a pod of three or four whales cavorting. Angus squared up on the edge of the cliff and barked furiously. I laughed – he was probably the first Westie to challenge an Orca. The huge mammals paid him no heed and continued spouting off and sounding as they made their way down the channel to the open Pacific.

As I paddled steadily along the coastline towards Dean Channel, seagulls gathered overhead in large numbers, their shrieks filling the air. They had spotted a school of fish. Some of the birds were quite aggressive, swooping down and knocking off my hat. Angus, crouched astride the canoe cover in his role of a canine Walter Mitty, took on gull defence. Growling and barking belligerently, he rose on his haunches. In an impressive feat of derring-do he actually leaped at low-flying gulls, missing them by inches. His tactics worked: their dive-bombing ceased. He either didn't know what fear was or he was just plain dumb.

Ignoring my pleas to sit down, he would go on a walkabout around the gunwales. Since the wood support was only an inch and a bit wide, this was a formidable piece of gymnastics. I was sure he would lose his balance and didn't relish hauling a bedraggled Westie back on board, but he never missed his step.

Dean Channel is marked by a light at Edward Point, but I managed to miss it. The wind had risen from the east, allowing me to scoot along all day at a fast clip with the sail up. I had been so pleased to be making up for lost time. Furious at having missed a prominent mark, I decided it was time to pull in at a small clearing and set up camp. Already the light was beginning to fade.

Next morning I met a fisherman heading out in a Boston Whaler to the fishing grounds. When I hollered across, he told me I had gone past the channel. As I headed back, the winds rose, creating a nasty swell and choppy conditions that sent the canoe rolling. It was a struggle to maintain course. Angus looked at me askance, figuring it was all my fault. He was right. As I searched desperately for the entrance to Dean Channel, pelting rain set in, reducing visibility to a few metres.

I pushed Angus under the slipcover as I fought the drenching downpour. It was difficult to imagine that conditions could get any worse – but they did. The tide started to come in, producing a race that was overwhelming. It was maddening: there was no way to make headway. The choppy waters sent the canoe wallowing from side to side creating a helter-skelter ride that soon had me feeling groggy. I was kicking myself – if I hadn't missed the channel yesterday, I would be in sheltered waters. It was also getting dark.

Across the gunwale through the blinding rain I made out a pile of rocks on shore. But my elation at finding a refuge was short-lived. The rocks were covered in slimy seaweed, making it almost impossible to find a handhold. Eventually, I leaped ashore with a line and wrapped it around a smaller rock to secure the canoe. Then, I attempted to clamber up, holding Angus in my arms. At the halfway point I slid back into the sea. This time I tucked Angus in my backpack and managed to slip and slide to the top. There I set him down to fend for himself. But no sooner had I straightened up than once more I slid back down into the water.

The powerful current and angry waves pummelled me against the rocks. I was exhausted. This was a dangerous situation to be in, particularly now that darkness had fallen. Grasping at the seaweed to catch my breath, I made a huge effort to haul myself out of the water. This time I succeeded. Reaching the top of the rock once more, I moved around cautiously on my knees.

Here I was on pile of seaweed-covered rocks. Why hadn't I made camp earlier? A mountainous shoreline jammed with logs would have been paradise compared to my present abode. I spread out my ground sheet on the seaweed, then placed my tent on top. I would use it as a blanket since there was no way I could set it up. Opening the flap I slid my sleeping bag inside, and to Angus's chagrin, pushed him in too. Squirming like a snake I inserted myself.

When I checked my chart by flashlight I figured I was only a paltry eight kilometres from Mackenzie's Rock: thank God for that. Sleep or no sleep, I would be up at early light and out. Lying back in my confined quarters on a pile of rocks, I felt drained. The crucial piece of my equipment, the canoe, was swinging back and forth on its tether below. At least it was secure, and the thick covering of seaweed prevented damage to the canvas.

This was not how I expected to spend my last night of a four-year cross-country marathon. Weary and fed up, I didn't want to face any more challenges. Four years of unpredictable storms and high-anxiety situations, ending with today's fiasco with my body bruised from pounding by waves, had taken their toll. My resiliency was almost gone. I vowed that tomorrow I would break the world's canoe speed record to cover the last kilometres.

The weak light of a grey watery dawn appeared. It was July 21, 1993, one day before the bicentennial. This was D-Day. Despite the lack of sleep, I rose eager to get going. Hastily rolling up my sleeping bag and enticing Angus into my backpack, I slithered down to the canoe. Angus did not appreciate his undignified position, but I left him in the canoe and climbed back up to get the rest of my gear.

Before shoving off, I paused to say a prayer of gratitude for having survived four years slogging across tough country. Aided by a soft wind, the flag of St Andrew, Scotland's ancient emblem, fluttered from *Spirit of Mackenzie's* stern. I plunged the paddle deep and made towards Mackenzie's Rock. The end of my odyssey was in sight!

With a gentle breeze from the east, the final leg proved to be the easiest. Faintly visible through a light mist creeping down from the nearby hills, an island on the North Bentinck Arm loomed two kilometres distant. Small craft were bobbing just off the island.

Drawing closer, I could see people, some in voyageur costume, gathering on the shore. They must be the students from Lakehead re-enacting Mackenzie's journey. Unable to resist a touch of melodrama, I cupped my hands and shouted across the water. My voice, magnified by the nearby fiords, resounded with a roar. "Are you Mackenzie's men?"

In the spirit of the moment, a great cheer arose. Resonating from the hills, their reply bounced across the water: "Aye, we are."

Tears ran down my face as I grabbed the flag from the stern and waved it to and fro, shouting, "Scotland forever." For good measure I called out the Mackenzie clan motto: "*Cuidich n' righ!*"

Angus, perched proudly on the bow, looked the image of the Westie on the Black and White Scotch bottle. The students on the beach offered their congratulations and helped me haul out the canoe. Angus bounded about barking, delighted to be on firm land with lots of trees.

Jim Smithers, the expedition leader, grasped my hand. An invitation to share lunch with the company followed. After I unloaded my packs, some of the lads grabbed my canoe, carrying it up a steep slope and setting it carefully down. They seemed awestruck at the contrast between the midget-sized *Spirit of Mackenzie* and their huge 12-metre fibreglass voyageur canoes. Picking out a grassy spot, I set up camp on a bluff overlooking the water. As I chucked my sleeping bag inside the tent my attention was drawn by a splashing noise out on the sound. Another pod of whales was frolicking a mere 50 metres out from the Rock.

I was eager to view a replica of the words the famous explorer wrote on the edge of the cliff face. I made my way around the small island, believed to be Mackenzie's most westerly point in his voyage from Montreal, and now a tiny provincial park. The realization was dawning slowly that my four-year marathon was now complete. Climbing down to a narrow ledge about 30 metres above the sea, I made my way to the large rock on which 200 years previously Mackenzie had written in vermilion and bear grease his famous inscription: "*Alexander Mackenzie from Canda by Land Twenty Second of July One Thousand Seven Hundred and Ninety Three.*"

Thus ended the quest for a North West Passage. It had taken some 300 years, during which the existence of such a route had tantalized legions of adventurers contemplating the vast riches of Cathay. The possibility of a passage to the Orient traces its origin to Columbus when he sailed to the Americas in 1492 in the *Santa Maria*. Mackenzie proved such a scheme was impossible as he paddled a humble birchbark canoe into a lonely Pacific inlet on Dean Channel.

He recorded the moment for posterity: "Here my voyages of discovery terminate. Their toils and their dangers, their solicitudes and sufferings, have not been exaggerated in my description. On the contrary, in many instances, language has failed me, in the attempt to describe them. I received, however, the reward of my labours, for they were crowned with success."

Looking across the sea from my lofty perch, I thought of the number of times I had dreamed of this moment. What I'd expected to find on my travels into the wilderness, I don't really know. My boyhood dreams of adventure in the Canadian North had spurred me on. Certainly, my voyage had proved a panacea for the disappointments of life. Despite my disenchantment, my travels had brought me to a distinct appreciation of our country and how fortunate we are to live in such a land.

The wilderness, as long as the ego does not embrace the notion that we are out to "conquer" it, serves as balm for a wounded spirit. My encounter with Old Sasquatch on a Lake Winnipeg fish camp had amply demonstrated that. In my own case, the journey served to melt an icy intellectual mountain in whose shadow I had lived for too many years. Much beauty had passed before me, often majestic, tinged sometimes with an aura of peril. But every explorer knows that danger synergizes with grandeur.

At times I had been so overwhelmed by nature that it moved me to tears, filling me with gratitude for a Creator who endowed our world with such a legacy of beauty. It is easy to understand why native spirituality is so bound up with the natural world. For First Nations people, the environmental tragedies they have endured are all the more deeply wounding since they disrupt their basic spiritual belief system.

My travels had been punctuated by seemingly insurmountable obstacles, abysmal weather, impassable terrain, swirling gales, torrential rains, and encounters with dangerous wildlife. Such experiences are part of life and served to sharpen my alertness. Some encounters provided awesome and fearsome learning episodes. These were filed away in my survival kit for future reference. However, it was the eclectic collection of people who crossed my path that contributed most to my learning. Some individuals, scarcely able to construct a sentence in English, nonetheless possessed an eloquent command of the language of the heart. Many were characters, with an enviable understanding of life. From their distilled wisdom my wounded spirit received healing.

In the profound stillness of the glacial landscape, there had been ample time to meditate on the meaning of life. Thoreau had it right: "In wildness is the preservation of the world."

Occasionally, particularly in northern Alberta and B.C., there had seemed to be not another living creature in the world. Encased in such a cocoon of solitude, many of my negative and positive experiences were revealed as but a part of the natural rhythm of emotions that all of us encounter in our personal journeys. Intuitively I was aware that golden times lay ahead. But even at the outset of my venture I had vowed to take it one day at a time. This attitude brought me safely to the end of the trail.

In retrospect I found it hard to comprehend that in four years of paddling, the canoe had never tipped. Or that my paddles, swept out into the vastness of turbulent Lake Winnipeg, had turned up three days later side by side on a stormbound beach. These were inexplicable events that defied all attempts at logical explanation.

As we slog through tough times in the routine of daily life, it is hard to believe that serene peaks can lie over the horizon. It had been my privilege to realize my boyhood fantasy of travelling through a country of such magnificence. Youthful dreams can provide the drive and enthusiasm to overcome many difficulties. They had proven strong enough to take an old guy like me across the vastness of our land.

When Voltaire scornfully dismissed Canada as "a few acres of snow," he displayed the ignorance of strangers who see this country from afar, with but not through the eye. Our beautiful country is best appreciated from a vehicle with the appropriate spiritual bona fides, a canoe. It is a land that bestows a bounty on those fortunate few who take up a personal pilgrimage in search of wholeness. This spiritual quest to understand our world and our place in it is precisely what our aboriginal neighbours have done since time began. Despite the onslaughts of an uncaring technology, the land retains its uniqueness.

Continuing my walk around the island I came upon a plaque commemorating Mackenzie's landing. As I finished reading the story of his arrival on the Pacific shore, I picked up a small rock as a souvenir of my trip to the Rock and stuffed it in my pack. I was taken aback when a voice suddenly boomed in my ear.

"Quite a guy, wasn't he?"

My jaw dropped. Facing me was Alexander Mackenzie himself. Or, to be more precise, a young man dressed like him. Dwayne Smith laughed heartily at my discomfiture. "I'm with the students from Lakehead. I'm playing Mackenzie at the bicentennial celebrations tomorrow."

Dwayne, who was from Newfoundland, told me that he was an admirer of Mackenzie, having read up on him before taking up the role. "But wasn't he also rather a dour character?" he asked.

I rose to the defence. "On the contrary – nobody liked a good time better. He was the life and soul of any party and could drink the best of them under the table." In the spring of 1797, just before the Nor'wester canoe brigades were leaving Lachine, Mackenzie and William McGillivray had lunch with George Landmann, an officer of the Royal Engineers. Landmann's journal contains his graphic description of this event:

> We sat down, and without loss of time, expedited the lunch intended to supersede a dinner, during which time the bottle had freely circulated, raising the old Highland drinking propensity, so that there was no stopping it; Highland speeches and sayings, Highland reminiscences; and Highland farewells, with the doch and dorich, over and over again, was kept up with extraordinary energy, so that by six or seven o'clock, I had, in common with many of the others, fallen from my seat. To save my legs from being trampled on, I contrived to draw myself into the fire-place, and sat up in one of the corners, there being no stove or grate … I there remained very passive, contemplating the proceedings of those who still remained at table, when at length Mackenzie … and McGillivray … were the last retaining their seats. Mackenzie now proposed to drink to our memory, and then give the war-whoop over us, fallen foes or friends, all nevertheless on the floor, and in attempting to push the bottle to McGillivray at the opposite end of the table, he slid off his chair, and could not recover his seat while McGillivray, in extending himself over the table in the hope of seizing the bottle which Mackenzie had attempted to push to him, also in like manner began to slide to one side, and fell helpless on the floor.

Around a campfire on Mackenzie's Rock, Dwayne and the other young voyageurs and I ate our supper, passed the bottle, and had a sing-along of old French-Canadian canoe ballads. From their exuberance it was evident that these present-day voyageurs could hold their own with Mackenzie's men.

However, all was not serene. In talking to several of the students I learned they had been forbidden to sing the national anthem at the re-enactment celebrations the following day. "But that's incredible," I exclaimed. "Why on earth not?"

"Apparently the Ottawa politicos are afraid we'll upset the First Nations," one student replied. From the chorus of catcalls around me it was evident they were upset at this piece of politically correct folly. While I seldom if ever find myself surprised at the ineptitude of bureaucrats, this mean-spirited directive left me fuming.

Many of the students were interested in Mackenzie and queried me intensely. They were fascinated to learn that when he had completed his book in 1801, French spies translated it into French, then smuggled it out of England. It was delivered to Napoleon, then languishing in exile, who astutely recognized the value of Mackenzie's navigational data. Orders were smuggled out of prison to his senior marshal to construct a plan for an invasion of Canada via the Mississippi. This daring bid to retake New France would require American collusion. The plan was withdrawn when Napoleon decided to embark instead on his disastrous foray into Russia. It is intriguing to speculate whether he would have fared better in Canada.

Next morning after breakfast I made my way up the rocky promontory to watch the re-enactment of Mackenzie's landing. Hereditary chiefs and elders arrived by boat and climbed the steep path. Some were descendants of the welcoming party that had met Mackenzie 200 years before. They stood looking out across the sound in their dramatic black and red button blankets, the men in full head-dress. The students began arriving in their replica canoes at the dock below. Vessels of all shapes and sizes were anchoring just off the Rock. Well out in the sound, HMCS *Mackenzie* was an impressive sight against the backdrop of the foothills.

In his role as Mackenzie, Dwayne Smith exchanged greetings with the chiefs. Then to my delight, the students started to sing "Oh Canada." It began faintly, somewhat disjointed at first. As more people joined in from the many boats anchored off the Rock, it swelled to a resounding chorus, rising to a crescendo that bounced off the nearby hills. It was a moment I shall not forget. Belting out chorus after chorus, I was proud to join the ranks of these young patriots thumbing their noses at an insensitive bureaucracy that had forbidden them to express their love for their country. As the anthem ended, cheers and whistles from crew and passengers lining the decks of the many boats signalled their solidarity with the students.

A lone piper perched atop a large boulder, a Seaforth Highlander in Mackenzie tartan, wore the same badge that my hat sported. Soon the skirl of bagpipes filled the air. At the sound of the plaintive notes a reverential hush settled over those gathered on the Rock and in the nearby boats. Then the piper played "Mackenzie's Lament," a dirge that tugged at the heartstrings.

Two hundred years to the day, the great explorer and his band of adventurers had stood where we were now. They had survived a journey of some 8,000 kilometres, facing indescribable hardships, their lives frequently hanging on a knife-edge. My own journey, carried out with ready access to modern conveniences, could never approach the hardship they endured. But I wondered what Mackenzie and his crew would have made of some of the dangers the present-day voyageur must face, like petrified forests and lakes such as Cedar Lake in Manitoba and Williston Lake in B.C.

Later that day I had the opportunity to meet with the captain of HMCS *Mackenzie*, Commander Henri Phillipe Lebel, who filled me in on the history of his ship. When it was built during the Cold War with a complement of 258 officers and men, it was the pride of the navy. Sadly, its presence at the Rock was to be its last official duty before being scrapped. Earlier I had learned from John Fraser that the ship had in fact already been decommissioned and mothballed. Only through his personal intervention, and in the teeth of fierce opposition from Ottawa, was it re-commissioned for the final task of honouring its namesake.

Commander Lebel invited me to travel on board to Bella Coola. I accepted with alacrity, delighted to travel in luxury along the coast instead of slogging it out with the elements. Heading back to dismantle my tent and pack up, I stumbled across a flat rock covered with petroglyphs. They were similar to the stone carvings I had seen earlier and were believed to trace their origins to Polynesia, left perhaps thousands of years earlier by explorers as daring as Mackenzie.

A couple of the lads offered to carry my canoe on board the warship. Since I had a hefty pack and Angus in my arms, I accepted their help gratefully. The captain sent a tender to take us across the sound to the ship. A fast run across the water in a high-powered Zodiac drew us alongside. A shrill whistle greeted me as I ascended the gangway. After doffing my cap to the quarterdeck, I was escorted by a petty officer to the officers' wardroom. To his chagrin, and despite low-throated growls of protest indicating that he was a Westie and not just a dog, Angus was led away by a crew member to some broom closet. On Canadian warships, even Westies travel steerage.

Coffee and sandwiches in the well-appointed wardroom while watching the coastline unravel made me feel like a VIP. Among those on board was Jerry MacDonald, editor of the *Quesnel Cariboo Observer* and very knowledgeable about western Canadian history. He regaled me with stories of the early West, particularly the overlanders' epic struggles to settle in the territory. Jerry's account of the hardships endured by early homesteaders around Peace River Country was fascinating.

He interviewed me on my experiences and later published several pieces in his paper under the title "One Man's Unbelievable Tribute to Mackenzie." He was ticked off that there had been no recognition for me by the Mackenzie bicentennial committee during the ceremonies. "Why they didn't even give you a plug? Your solo trip was an incredible achievement and puts their effort in the shade."

Shrugging, I told him it was par for the course. I related my experience with their coordinator in Thunder Bay who complained, "You're stealing all our publicity." After that experience, nothing would surprise me. The committee had clearly been miffed that my solo voyage was getting too much press, taking the edge off their million-dollar, publicly funded event. But I told Jerry how impressed I was when the young people had ignored their handlers and gone on to sing the national anthem. I added how disgusted I was that federal representatives were absent at this important national event, having scurried for cover, terrified they might tarnish their image by being involved in an "incident" on the Rock with the aboriginal people. (Later I learned that John Fraser, Speaker of the House, sadly was unable to attend, having been hospitalized with heart problems.)

It was a short journey to Bella Coola. After liberating Angus, we piled onboard the tender. Roaring across the harbour, it pulled up at the dock with a great swish, throwing foam in every direction. As I was gathering my gear, someone handed me an envelope. Preoccupied, I stuffed it in my pack.

After checking in at a motel, I arranged for storage of my canoe and gear as well as transport to Victoria. Before I headed home, I planned to spend some time there with my daughter, Maureen, and my grandchildren. After supper I made my way to the Bella Coola Exhibition Park where I watched the fireworks display signalling the end of the Mackenzie bicentennial celebrations. It had been a most eventful day, but I felt weary now, with an anticlimax hangover.

Just before going to bed I remembered the envelope that had been passed to me earlier. To my surprise it contained a fax from the office of the prime minister. I read it in amazement:

On behalf of the Government of Canada; I wish to extend warm congratulations to you as you complete your epic journey across this great land by canoe.

On this day, we commemorate the 200th anniversary of the arrival of the great explorer, Sir Alexander Mackenzie at Bella Coola. You have chosen to commemorate this event in a way that most people can only dream of. As one who hails from the same region in Scotland as Mackenzie, you have successfully retraced his path, alone, with only moral support, having started four summers ago in Montreal. You have survived several brushes with danger, but you have the advantage of having seen Canada from what today is a unique vantage point, that being the seat of your canoe. Many of us envy you this advantage.

For reliving and recapturing the hearty spirit of Canada's early explorers and pioneers, Dr Donaldson, we salute you today.

Yours sincerely,
Jean Charest, Deputy Prime Minister

There was a second fax in the envelope, signed by the Valcovs, Anne, Bob, and my grandchildren Christiana, Katherine, Elizabeth, Alexandra, Gregory, and Jennifer in Aylmer, Quebec. It touched me deeply:

Dear Grandpa:

We wish we could be with you today at Bella Coola to celebrate your monumental achievement, that of single-handedly retracing the footsteps of that other great Inverness Scot, Sir Alexander Mackenzie, from Montreal to the Pacific by canoe. Of course, he did it the easy way as he took along some friends and relied on skilled local guides for assistance. It is also widely known that he at least had some private-sector support. You, by contrast, have never been known to do things the easy way.

Your family has, we hope, performed our role as effectively as possible during your expedition. Our job was to worry. We worried when you announced you intended to embark upon your venture. We worried when you actually left. We worried when you turned up with your face burnt by the sun and your hands swollen and blistered. We worried when we heard you were almost capsized in the wake of a laker on Superior. We worried when we discovered you had been held at gunpoint by a madman near Buffalo Narrows. We worried when you were caught in a freezing blizzard at Peace River. We worried when you had to negotiate the tricky whitewater west of the watershed. Now we are worried about what you are going to do for an encore.

All of us simply want you to know that we are very proud of you and what you have managed to accomplish. Your spirit and determination are an inspiration to all those you have met along the voyage and especially to us, your loving family.

PART 5

SONG OF THE MACKENZIE 1997

FROM FORT SMITH

TO TUKTOYAKTUK

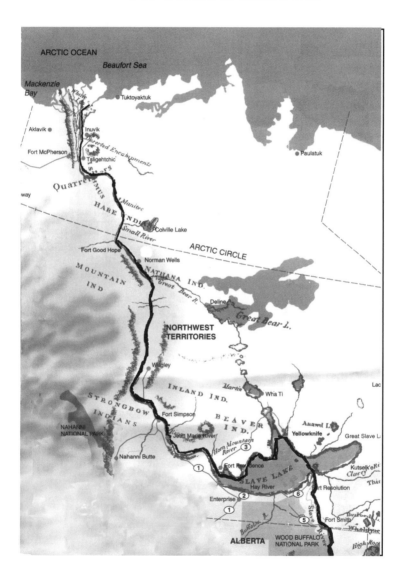

The Ramparts draw *Spirit of Mackenzie II* along the mighty Mackenzie River to the Beaufort Sea.

Enormous ice blocks during spring runoff cause devastation along the Mackenzie's bank, as this precarious log cabin testifies.

Spirit of Mackenzie's paddle is presented to the archive collection at the Prince of Wales Heritage Centre in Yellowknife.

Part 5:

Song of the Mackenzie

Four years after crossing Canada from the St Lawrence to the Pacific by canoe, I stood on the banks of the Slave River at Fort Smith, downstream from the Rapids of the Drowned. The bleak name commemorated an incident when five men of fur-trader Cuthbert Grant perished attempting to negotiate the white water. Though I was relieved to be able to bypass the rapids, the river, swollen with spring runoff, was intimidating. Blocks of ice the size of houses were scattered on the banks alongside trenches where their bulk had deeply gouged the earth. The water had pushed debris 50 metres up the banks in some places.

It was June 1997, and I was about to undertake my first canoe trip since 1993. This would be the second phase of the marathon in which I was replicating Mackenzie's expeditions of 1789 and 1793. My survival skills were rusty; however, I was comforted by knowing from previous experience that my anxiety was typical of the first day out. Drawing a deep breath, I pushed the canoe into the water, then leaped onboard. The current pulled me into the river.

Thus began my journey towards Fort Resolution on Great Slave Lake. After crossing that lake I would enter the mighty Mackenzie River, its twisting course leading to Tukotoyaktuk on the shores of the Beaufort Sea nearly 2,000 kilometres to the north. I filled my lungs with fresh northern air, its crispness banishing the cobwebs of southern climes.

My first-day euphoria was jolted as the sky erupted in a crescendo of noise. A helicopter raced along the banks, the downdraft bending trees like bows and generating waves that wildly rocked the canoe. From the open door a man scanned the riverbanks with binoculars. The helicopter swept quickly out of sight. What were they searching for, I wondered uneasily.

The Slave River, named after the Slavey Indian tribe, has long been the route to the North preferred by aboriginal people – indeed, it is a key transportation link. This powerful river, really a combination of the waters of the Peace and Athabasca, empties into Great Slave Lake, a vast inland sea of 28,400 square kilometres, the second largest lake in North America. Some 480 kilometres long and up to 109 kilometres wide, it joins the Mackenzie River, which emerges at the sea.

To the west the lake's shores are heavily forested, but the east side is largely tundra. Because of this, bitingly cold easterly winds lash the lake, producing waves that create a traveller's nightmare. I passed riverbanks thick with jack pine and spruce but also, to my chagrin, with extensive stretches of thick mud that recalled my dismal experience on the gooey banks of the North Saskatchewan River.

The lowering clouds looked ominous. Sure enough, a couple of hours later, icy rain began to fall, then became torrential. I called it a day and, pulling into a reasonably mud-free stretch, soon had a brew underway. Despite the rain I felt my first day had gone well. Even after my four-year sabbatical from canoeing, I was in pretty good form.

The rain stopped after I'd finished setting up camp. To my surprise, I heard the faint sound of an outboard motor. An aluminum boat swung into view, with two men in it. One of them hailed me. "Hi, fella, mind if we join you?"

I hollered back, " Tea's on the boil. Glad for the company."

After securing their boat, they made themselves comfortable on a sodden log, I used some dry kindling to light a fire. Robert Ekinla and his friend Jim were from Fort Resolution. They were on a fishing trip but hadn't had much luck.

"There's too much pollution," Robert said. "Lots of fish are deformed. You have to chuck them away and take the good ones – when you can find them. It's likely going to get worse when they build that new paper mill at Peace River."

I sighed at hearing yet another story of pollution of once-pristine waters. The root cause was invariably government failure to enforce regulations on industrial discharge of toxic effluents. The addition of another pulp mill would be a cruel blow to an already seriously polluted waterway. The Peace-Athabasca delta is not merely a sanctuary for rare wildlife but also one of the wonders of the world.

Robert sipped his tea. In soft voice, he said, "You know, John, there's an old Indian prophecy that some say is Cree, but is more likely Dene, that describes this constant encroachment on native land: 'Only after the last tree has been cut down, only after the last river has been poisoned, only after the last fish has been caught: only then will you find out that money can't be eaten.'"

The two men left as the wind rose and it turned bitterly cold. I cooked supper inside the tent. Watching the water boil, I asked myself why, after four years of hard slogging east to west in a canoe, from

Montreal to the Pacific Ocean, I was once again following Mackenzie's trail, this time North of 60.

On a visit to Scotland in the fall of 1996, I had presented the Mackenzie museum with a piece of rock from Mount Mackenzie in the Rainbow Mountain ranges of northern British Columbia. When it was suggested that my canoe would make a welcome addition to the museum's growing collection of Mackenzie artifacts, I readily assented – anything to increase Scotland's awareness of Mackenzie. Sadly, in the land of his birth, there is little knowledge of the great explorer.

After his return to Scotland and following a brief spell as a politician, a profession he detested, Mackenzie retired to the Scottish Highlands. He married Geddes Mackenzie, a lovely young woman whose parents had left her considerable property. The couple settled in Avoch, a small village on the banks of the Moray Firth near Inverness. He died there and is buried in the village churchyard, his grave flanked on either side by Canadian and Scottish flags.

While I appreciated the honour of the request to display my canoe, Mackenzie had made two great voyages across the continent in search of the North West passage, whereas I had only completed one. In 1789 he had journeyed down the Deh-Cho – the "Big River," as aboriginals called what later became the Mackenzie – to the Beaufort Sea. His second voyage in 1793, the one I'd completed, took him to the shores of the Pacific.

After returning to Canada, my resolve grew to repeat Mackenzie's 1789 voyage to the Arctic before putting my canoe into retirement. It did cause me some concern that I was now well into my sixth decade. But what the heck, my health was excellent, and I had recently passed the stiff annual pilot medical. Besides, T.S. Eliot said, "Old men ought to be explorers." Assuring myself that there was nothing to worry about, I checked my camping gear, went over my maps, and planned my strategy for canoeing to the Arctic. My canoe had been in a garage. I wiped away four years of dust and cobwebs and thoroughly cleaned and polished it. Since this was to be its second voyage, I altered the name to *Spirit of Mackenzie II*.

Despite a chilling wind that first night, I slept well. Skipping breakfast, I launched into a fast current. I spotted several eagles' nests anchored precariously on tall pines along the river. The residents looked down at me with imperturbable, stony gazes. At mid-morning I pulled in for coffee. As I was hauling the canoe out of the water, I became aware of a strange noise from a clump of bushes. A large bird-like creature broke through the thicket and rampaged towards me. I ducked as it leaped over me, but even then it missed my head by inches. The downdraft as its huge wings beat the air was startling. I reeled in panic while my brain scrambled to process the information. For a moment I thought that I had been attacked by a flying ostrich!

Watching the massive bird climbing steadily over the treetops, it dawned on me: I'd had a face-to-face encounter with a whooping crane! I recalled reading about them at the NWT Interpretive Centre. Distinguished by a bugle-like call, the rare birds are over 1.5 metres tall, with long legs, a red and black head, and a wingspan of over two metres. The Slave River borders the Wood Buffalo National Park, where whooping cranes have their nesting grounds. Very few birds are left. The one I'd encountered was likely returning from wintering down south.

About 15 kilometres downstream the light rain became a downpour. Just as I was approaching Salt River, a huge chunk of soggy bank broke off, almost swamping me. It was time to pack it in for the day.

Today Salt River is only a speck on the map, but in the eighteenth century it was a thriving community. The river's salinity comes from springs of salt water that empty into flat prairie on the west side of Slave River. Curiously, the rivers emptying from the east are clear and clean, thanks to the filtering action of the rocks of the Canadian Shield.

At one time the settlement had a Hudson's Bay post that traded salt as well as furs. Francois Beaulieu, a Métis and one of the North's many colourful characters, became head trader. He accompanied Mackenzie to the Pacific in 1792 and also acted as a guide for the Franklin expedition in 1825. A chief of the Yellowknife tribe, he had seven wives and carried out vendettas with the Dogrib, Slavey, and Sekanis tribes. An incredible fighter, he is said to have killed twelve men with his bare hands. The Beaulieu River draining into Great Slave Lake is named after him. Many of his descendants, one of whom I met at Fort Resolution, live on the lake's shores.

I launched next day as a misty dawn was breaking. After a few hours a clammy fog descended, then combined with icy sleet, making navigation difficult. Ten kilometres on, the river abruptly divided into several convoluted channels. At one point where it flows into a small creek, I was taken aback to see a large cross on a small hill. I later learned that it was a memorial for five men who drowned nearby.

The sleet turned to heavy snow in early afternoon, forcing me to call it a day. On the soggy ground, setting up the tent was impossible. To raise it off the mud, I gathered several stout pieces of wood and covered them with branches to improvise a platform. Though the tent floor was lumpy and uneven, I still managed to get a decent sleep.

Fog, sleet, and rain were the norm for the next three days, with occasional relief from this monotony when it changed to snow. Respite came on Day 4 when the weather briefly improved. In brilliant (albeit chilly) sunshine, it was delightful to see such diverse wildlife. Eagles soared high overhead or nested atop tall pines. Black bears were abundant. Moose, sometimes in groups of as many as eight, made their way along the riverbanks, giving me only a cursory glance.

On occasions, white pelicans fishing for their supper would appear through a mist, but spotting me, they would soar up from the river. These beautiful birds make their nesting grounds on a small island in the Mountain Rapids upstream at Fort Smith, the only river-nesting pelican colony in the world. Unfortunately, their fame is contributing to their demise, as sightseers in helicopters roar low overheard their habitat.

When conditions were good, I would head to shore, laying out my damp clothes and basking in the June sun while they dried. Since the two fishermen from Fort Resolution, I hadn't met another living soul on the river – nothing but spruce forest and interminable silence. It was a silence broken intermittently when giant chunks of bank fell into the water with a resounding splash. Terrified of being trapped or upturned, I stayed well clear of the shore, until a fierce opposing current forced me to seek the helpful back eddies alongside the bank.

The Slave River delta where it meets Great Slave Lake seemed to stretch to infinity. I gazed perplexed at the many serpentine channels that confronted me. There was no clue as to which one would take me into the lake and Fort Resolution – Fort Res, as the natives called it. Eventually I headed for the left side of the river. It didn't take long to realize I'd chosen the wrong channel, resulting in a circular paddle of some 15 kilometres. I needed to make for the Resdelta and Sawmill channels. Finally, the Nagle Channel would take me across Nagle Bay to the fort.

Backtracking to get on course, however, was something else. The current was running a fierce six knots. Navigating at such speed while watching for debris or sweepers ahead was onerous. More danger lay in the large ice floes constantly barrelling downriver, and I was on high alert, swerving to avoid them. Miscalculation could be catastrophic. Snow again started falling heavily, encasing me in a snowy cocoon. It piled high on the bow, blocking my vision. So much for springtime in the great North!

Camp that night was once more a piece of soggy ground. After a day in canoeing hell, I didn't care. I was just glad to be off the water. Next morning I made my way out into the delta. My morale zoomed as the sun made a welcome reappearance after several days' absence. It was time to strike out for the 17-kilometre paddle to Fort Resolution.

I had travelled about 10 kilometres when I became aware of an enormous white expanse stretching across the lake. It was an incredible panorama. Finally it dawned on me that the entire lake was frozen, except for an open stretch three to five kilometres out from the shore – lots of room for a canoe. The sun on the surface was blinding, and I searched frantically for sunglasses. It was June 9, the precise date in 1789 when Alexander Mackenzie and his crew looked on an identical scene. He too reported that the lake was frozen except near the shore: "We found a great change in the weather, it being excessive cold." It was an observation I could relate to.

Despite the sun, the breeze coming across the vast lake made me dig out on an extra sweater. One benefit of the cold breezes was that they forced me to put on frequent bursts of speed to warm up my chilled body. My deep paddle strokes soon brought Fort Resolution into view. Tying up at the dock, I made my way to the band office to obtain permission to use the campground.

At the office I learned about the contamination problem from PCBs and other pollutants threatening the livelihood of local fishermen. Fish, a staple for the community, are so contaminated they pose a health risk. Only after prolonged pressure by the aboriginal administration is this serious problem being investigated by Environment Canada. For years, everyone on the reserve had been aware that the huge mill downstream at Peace River was polluting the Slave and Mackenzie rivers and ultimately the Beaufort Sea. Pulp mills are required by Canadian law to monitor the effects of their effluents on the environment and to keep government informed. The chemical and biological analyses are contracted out to "partners" who provide results on an "opinion-on-demand" basis to corporate clients. Inevitably such studies conclude that the Peace River is healthy, despite a plethora of evidence from native fisherman, trappers, and scientifically credible non-partisan studies. From my own experience as an environmental consultant, I found it a situation all too prevalent.

In the general store as I was picking up supplies, a man introduced himself. "Ed Lafferty. I live above the store. Heard about your trip down the Slave. Come on up for coffee." I followed him up the stairs to a comfortable apartment. Ed introduced me to his family while his wife placed a huge mug of coffee in front of me. "You know, John, you've set a lot of tongues wagging," Ed said with a big grin. "Some fishermen saw you paddling against the flow in a river crammed with ice floes and can't figure how you made it. Most of us guys have a hard time running power boats against that current!" According to Ed, one fisherman had remarked, "He might look like old sasquatch, but he's some guy!" I laughed heartily at the compliment.

On a more sombre note Ed added: "The Slave River and the delta are treacherous for anyone in a boat, never mind a canoe. Last week one man perished attempting to run Rapids of the Drowned. He was an experienced guide and champion canoeist. They found his companion a couple of days later on an island, half dead from exposure." I now realized why the helicopter had been combing the riverbanks as I began my trip. I could only stare at Ed, shocked.

Ed had been a guide for many years on Great Slave Lake delta before going into business for himself. He built a lodge on Buffalo River for canoe trippers as well as American visitors flying in. He invited me to stay there when I finished my trip. "It's on the house, no sweat." Ed told me he does a fair amount of duck hunting, but instead of using blinds and decoys, he has a trained eagle that acts as "pointer." The bird scouts from above, then guides Ed to flocks of wildfowl. He found the eagle when it was very young, drowning in the lake: "Likely zoomed in to grab a fish and misjudged the height. I took it home. It kind of attached itself and follows me everywhere. I just have to whistle, and down it comes to perch on my shoulder like a parrot."

Ed invited me to a feast that evening at the community centre. When I got there, I met up again with Robert Ekinla, one of the fishermen I encountered coming down the Slave River. Robert told me my canoeing and bush skills in crossing the country, particularly through the delta, were looked on with great interest in the community. "It's because of the great loss of such skills by our people," he explained. Then a smile lit up his face. "But we are now learning all over again."

As I prepared to launch next morning, a lady hailed me from a nearby building. "Come on in for breakfast before you head out." The building turned out to be a seniors home, and the lady was Eva Villeneuve, Robert Ekinla's wife. As I sat down to a huge plate of eggs, sausage and pancakes, she warned me to watch myself on the lake. "It can be very tricky, and the waves are powerful." As I was leaving, she handed me a much-appreciated package of bannock for my journey.

With a brisk easterly blowing, I soon had the sail up and set a course for Hay River. The sky was icy blue and the air was invigorating. Scolding gulls wheeled and shrieked overhead. I saw lots of sandy beaches along the lakeshore. I must have travelled 15 kilometres under sail. It was great to be free of the muddy Slave River. But before long I found that, while the rollers weren't as large as those on Superior, they still pack a mighty punch. Ten kilometres east of Hay River, the weather turned nasty. Waves started to break over the canoe, causing it to stagger and reel. A rogue wave from the side slammed into the canoe dead centre, spinning it around 180 degrees. Water cascaded over the spray covers. I was struggling to get back on course when another roller struck me in the chest, winding me and nearly knocking me overboard. The icy water soaked my clothes.

The canoe rolled and reared until it seemed the only thing above water was my head! Without the spray covers the waves would have spilled in and capsized me for sure. I paddled furiously to get warm. I could see a frothy mass of breakers close to shore. Manouevring for a landing, I was taken by surprise at the ferocious surf extending well offshore. Sandbanks reached well out into the lake and the water was only centimetres deep. This meant dragging the canoe quite a distance to the beach. Following a brisk towelling and change of clothes I put the stove on for a brew. Tea never tasted so good.

Next day, I dragged the canoe well out into the water for launching. I was acutely aware of all the hazards I needed to be on guard for: blinding fog, intense cold, fierce winds, but especially maverick high rollers coming from any direction. I passed several wrecked boats, one about the size of a tugboat, buried in the sand, silent testimony to the dangerous conditions that could prevail. This lake was even more formidable than Lake Superior. It certainly was colder. On Superior, while waves could be enormous, it was possible to go with the flow by surfing along the waves on their lee side. This strategy wasn't possible with the short-breaking, unpredictable waves of Great Slave Lake.

Hay River was enshrouded in a dismal blanket of fog, making it near impossible to see the harbour entrance. As I was bounced around on large breaking waves, a blood-curdling shriek startled me, and a coast-guard boat, engines pounding, passed me with metres to spare. I paddled desperately. Two more boats passed close by before I reached the security of the inner harbour.

I pitched my tent in a newly built campground, greatly relieved to be off the lake. The sun was well up when I awoke to a crystal clear sky and headed into town. Gateway to the South Mackenzie, Hay River has a population of about 3,000, mostly Dene, Slavey, and Métis, and is considered the transportation hub of the Western Arctic. From here long barge trains towed by powerful tugs make their way down the Mackenzie to the Beaufort Sea to serve small communities in the Arctic.

Following a hearty breakfast at the Ptarmigan Inn, I set a course towards the western end of the lake and Fort Providence. The weather was now perfect, the lake serene. A moderate 10-knot easterly wind filled my sail, speeding me towards my next goal: the mighty Mackenzie.

It was difficult to know where the western end of the lake left off and the river began. This situation caused Mackenzie endless difficulties. His crew searched for four days among huge icebergs and thick fog to find the river he mistakenly thought would take them to the Pacific. They repeatedly canoed up channels that went nowhere. Red Knife, their guide, was unable to recall where the main channel was. His memory improved remarkably when English Chief, the leader of Mackenzie's Chipeweyans, threatened in a rage to shoot him. He meant it, too.

Gingerly skirting clusters of icebergs in the narrowing channel, I searched for clues to indicate I was leaving the lake behind. As I rested my paddle for a moment, the canoe continued moving forward. The current increased until I was zipping along. I was elated. I'd left Great Slave Lake and had now entered "Deh-Cho" – the Big River.

I pulled up at the dock in Fort Providence, a Dene community of about 600 on the Mackenzie's north shore. As I strolled around, a young woman mowing the grass saw me admiring a small church nearby. "If you'd like to have a look at the tapestries inside, I've got the keys," she called out. Opening the front door, Kim told me she was the unofficial caretaker. "If you like, you can camp behind the church." I was delighted at the offer. Inside, I admired the exquisite embroidery of several hangings, which she told me had been done by local artisans. One tapestry had words I found most moving. "That's a poem by Chief Dan George," Kim said. "He's very popular with our community." It read:

> Oh Great Spirit whose voice I hear in the winds, whose breath gave me the world, I come to you as one of your many children.
>
> I am small and weak. I need your strength and wisdom.
>
> May I walk in beauty, make my eyes ever behold the red and purple sunset.
>
> Make my hands repeat the things you have made and my ears sharp to hear your voice.
>
> Make me wise so that I may know the things you have taught your children, let me learn the lessons you have hidden in every leaf and rock.
>
> Make me strong, not to be greater to my brothers but to fight my greatest enemy, myself.
>
> Make me always ready to come to you with clean hands and straight eyes so that when life fades as the fading sunset, my spirit may come to you without shame.

The Mackenzie was unlike any river I had travelled on. Ostensibly passive and serene, it was tinged with an aura of enormous power still relatively unsullied by man. It was thrilling to launch into such a river early next morning.

Near this point Alexander Mackenzie had fixed his position at 61 degrees, 40 minutes north, the same latitude recorded by Captain James Cook of the Royal Navy 11 years earlier. Cook noted in his log "a great river was emerging from the interior of North America into the Pacific Ocean." Mackenzie, sure that his present location was "Cook's River," became convinced that it would change its northward direction to westward. Later he was to find out that "Cook's River" was only a minor waterway, known as Cook Inlet. Today, it is the site of Anchorage, Alaska.

My first day on the great river was spent paddling – or, rather, poling – through high grass and water aspen, an exhausting chore. The thick weed created a barrier for over 30 kilometres, forcing me to take lunch and supper onboard. Late in the evening I hacked my way to shore in desperation and set up camp.

The next day shortly after I launched, a tugboat passed me, hauling several barges. In the narrow passage the boat train set up fierce hydraulics. I headed for the bank until the turbulence subsided. Further on, the river widened into Mills Lake, a shallow body of water with the reputation of being dangerous even in moderate winds. At the moment, with the winds light, it appeared calm.

My first taste of the powerful blasts blowing across the tundra came next day as the Mackenzie mountain range came into view. With icy gusts up to 70 kilometres, I racked up 15 kilometres before calling it a day. To make matters worse, I camped in a swamp with serenading frogs and hordes of mosquitoes that kept me awake most of the night. The following day was wind, wind, wind. After only eight kilometres, I packed it in, exhausted and frustrated. This river was as temperamental as Lake Winnipeg – miserable, spiteful, and frequently throwing tantrums.

Yet in the morning all was calm and serene again. The sun sparkled on a mirror-like surface, and an occasional fish jumped. It seemed inconceivable that it was the same river. Paddling was easy, and before long I pulled into the tiny Slavey community of Jean Marie River. Although there are only a hundred souls in the village, its resourceful women have earned it an international reputation for craftwork. Using moose hair, skin, tuftings, and porcupine quill-work, they create authentic products such as moccasins, purses, and decorative items.

Walking through the village, I was intrigued to hear someone singing. Peering in a window, I could see an elderly native lady busily engaged in sewing a pair of moccasins. Seeing my face, she looked startled, but then beckoned to me with a friendly wave. "Come on in." Mary Hardstick, a pleasant smile on her weathered face, introduced herself. "Sit down. I'll put the kettle on."

As we drank tea, she told me she had lived all her life in the village. "My dad was well known as a fine canoe builder, beautiful birch-bark canoes. When I was a girl, I used to try out all the canoes … they don't make canoes like that anymore." She sighed. "We did all our fishing and hunting using canoes then. The Deh-Cho was good to us. We had a saying then, if you drink Deh-Cho water, you will always return." She chuckled as I told her I drank gallons of Mackenzie water in my tea, so likely I'd be back.

I launched again into placid water, but the current was strong and whisked me towards Fort Simpson. A few kilometres upstream from the town, the speed of the water increased dramatically as I approached the junction of the powerful Liard River. Fort Simpson, on an island in the river, was set up in 1804 as a Hudson Bay Company post. Because of the vast resources in the Mackenzie District, the town flourished. Unlike most northern communities, it has excellent soil, allowing vegetables to be grown and livestock raised. The HBC even opened an experimental farm.

I set up my tent in a campground about two kilometeres from the fort. Later, I walked into the town of about 1,000, where I visited a craft shop run by an English ex-pat, Peter Shaw. A general dogsbody in the community, Peter was a builder, coroner, and ambulance driver, as well as local historian. Over coffee he filled me in on highlights in the community's history.

"We've had lots of characters in Simpson," he told me. "However, none of them likely could hold a candle to Robert Campbell." Peter referred me to a section of James K. Smith's *The Mackenzie River* on the career of this unique character.

A fiery Scot, Campbell was not only chief trader for the HBC but also a courageous explorer. His voyages down the fearsome rapids and whirlpools of the Liard River to set up posts in isolated regions are legendary. Campbell never received the fame of giants like Mackenzie or Fraser, but as an explorer and adventurer he was exceptional. He pioneered trade north-west of the Mackenzie to the Pacific, battling a river whose dangerous waters had sombre names like Hell's Gate, or Devil's Portage, and undertaking voyages that had killed many other Company men. His travels brought him up against natives who had never seen a European and whose first inclination was to kill him. In fact, he was saved from death at least three times by a remarkable woman who took a fancy to him, the chieftainess of the Nahanni tribe. She was held in great respect because of her wisdom and prowess in battle. After she rescued him from several potentially deadly skirmishes, Campbell declared, "I have seen many far-famed warrior Chiefs with their bands in every kind of mood, but I never saw one who had such absolute authority or was as bold and ready to exercise it as that noble woman. She was truly a born leader, whose mandate none dared dispute."

Campbell marked his retirement from HBC by snowshoeing up the frozen Mackenzie from Fort Simpson all the way to Montreal, a distance of over 5,000 kilometres.

I was sorry to leave Fort Simpson but not its campground with its hordes of insects relentless in their search for victims. Shortly after launching, I ran into thunderstorms. My clothes eventually became sodden, and I reluctantly I pulled onshore to dry out. No sooner was I back on the water than another heavy thunderstorm developed. I searched diligently for a campsite and was rewarded with a sandy beach near Mount Nahanni. After supper, I sat on a stump taking in the snow-capped Mackenzie Mountains reflected in the mirror-like river, a magnificent setting I am unlikely ever to forget. It was near here that Mackenzie learned from a native guide that these mountains contained "great numbers of bears and small white buffaloes." While this description perplexed him, eventually he figured that the "small white buffaloes" were likely mountain goats or Dall sheep.

The weather looked fine next morning, and before long I was passing the inlet to the Nahanni River. In the distance, the caps of the Franklin and McConnell ranges were now visible. With the sail up, I was soon whizzing alongside a majestic mountain range. I made coffee on board and was sipping contentedly when – thump! – I ran into a large deadhead. No damage, except for my ego and coffee-sodden shirt. Obviously I was getting careless with my lookout duties. Camsell Bend brought a distinct change of scenery for a short stretch: instead of boreal forest and tundra, it was now hills and valleys thickly covered in poplar and black spruce.

When the tiny hamlet of Wrigley came into view I was gob-struck. I must have travelled 90 kilometres in two days! Because of the long northern days in late June and since I didn't carry a watch, I had no idea how long I'd been paddling. Wrigley is perched on a bluff on the river's east bank. The economy of this Slavey community is strictly trapping, hunting and fishing, evidenced by carefully folded nets in the fishing boats at the dock. I found little there, not even a telephone, and left after an hour ashore. Downstream a short way was an impressive cliff about 300 metres high, known as Roche Qui Trempe. As I passed the huge bluff, I saw two moose on the beach and gave them a friendly moo. I received disdainful stares in return.

Twenty kilometres further on, the landscape was suddenly blighted. The left bank was blackened from a recent fire to the water's edge. Charred forest stretched for dozens of kilometres, a scene of utter desolation.

Near Fort Norman, the current became very swift, and I was finally able to hear "the song of the Mackenzie." It was a gentle hissing, "a kettle moderately boiling," as the explorer recorded two centuries before. At the mouth of the great Bear River five kilometres ahead I could see huge cliffs. About 500 metres high, they were adorned with bizarre red clay patches near the top. According to Dene mythology, in ancient times a giant, desperate for warmth in a long cold winter, killed three huge beaver and stretched their red pelts there on Bear Rock.

Overlooking the river in Fort Norman was a pretty little Anglican church, one of the oldest in the valley, built around 1860. St Therese Catholic Church further along the street was founded about the same time. As I was looking it over, one of the nuns, Sister Celeste, introduced herself and invited me for coffee.

"Why don't you camp on the grass," she said as we sat at the kitchen table, giant-sized mugs in our hands. "You're more than welcome to use our facilities, and take a shower or bath. There's lots of towels." I headed straight for the bathroom. It was the first decent wash I'd had in weeks and I soaked my muddy carcass luxuriantly in hot water.

Making my way back to the dock to pick up some gear, I met Sister Margaret, another nun in a grey habit, hurrying along the path pursued by mosquitoes. We stopped for a chat. Principal for twenty years of a school in Princeton, New Jersey, she was staying at the convent for the summer. She imparted this information while swatting and slapping mosquitoes. "It doesn't seem to matter whether I spray or not – they never leave me alone," she said in exasperation. Remarkably, it was true. The whining horde ignored me as they bloodthirstily attacked her face, neck, and hands. With a groan of despair she abruptly terminated our conversation and fled for the safety of the church.

Preparing to leave the next day, I watched fishermen landing their catch at the harbour. A Dene elder standing beside me told me that the fish were caught in Great Bear Lake. "Our people travel around the lake following the caribou, but the fish are a staple. God knows how long we'll be able to do that." When I asked what the problem was, he said sadly, "Our land is poisoned. The community at Deline is a village of widows. Most of the men who worked as labourers have died of cancer. There is talk of contamination of our land, even our ancient spiritual gathering grounds. The government is finally coming around to admit what we have long suspected."

Despite hearing numerous accounts of environmental disaster inflicted on First Nations people across the country, I was shocked at his testimony. During my short stay at Fort Norman, others had told me similar stories. I recalled CBC news reports of health hazards among the Dene people at Great Bear Lake related to radioactive contamination of the north shore. There had been feature stories in the *Calgary Herald* and the *Globe and Mail*.

Great Bear Lake is the largest freshwater lake in Canada, 310 kilometres long and 40 to 175 kilometres across. Because of its depth, some 413 metres (1,356 feet), it is the finest lake in North America for trout fishing. Great Bear River (Sahtu De) drains it for 160 kilometres, finally flowing into the Mackenzie. Its name is derived from the many bears that roam the shores. The Nor'westers built a post here in 1800, and Sir John Franklin built another in 1825 on the southwest shore.

Ringed by mountains, the lake is a paradise for anglers, mainly fly-in Americans. However, there is a dark side to the lake that until recently was Canada's most closely guarded secret. Some 800 Dene people live in the community of Deline, formerly Fort Franklin, on the shores of Sahtu (Bear Water). During World War II, in a top secret agreement between the U.S. and Canada, uranium and radium mines were reopened by Eldorado Mines on the north shore, and the products shipped south to Port Hope for refining before being transported to the U.S. Canadian uranium was supplied to American and British scientists involved in the Manhattan Project. This highly secret project, carried out in research labs at Los Alamos, with testing grounds in Nevada, was designed to produce the world's first atomic bomb. Fissionable material from the mines at Port Radium on Great Bear Lake was used in the bombs dropped by the B29 bomber Enola Gay in August 1945 on the Japanese cities of Hiroshima and Nagasaki.

Dene workers were paid three dollars a day to haul uranium – incredibly, in burlap sacks – which was ferried by barge across the Territories to Fort McMurray. Anecdotal reports indicate that pilots on the barges developed radiation sickness. Fourteen Dene out of the 30 who worked as miners at Port Radium died of lung, colon, and kidney cancers, according to the NWT Cancer Registry. Top-secret documents, declassified and made available in the U.S. but not Canada, indicate that the extreme danger in handling uranium was known to Canadian and American authorities when the mine was operating. Nonetheless, appallingly, neither government shared that critical health information, and both aboriginal and non-aboriginal workers treated the uranium casually, even to the extent of sleeping on the sacks or putting bits of ore in their pockets. The Dene were given a few sacks of flour, lard, and baking powder in exchange for the right to mine the ore then selling for $70,000 a gram on the international market.

In a book about Eldorado, the Crown company that ran the mine at Port Radium, historian Robert Bothwell provides a scathing indictment of the Canadian government's policy to withhold health safety information: "The profound and deliberate falsification of nuclear hazards began at the top."

Louis Ayah, a respected elder and prophet known as "Grandfather," predicted to the Dene community before his death in 1940 that "the waters in Great Bear Lake will turn foul and yellow poison would flow towards the village. There would be hard times and deaths."

As the next day was beautiful, I decided to have a wash and a swim before leaving Fort Norman. This daring adventure was only possible because of the rare absence of mosquitoes and blackflies. Invigorated, I launched into a strong current and with the sail up made good progress towards Norman Wells.

The Wells, as it is called by the locals, aptly known by the Dene as "Le Gohlini" ("where the oil is"), is a typical company town. It was the epicentre of the "oil rush" that began at Fort Norman in 1920, changing the economy of the Territories forever. This small community now has an airport, hotel, several restaurants, and a reputation as the only oil-refinery town on the Mackenzie. The oil was known to the Dene for generations, but it was only in 1919 that they revealed its location to surveyors for Imperial Oil.

Following the destruction of the U.S. fleet at Pearl Harbour in late 1941, the necessity for bases in Alaska and Northern B.C. was quickly realized. However, it took the perceived threat of Japanese invasion of the Aleutian Islands, a chain off the Alaskan coast, to spur the construction by the U.S. Army of a 1,000-kilometre pipeline. When completed, it ran through barren tundra and the Mackenzie Mountains from Norman Wells to Whitehorse in the Yukon.

Known as the Canol Pipeline, it would deliver refined gasoline to a series of airfields being built from Alberta to Alaska. The Alaska Highway, also under construction, would serve a pivotal role as a roadway for heavy gasoline trucks. However, when conflict ended in 1945, the project was abandoned. In recent years, the Canol Road built alongside the pipeline has found great favour with backpackers and hikers as a challenging wilderness trek to the Yukon and Whitehorse.

Late that evening I pulled into Norman Wells and camped on the beach. In the morning, I picked up the local gossip in the coffee shop. Talk was circulating that the company was closing down operations. After a stroll through the town, I made my way back to the beach. I had only paddled a few kilometres when I became aware of an odour like burning coal. Mackenzie had noted a similar smell in 1789, terming it "sea coal."

The river began to constrict markedly as the current took me towards the rapids a short piece downstream. The Sans Sault Rapids race over a long rocky ledge that starts from the east bank and runs into the midstream. In the spring at high water, they can be challenging, but portaging is not usually necessary. Since the west side is reputed to be the safer route, I decided to run the rapids there. Several drowning accidents have occurred on the east side.

Haystacks about two metres high covered me in spray. I was relieved that there were few rocks – at the speed I was travelling, they would wreck the canoe. The powerful hydraulics made for a tricky passage. My progress was further complicated when the wind rose fiercely, pushing me towards the centre of the foaming cataract. Only furious paddling saved me from being swept into serious white water. Even then, I found myself trapped between two sandbars. It was near impossible to swing the bow around, and I almost overturned in the attempt. It was a close thing.

I was beginning to relax when the damned wind came up again suddenly. My troubles weren't over yet. Gusts of about 50 kilometres, a swift current and high, confused waves were forcing me into the main rapids. It took a major effort to maintain control, and again it was a burst of rapid paddling that finally set me free. I pulled over to the left bank, making a rough landing on a narrow beach. As I stepped out, the paddle slipped from my hand, speeding off downstream. I swam frantically after it and managed to grab it. Turning back, I was alarmed to see the stern of the canoe being steadily turned by the current. In a flash it was swept downriver. I was able to catch it only by a great burst of speed. I pulled it to shore, where I lay absolutely pooped.

Setting up camp that evening I received another rude surprise – my tent zipper broke! This might seem a trivial inconvenience, but huge numbers of voracious mosquitoes and venomous blackflies frequent the Mackenzie. Anything preventing my keeping them at bay from my living quarters was a disaster. My heroic efforts at repair were of no avail. Even my ubiquitous duct tape proved ineffective. The tent door yawned, allowing squadrons of pesky varmints to invade. I covered myself tightly in my sleeping bag, spraying myself and the tent with highly potent, U.S.-military Off. All my efforts were useless. The hordes insinuated themselves, making life and sleep impossible.

In the morning I treated my bites with lotion, then launched onto a motionless river. Brisk paddling eventually relieved my discomfort. Soon I was able to see the outline of the Ramparts Canyon about 10 kilometres ahead. The limestone gorge reminded me of Mayan ruins. During times of tribal wars, the cliffs, rising to some 80 metres, had made excellent vantagepoints for the Dene. Considered one of the most spectacular sights on the Mackenzie River, the Ramparts, about 12 kilometres long, are indeed impressive. It was at this spot in July 1789 that Mackenzie pulled onshore and befriended the Slave and Dogrib peoples. They gave him gifts of Arctic grayling, northern pike and whitefish.

James K. Smith notes in *Mackenzie River* that Mackenzie's crew became alarmed after an Indian spoke of a hostile people called "Eskmeaux" living downriver. One informant displayed his knowledge of these people by performing an Eskimo dance in Mackenzie's canoe, right in the middle of the river – at which the crew told him to shut up and quit rocking the boat. "Before he sat down," Smith wrote, "he pulled his penis out of his breeches; laying it on his hand he told us the Eskmeaux name for it. In short, he took much pains to show us that he knew the Eskmeaux and their customs."

The still surface of the river reflected the canyon walls, creating an optical illusion that made it difficult to locate the entrance to the waterway. As I drew closer, the current picked up and I stopped paddling, letting the current take me through the channel markers. The river narrowed through the canyon, increasing the flow dramatically. I merely had to flick my paddle now and then to maintain direction.

Approaching Fort Good Hope I made out a statue high on a hill overlooking the water. I later learned that it was a monument to the Virgin Mary erected in the nineteenth century after she was said to have appeared in a vision to Dene tribal elders.

I walked up a steep hill towards the picturesque village. In the coffee shop I learned the community's main attraction was the murals that decorate Our Lady of Good Hope Church. On the way back to the dock I stopped by the church, where I met Don Goodman, a retired mining engineer. He and his wife live in the Mission House. Because of the shortage of priests in the Mackenzie District, Don has been deputized to conduct services. He opened the church for me, explaining it was built in 1878, and showed me the beautiful murals on the ceiling and walls. They were painted by Father Emile Petito, a versatile priest who was responsible for mapping a great deal of surrounding territory.

I picked up some groceries at the Northern Store. The outlandish prices were the norm for the far North where all supplies come in by air or river barge. Setting up camp on the beach, I tackled my tent closure problem once more. This time I taped two garbage bags across the door opening. I didn't think it would be effective. It wasn't.

An hour or two out of Fort Good Hope I encountered strong wind and high waves. Just as water started sloshing around my feet, I saw a cluster of islands ahead and headed for them. After supper, I emptied the canoe and traced the leak to the stern section. I covered it in duct tape, then checked it out on the water. I was pleased when it stayed bone dry.

Next morning a heavy mist enshrouded the river. Vigorous paddling soon warmed me up. In late afternoon the mist gave way to heavy sleet. A short time later, as blowing snow enveloped the canoe, I crossed the Arctic Circle. The weather was certainly appropriate for the crossing. High up on the east bank a tattered sign denoted the location of the circle at 66 degrees latitude. Like the magnetic North Pole, it moves about 100 metres a year, so it was doubtful that the sign was still relevant. Unlike crossing the equator, always a fun ceremony on board ship, rites of passage to the frozen North are now given little attention. But at one time the crossing was widely accorded great pomp and ceremony by northern peoples like the Vikings and Laplanders.

Further downriver I passed Little Chicago, once a wintering place for American prospectors on their way to the Klondike gold fields. Like many areas around the Mackenzie, it was ravaged by fire, and the few buildings that marked the hamlet's presence were destroyed.

Towards evening I spotted a cabin on the bank and decided to check it out. The door was open, and tools and an outboard motor lay on a bench. Since my stove had been giving me some trouble, I fetched it from the canoe and used some machine oil on the moving parts. It worked fine. I also helped myself to some matches as I was running low, leaving a can of Irish stew as a sort of trade.

Twenty kilometres downriver I set up camp on a delightful sandy beach. I attempted once more to patch up the tent door by using the fly cover. I attached it to either side of the door with duct tape and left its zip and netted opener in the middle. Crossing my fingers, I hoped I could now get some peace from bugs. There was already a heavy concentration of mosquitoes around the camp, but thanks to a resolute dragonfly that rapidly disposed of them, none approached me. Bizarre as it seems, I count myself lucky to have developed a harmonious relationship with these wondrous winged helpers of weary travellers. Only the previous day I had rescued a dragonfly from the water and laid it on the canoe cover to dry. It didn't move for several hours and I figured it was probably dead. Just before docking I was surprised to see that it had flown off. Who knows whether this was the same one, returning the favour! That evening as I lay in bed, the insidious hum of the mosquitoes was all around the tent. Eureka! none invaded my chambers.

Refreshed and bite-free in the morning, it was a pleasure paddling on a serene river. My only problem was the complete absence of any landmarks onshore. I didn't have a clue where I was. Not for the first time, I realized that dead-reckoning navigation has its faults, and I was almost wishing I had a GPS on board. I stopped for tea break near a trapper's cabin, climbing up the steep embankment to have a look inside. The log cabin was tidy, with several moose hides drying as well as numerous dried fish on racks outside. However, no one was around.

Further downstream I was taken by surprise as away in the distance there appeared to be a boat crossing the river. A few kilometres later I could see that it was indeed a boat – a ferryboat. This had to be Arctic Red River. I'd been convinced I still had at least 60 kilometres to go before reaching this hamlet.

When I stopped and talked to the ferryman, he told me the crossing is a connection point for traffic travelling to the Dempster Highway that connects to Inuvik as well as Dawson City in the Yukon. At one time both the HBC and the Northern Trading Company had posts here, and the RCMP also had a detachment. In fact, Canada's greatest manhunt for the " Mad Trapper of Rat River," Albert Johnson, reached its peak when Johnson killed a Mountie here during a gun battle.

Opening his thermos and pouring himself some tea, the ferryman selected a sandwich from his lunch pail. Leaning on the deck rail, he told me that a couple of years before he was crossing the river when a female passenger jumped overboard in an apparent suicide attempt. He turned the boat, lowered the ramp, and deftly scooped her up. She later recovered in hospital and returned to thank him.

As I scanned the riverbanks I was moved by the utter tranquillity. The mighty Mackenzie was so peaceful it resembled a benign lake. But the ferryman warned me, "Don't be fooled – she's most deceptive." At this point where the Arctic Red River enters the Mackenzie, spring runoff conditions are fierce. Enormous ice packs are pushed as much as 70 kilometres upstream. The Gwich'in people have always called the river "Tsiigehnjik," or "River of Iron," the ferryman said, suggesting that the name arises likely from the black shale cliffs that define the river valley, at times emitting brilliant displays of red, purple and yellow. Well into the twentieth century, he added, the Gwich'in made an annual migration up the river to hunt and fish. The river is some 450 kilometres long and arises from glaciers in the North Mackenzie Mountains. The valley is sheltered, with white spruce some 600 years old, the oldest trees found within the boreal forests of Canada. Despite the inhospitable appearance of the landscape, Dall sheep and caribou migrate through the mountains and large numbers of grizzly bears prey on the caribou herds. The river provides excellent fishing, particularly for northern pike.

As the congenial ferryman prepared for another crossing, I set up camp near the dock and then climbed a steep hill towards town. It being Sunday, the stores were closed, but I visited the mission church, then spent a lazy day watching youngsters fishing and listening to some elders who were sitting on the dock. Later, I walked along the river, admiring its sheer tranquillity before turning in for the night.

I was awakened suddenly by a voice bawling in my ear, "This is Barney. Are you asleep?" I mumbled that I was awake now. Through the fabric I made out the shape of a grizzled old-timer. When I stuck my head out, he said, " It's a great thing you're doing. I know what it's like to be in the bush. Come up to my house tomorrow. You're welcome to a bath and a shave. Can't miss the house." With these remarks the shadowy figure melted away. Lying back again, I mused over the unlikely possibility of such a generous offer being made down south.

Next morning I made my way up the hill to the coffee shop. Everyone knew "Barney," and gave me a barrage of directions to his house. Barney greeted me at the door and we introduced ourselves. Ushering me in, he gave me advice on using the coffee percolator and other kitchen appliances as well as telling me where the food was kept. Then he told me he had some business in the village and left me to it. I was dumbfounded. Here I was, a total stranger, given the free run of his home. In a world where meanness of spirit is becoming a norm, northern hospitality is a heartwarming change, especially when it comes within the wrapper of implicit trust.

It was wonderful to soak off the caked Mackenzie mud in a hot bath. Later, I relaxed on the chesterfield with coffee and toast, listening to CBC Northern Radio from Inuvik. I brewed more coffee, figuring Bernie would be back shortly, then left him a note of thanks. But this wasn't the end of my experience of Gwich'in hospitality. Back at the dock, a man was waiting beside my canoe. "I'm Victor," he introduced himself. "I brought you a jug of fresh water and some bannock the wife made. Figured you could use it." After chatting a while, Victor invited me for lunch. I couldn't refuse: they were having fresh whitefish.

Bernie and Victor were like many hospitable people in the North, but Gwich'in hospitality was something else. One thing these generous individuals had in common was a great love for their land and deep nostalgia for the old life they had learned from the elders. The elder plays a prominent role in First Nations culture by passing on past knowledge. Accordingly, as an elderly stranger using a craft derived from their culture and living in the bush, I think I kindled longings for their lost heritage. Sadly, bushcraft, canoe construction and other native skills had been compromised by a plethora of ill-conceived dams, the DEW line, and environmentally and culturally degrading megaprojects that brought them little financial rewards.

The current was swift and my progress downriver speedy. However, high winds in the afternoon exhausted me. I set up camp on the steep riverbank with difficulty. During the night there was a frightening storm. The ground turned sodden and began falling into the river. I was seriously concerned a landslide could take away my entire campsite – and me with it!

As I darted out to check, an enormous gust lifted the tent, with all my gear, rolling it down the embankment and into the river. Frantically, I dragged my canoe down the bank, the ground crumbling beneath me. It felt that any moment I could tumble into an abyss. Shoving off into the river, I paddled furiously after my runaway abode, now in mid-stream! Lashing a rope around one of the tent supports, I pulled it to shore and dismantled it before another gust could hurl it into the water again.

Hurriedly packing everything into the canoe, I set off, desperate to find shelter from the gale that had turned the river into a foaming mass. Finally I saw what looked like a large island and made great speed for the lee side. Dumping tent and gear on the ground, I set about to restore order to the sodden mass.

When the wind moderated, I set out again, spreading some of my gear on the spray cover to dry. About 30 kilometres downriver I made out a profusion of islands that must be the beginning of the Mackenzie delta. I searched my wet, torn chart to make some sense of the navigational maze that confronted me. During the winter when I had planned the trip, I realized that my greatest challenge would be finding my way through the thousands of islands and sandbars making up the enormous silt dump of the Arctic tundra. How to steer through this some 200 kilometres to Inuvik before my food ran out, with great chunks missing from my chart, was now my primary concern.

When Mackenzie was confronted with the numerous channels on the formidable delta, he took a sighting and was dismayed to find his position further south than he anticipated. For the first time he realized that the river unquestionably ended in the Arctic Sea, not the Pacific. This was a cruel blow, made worse by growing concern about dwindling provisions, but he took it in stride.

For the next two days I fought to overcome an anxiety that threatened to overwhelm my reason. I decided to allow the current to push me downriver until I could work out my position, figuring I couldn't wander too far off course that way. Late in the afternoon, as I searched for a decent campsite, I was astonished to hear the throb of an outboard motor. Suddenly around a bend a large aluminum boat roared into view. I held my paddle high and waved it madly.

The boat slowed, pulled across the water, then cut the motor and drew alongside. There were two occupants in the powerful cruiser, a man in his early forties and his son. "We're heading towards Arctic Red River to visit relatives," the man said. After I explained my predicament, he pointed out that I was in the wrong channel but gave me explicit directions on navigating through the island maze to Inuvik. After a few more pleasantries, he pushed off and roared away upstream. It was a great relief to continue paddling knowing I was now travelling in the right direction. My spirits rose steadily as I propelled the canoe swiftly towards Canada's most northerly town.

A modern town of nearly 4,000 people, Inuvik's motto, "Never Say Die," is a reminder of how the community, formerly known as Aklavik, was rescued from disaster when in the spring runoff one year it was almost swept down the Mackenzie River. The town was relocated to its present site and renamed Inuvik. It is now considered the main transportation hub for the western Arctic, as well as the main headquarters for the oil and gas exploration taking place in the Beaufort Sea and Mackenzie Delta.

Building a town from scratch on permafrost was a major challenge that necessitated building on piles. The situation arose because of the presence of numerous ice lenses, or frozen groundwater, where the water has collected underground. These areas of "blue ice," as they are known, served as foundation areas. In fact, a book written on the building of Inuvik is titled *On Blue Ice*. Unfortunately, if the ground warms up, the ice melts and there is no longer any structural support. A few years ago a huge section of road close to a sewage lagoon dropped almost 10 metres.

The building of Our Lady of Victory Church epitomized the architectural challenges to be overcome in the high Arctic. The majority of the buildings in the town are shoebox-like structures in various colours resting on wooden piles. The "igloo church," as it is widely known throughout the Arctic, is clearly recognizable from its circular structure, in addition to a striking Byzantine dome capped by a cupola with a large cross on top. The church is also renowned for a series of murals on the interior depicting the Stations of the Cross. This building stands in marked contrast to all of the others, and it is easy to understand why it is a major tourist attraction. I learned later that the secret of the building's construction lay in its ability to prevent heat from the building seeping into the permafrost. This is because of the double-shell construction embedded in a structural foundation shaped like a large saucer containing gravel.

The church was closed when I reached it, but I decided to return later. Meanwhile, across the road was the Mackenzie Hotel: time for coffee. The smoke-filled dining room was packed with noisy patrons, and conversation bounced off the walls. Sipping my coffee and munching toast, I was startled as a voice boomed in my ear.

"Heard on the CBC about your fantastic trip following in the steps of Alexander Mackenzie." A well-dressed man in his fifties pulled up a chair and sat down. "I'm the manager. I just wanted to extend a welcome to Inuvik." He spoke with a slight German accent and said he had emigrated from Germany with his wife a few years before. He was intrigued when I told him that one of Mackenzie's crew members was German.

We spent some time discussing politics in the Arctic. When I was about to leave, he told me, "You're welcome to stay in the hotel. Compliments of the house." I was taken aback, but readily assented. Before I left to pick up my gear, he told me that there was a message for me from the local radio station.

Later on I called in to the community centre to view an exhibition of native crafts and spent a pleasant hour browsing over the exquisite carvings. One of the artisans presented me with a unique gift: fragments of a tusk from a 12,000-year-old mammoth uncovered from an area near the Richardson Mountains. At one of the displays I fell into conversation with Dr David Malcolm, director of the Arctic Science Centre down the road a short piece. David invited me for a tour and was a most genial host, showing me over the laboratories and describing a variety of environmental projects being conducted there. He was also a keen canoeist, and took me home for lunch where he regaled me with tales of the northland. Later, he dropped me at the CBC where I had an interview with staffer Elizabeth Hoath, about my experiences canoeing the Mackenzie. I was delighted to get the opportunity on air to thank all of those who had been so helpful to me on my trip through NWT, particularly Victor and Barnie from Arctic River. I was also thrilled to learn from Elizabeth that I had been invited by director Chuck Arnold to present one of my paddles to the famous Prince of Wales Arctic Centre in Yellowknife.

Arriving on July 31 in Tuktoyaktuk a bit over 100 kilometres north, I dipped my feet in the Beaufort Sea. According to the tourist board, this feat entitled me to an "Explorer" diploma, stating I was "one of the few" to do so! I was intrigued by the numerous pingos dotting the landscape – peculiar mini-hills about 70 metres high, covered with blue ice and tundra vegetation. Though they were taller, they reminded me of the huge ant hills found in Australia's Northern Territories.

While Tuktoyaktuk's population today is almost 1,000, it was once at least double before being severely reduced by influenza brought to the area by American whalers. Although many of the Inuit still enjoy the traditional hunting and trapping lifestyle, the oil, gas, and transportation industry is now an important part of the economy.

Gazing across the water through thin fog at the mouth of the delta of Mackenzie Bay, I searched for the small island that Mackenzie called Whale Island. He named it after his crew's unexpected encounter with several whales following them in their canoes. The whales were white, causing Mackenzie to wonder whether they were perhaps porpoises. It was the most northerly point he and his men reached in 1789. He had covered an incredible 2,000 kilometres in two weeks! He didn't realize they had actually reached the sea until the tide rose during the night and flooded their tents and baggage. There is some indication that "Whale Island" was Garry Island, since this comes closest to the position Mackenzie recorded (latitude 69 degrees).

The arrival signalled the end of the expedition that the great explorer had hoped would lead to a navigable route to the Pacific. Not surprisingly, he termed it "disappointing." His comment has been taken out of context by several authors who speak of Mackenzie's "River of Disappointment." There is no evidence that he called it this. In fact, he is known to have referred to it on occasion as the "Grand River" – interestingly, Grande Riviére is the term used by the voyageurs for the Ottawa River. Certainly the panorama in some parts of the Mackenzie is similarly breathtaking.

As he was fluent in French, likely he was simply echoing his crew's observations. In addition, he frequently referred to the Arctic Ocean as the "lake." Since his native guides spoke often of the Arctic as "White Man's Lake," in this case too he was probably adopting their terminology.

Ironically, Mackenzie's achievement was most remarkable. He had found and charted a river whose length is eclipsed only by the Mississippi, but whose abundant energy sources and mineral riches, still relatively untapped, make it a major economic resource for Canada. His expeditions to the Arctic and the Pacific earned him the soubriquet the Prince of Explorers. Hugh MacLennan, in *Rivers of Canada*, considers him "one of the most interesting and attractive personalities in Canadian history … a giant."

In Tuktoyaktuk I fell into conversation with an Inuit elder who was readying his boat for a fishing trip. He told me that in his young days he would make his way out on the ice in the winter by dog sled, venturing as much as 300 kilometres from shore. When blizzards made navigation impossible, he said, "we would find our way home by closely watching the effect of the wind as it produced great furrows on the ice. We would figure out our direction by following those furrows which we figured would take us home." With some melancholy, he added, "Today they use snowmobiles, which are very fast. But when they run out of gas, they're big trouble. Some guys have frozen to death. Dogs will always get you home."

All the First Nations people I met with had great respect for elders, in contrast to the token respect our culture pays to the elderly. I believe this is one of the reasons why I was accorded such warm hospitality in all my travels in the North. I also found that northern people have a great yearning for the old life. My presence among them on a canoe expedition was perhaps a reminder of that lost heritage.

Returning to Inuvik, I left my camping gear with David Malcolm and caught a flight to Yellowknife, capital of the Territories. A city of some 18,000, it takes its name from the Yellowknife Dene who relocated here in the 1800s. The city has a fascinating heritage section downtown based on life in the 1930s. The carefully preserved Wildcat Café is one of the original buildings, the scene of many a barney when the city's residents were predominantly gold miners. Following Ragged Ass Street, a name that aptly sums up the miners' frequently riches-to-rags fortunes, I climbed a hill and had a magnificent view overlooking the city and the blue waters of Great Slave Lake. Later, I spent some time examining the impressive Pilot's Monument commemorating the bush pilots whose daring flights in the 1920s and '30s opened up the North. The large role that aviation plays in the city's economic life is expressed even in its local theatre. It not only produces plays in which aviation is prominently featured but stages them right at the water's edge. Authentic bush-plane sounds from aircraft landing and taking off along the busy waterfront lend unique authenticity to the productions.

In recent years the city has become known as the country's diamond centre. The labour for Canada's first diamond mine, some 300 kilometres northeast, is supplied by the city. Local jewellers are now trading in glittering Arctic diamonds.

But the new legislative buildings are easily the big eye-popper. When I made my appearance outside this novel structure, a commissionaire directed me to the premier's office. The PM's chief of staff, Ernie Cumerford, welcomed me on behalf of the premier and gave me a tour. After showing me around the impressive assembly room, he took me across to the Prince of Wales Heritage Centre, which features a magnificent Arctic museum. It was in its foyer that I handed over the precious paddle that had powered me some 12,000 kilometres. As the museum director told me later, it is the only manufactured artifact in the collection of several hundred natural specimens.

The trip to Yellowknife, with the presentation of my paddle to the museum, and my visit to the young legislative assembly, made it a day I would long remember. I was particularly thrilled on learning that Air Canada was going to fly *Spirit of Mackenzie II* to Scotland to Mackenzie's burial place at Avoch. There it would be given a place of honour in an exhibition dedicated to the Prince of Explorers. It was wonderful news and a great finale to my voyage through the Territories and the communities "North of 60."

Sir Alexander Mackenzie's burial place in the picturesque churchyard at Avoch, Scotland.

Avoch House, once the residence of Sir Alexander Mackenzie and his family.

Canadian High Commissioner Jacques Bilodeau, Avoch Historical Association President Magdalene Maclean, and the author aboard the *Spirit of Mackenzie II* at the exhibition of Mackenzie artifacts at Avoch.

Epilogue

The following year I was delighted to receive an invitation from the Avoch Heritage Association to attend an exhibition in Scotland. Featured would be displays on Mackenzie's life and travels in the Canadian wilderness. My canoe, *Spirit of Mackenzie II*, was going to be part of the exhibition. I was delighted to accept and made plans to attend.

Alongside the Moray Firth on the Black Isle in the county of Ross and Cromarty lies the picturesque village of Avoch. At one time a thriving fishing community, it was the haven to which Mackenzie retired after his years as an explorer in the Canadian wilderness. Following his marriage to "the most beautiful woman in Scotland," he and his wife acquired an estate and set up residence in Avoch House. The couple became very active in the social affairs of the area. Their home was frequently the centre for balls and banquets attended by nobility and captains of industry.

Mackenzie had a particular interest in the fishing community. From his own experience he was aware of the hardships and dangers of this risky trade. In those days, apart from Lossiemouth further along the coast (a delightful fishing town with incredibly beautiful beaches where I spent my young years), there were few harbours where craft could seek respite from the harsh weather along the northern Scottish coast. Sir Alexander's strong empathy with the fishing community took a practical bent when he arranged in 1814 for construction of a new harbour. He enjoyed his role as laird of the county, and both he and his wife, Geddes, carried out many charitable projects.

During a previous visit to Avoch, I had given a talk on my continental trek, to an audience predominantly of fishermen who displayed a great deal of interest in my canoe's ability to handle heavy seas and white water. During question period I was greatly taken by the understanding of the problems involved in long-distance canoeing. The compliments I received on surviving many difficulties touched me. Their recognition was not so much of my success in completing Mackenzie's voyages, but lay in the fact of my being brought up as a lad on the Moray Firth. I was one of their own. This was a great compliment coming from individuals who well knew the dangers of tricky waterways.

Making my way towards the highlands from Glasgow Airport, I stopped for lunch in the hamlet of Moulinearn. It was to the Moulinearn Inn that Mackenzie was taken in 1820 by his coachman after becoming seriously ill while returning from Edinburgh where he had been treated for kidney dysfunction, likely Bright's disease. Mackenzie died during the night, and his body was taken to Avoch for burial in the family plot. A plaque on the former site of the Moulinearn Inn records the details.

In Avoch one of the first places I visited was the home of Grigor MacIntosh, who for several years has taken on the jobs of caring for Mackenzie's gravesite and welcoming any Canadian visitors. A war veteran, he was a former sergeant in the Seaforth Highlanders. The regiment was raised in the highlands and renowned for its role in one of the great battles in Normandy in World War II. Grigor has welcomed Canadians including John Fraser, former Speaker of the House and also a former Canadian Seaforth Highlander. A Mackenzie fan, Fraser has been instrumental in enhancing awareness of Mackenzie in his own country and in Scotland.

As I settled in a comfortable chair, Grigor brought forth his finest ancient malt along with a set of exquisite silver drinking cups in an elegant travelling case. Like the good soldier he is, he took it in his stride when I told him I was a teetotaler!

I was surprised and delighted to learn that nearby Inverness is twinned with the town of St Valery de Caud in France. This arose because of the great impression the Seaforth Highlanders made on the citizens of that town. The Seaforths formed part of the Highland Division that fought with great valour at St Valery de Caud in Normandy in the summer of 1940. Surrounded by German forces under the command of General Hans Guderian, a brilliant tank commander, they were trapped, with the great cliffs overlooking the sea at their backs and the German army facing them. Three times the Germans offered honourable terms of surrender, but they were refused. The highlanders fought on until their ammunition and food was gone. Eventually, with no resources left, they laid down their arms. They had fought a courageous rearguard action and held out against overwhelming odds for an incredible three weeks after France surrendered and the British Army was taken off the beaches of Dunkirk. In tribute to their perseverance and courage, and in an unprecedented display of chivalry by a ruthless foe, the regiment was allowed to retain their rifles, fix bayonets and march through the town of St Valery with colours flying and pipes and drums playing. It was the first and last time in the war that such magnanimous treatment was accorded a defeated enemy.

Marched off to a POW camp, Grigor resolved there was no way he was going to sit out the war in jail. The stubborn Scot broke out of the compound, cutting his way through a wire fence and dodging the sentries. For several days he survived by living off the land. Avoiding his captors, he finally made his way to the railroad station, hoping to board a train to neutral Switzerland. His luck ran out when a policeman asked for ID.

My cousin, Ronald McHardie, also served in the Seaforth Highlanders and, like Grigor, was taken prisoner at St Valery de Caud. As they were marched through the streets to a POW camp, he was able to scribble his name and address on a cigarette package and throw it at the feet of a pretty girl, one of many onlookers watching this sombre procession. She picked it up and later was able to communicate this information to the French underground, which passed it on to London. Eventually, the British military communicated the details of Ronald's camp address to the International Red Cross. Having assumed he was a casualty, the family was delighted when a letter arrived notifying them of his whereabouts.

After leaving Grigor's delightful cottage, I made my way to the exhibition hall and viewed the various paraphernalia related to the great explorer's life. Of special interest was a life-size replica of Mackenzie the Heritage Society had commissioned. With some nostalgia, I looked over my canoe, *Spirit of Mackenzie II*, which had carried me through the wild and turbulent waterways of North America. It had a prominent place among other voyageur memorabilia in the display.

At a dinner that evening the deputy Canadian high commissioner, Jacques Bilodeau, presented me with a plaque, while the Heritage Association presented me with a highland drinking cup. It was a delightful experience to return to my native land and be honoured, particularly in the highlands where my ancestors have their roots.

Later I pulled off the highway at a small village near the market town of Elgin. The signpost indicated it was called Rothes. The name stirred a gripping nostalgia: I had lived there as a youngster. Driving through the village to the far end, I was saddened that Crossroads Cottage, which had been home to me in the war years, no longer existed. I was sent there to live with my favourite Aunt Maggie, away from the heavy bombing further south in Glasgow.

Both world wars had a devastating effect on the highlands. Scottish regiments seemed to bear huge, disproportionate casualties, particularly during the first war. The effects on my family were particularly brutal but only epitomized what was happening in wartime Scotland, where many members of the same family – fathers, brothers, uncles, cousins – volunteered. Like many similar highland communities, Rothes became known as the Village of Widows during the "war to end all wars."

While I was in Scotland I received a telephone call from Sir Sean Connery. He asked me, "Is there anything I can do to raise the profile of Mackenzie in Scotland?" I told him we were looking for financial assistance for the Avoch Heritage Association's forthcoming Mackenzie exhibition. Sir Sean suggested we contact his foundation in Edinburgh, which awards grants for worthy projects.

I called to arrange an appointment with the Connery Foundation, located in one of those delightful Edwardian terraces unique to Scotland's capital city. I was shown into the chief executive's office where I explained our funding request. I immediately recognized a bureaucrat skilled in maintaining a tight hold on the company cash. I decided right away on my strategy.

As I continued outlining our requirements for funding on behalf of the Historical Association, it was clearly evident from my listener's long-suffering expression that his mind was made up. His hands clasped in an ecclesiastical position, he was ready to deliver his let-down speech, one he was obviously skilled at delivering. "I'm afraid you must realize that we deal with hundreds of applicants – all well deserving – who request funding from our foundation. Unfortunately, it is impossible to fund all such deserving cases...."

He brought the interview to a close, rising from his chair. As we made our way to the door, the time was now or never. With as straight a face as I could muster, I administered my *coup de grace*: " Well, I am really sorry you cannot see your way to fund us. But ... well ... Sir Sean *did* suggest I contact you."

The executive stopped dead in his tracks. "What? Who did you say?" he spluttered. "Sir Sean Connery? I had no idea!" Regaining his composure somewhat, he placed his hand on my shoulder and gently turned me back to his office. Rummaging for papers on his desk, he found an application form. "Just fill this in. We'll get it expedited at once. Why, I had no idea you knew Sir Sean!" Not wishing to compromise my small victory, I did not elaborate on my brief acquaintance with one of Scotland's greats, but took the application and beat a hasty retreat.

I forwarded the details to the Avoch Historical Association, later learning that their application was successful. They received generous funding to allow them to continue maintaining Mackenzie's tomb and to assist them in obtaining several articles for their exhibition.

Flying back to Canada, I felt my visit to Scotland had been successful in helping to increase awareness there of the feats that Mackenzie had undertaken. In future, I hope it will be possible to see the Prince of Explorers' name listed along with the other Great Scots on memorial plaques at the new Parliament in Edinburgh. I was pleased that my five-year canoe odyssey had caused a stir in the Scottish media, sparking a number of articles about Mackenzie in the press. The BBC also did a two-way broadcast to Canada recounting Mackenzie's life in both countries as well as my own efforts in promoting the great explorer. A Scottish film company had filmed around Avoch and Moulinearn and was interested in producing a documentary on Mackenzie. In addition, Palm Tree Productions in Glasgow had a screenplay, *Voyage of Dreams*, based on one of the remarkable and little-known effects of Mackenzie's voyages across North America: a planned full-scale invasion of Canada by Napoleon's Grand Armee!

The launching of Mackenzie's book in London provoked great excitement in the new French Republic, remarkably inducing the French to consider and plan an attack on Canada to retake New France, or Quebec. In *Mackenzie of Canada: The Life and Adventures of Alexander Mackenzie, Discoverer*, historian M.S. Wade provides a fascinating account of this epochal event. He also uncovers previously unknown information about events that could have profoundly reshaped the history of North America:

The Rev. Dr D. Masson of Edinburgh, a friend of the descendants of Sir Alexander, states that Mackenzie's book was one of Napoleon's favourites, and that at his behest it was translated into French. A copy of it in three volumes had a place in his library during his exile in St Helena. Dr Masson had the privilege of examining these volumes, then in possession of the explorer's grandson, at the Deanery at Fortrose. There he was also given the opportunity of reading a most interesting manuscript, in autograph, by Napoleon which sheds new light on the emperor's secret schemes in the plan of his campaign against Great Britain. The reading of Mackenzie's *Voyages* gave him the idea of attacking the enemy nation in her Canadian possessions, not by direct assault but by a circuitous route, which he believed would be an effective surprise and prove infallible. Reference is made to this subject in a very interesting letter written by William Mackenzie of Gairloch, an old friend of Sir Alexander, to the latter's son, the heir of Avoch:

Leamington,
May 24, 1896

When in Stockholm in 1824, Lord Bloomfield, our minister there, did me the honour of presenting me to the King Bernadotte, father of the present king of Sweden. At the King's special request, the audience was a private one, and I was further especially requested to oblige by coming in my full Highland dress. The audience lasted fully an hour. Such an interest did Napoleon's first and most fortunate marshal take in everything which was Highland, not even the skean dhu escaped him, etc. etc. I now come to your family portion of the audience.

As we chatted on (old Bernadotte leaning upon my o'keachan, claymore), he was pleased to say, in that *sauviter in modo* for which his eagle eye so fitted him: "Yes, I repeat it – you Highlanders are deservedly proud of your country and your forefathers, and your people are a race apart, distinct from all the rest of Britain in high moral as well as martial bearing, and long, I hope, may you feel and show it outwardly by this noble distinction and dress. But, allow me to observe, sir, that in your family name and in the name Mackenzie there is a very predominant luster, which shall never be obliterated from my mind. Pray, are you connected in any way with Sir Alexander Mackenzie, the celebrated North American traveler, whose name and researches are immortalised by his discoveries in the Arctic Ocean and of the river which since then does honour to his name?"

I informed His Majesty that as a boy I had known him well, and that our families and his were nearly connected. This seemed to give me still greater favour with him, for familiarly putting his hand on my shoulder brooch, he replied that on that account alone, his making my acquaintance gave him great satisfaction. He then proceeded to tell Lord Bloomfield and me how your father's name had become familiar to him. And so much valued in his eyes.

He said that at one time Napoleon had arranged to distract the affairs of Britain by attacking her Canadian possessions, not by a direct descent upon them, but by a route which would take England quite by surprise and prove infallible. That route was to be the Mississippi, Ohio, etc, up to our Canadian border lakes. For this arrangements to be made with America – New Orleans occupied as a pied-a-terre by France, etc.

The organisation and command of this gigantic enterprise, as Bernadotte said, "was given to me by the Emperor with instructions to make myself master of any work which could bear upon it, and the facilities the nature of the country afforded. Foremost among these the work of your namesake (Sir Alexander Mackenzie) was recommended, but how to get at it, with all communications with England interdicted, all knowledge of English unknown to us, seemed a difficulty not easily to be got over. However, as every one knows, my then master, L'Empereur, was not the man to be overcome by such small difficulties. The book, a huge quarto, was procured through smugglers, and in an inconceivably short space of time most admirably translated into French for my especial use. I need hardly add with what interest I perused and re-perused that admirable work, till I made myself so thoroughly master of it that I could almost fancy myself (this he said laughing heartily) taking your Canada *en revers* from the upper waters, and ever since then I have never ceased to look upon the home and think of the author with more than ordinary respect and esteem."

After a short pause and a long-drawn breath, almost amounting to a sigh, accompanied by a look at Bloomfield and a most expressive "Ah my lord, que des changements depuis ce jours-la!" Bernadotte concluded by saying that the Russian campaign had knocked that of Canada on the head until Russia was crushed, but it had pleased God to ordain it otherwise – "et maintenant me voila Roi Suede" (his exact words as he concluded these compliments to your father). So much for old recollections of my sunny days of youth. –

Yours faithfully,
Wm. Mackenzie
(Gairloch).

To George Mackenzie, Esqre., Avoch

At the end of Napoleon's exile on St Helena's, his copy of the *Voyages* made its way to the U.K., ending up in the home of his granddaughter, who in 1931 presented it to the National Archives of Canada. When I was researching Mackenzie at the NAC, I came across it. I was thrilled to handle the volume with the imprimatur of the French Republic and to contemplate what a role the *Voyages* had in world events.

Now as I headed home over the Atlantic to my adopted country, I thought how unlikely it was that a guy like me from a Glasgow tenement could have paddled his way across the harsh, unforgiving, beautiful wilderness that is Canada. But my own experience was not so very different from many other Scottish exiles who came to this great country – particularly the many thousands who, after conquest by the English spelled the end of the clansman's way of life, embraced a new life in a new land.

I also realized that my journeys had brought about changes in me I had not been aware of when I first finished them. I had since had time to reflect. When I began on my pilgrimages, I found myself no longer with a career, my life in turmoil, shaken to my foundations emotionally and spiritually. Certainly, many dangers had followed me: cranky bears, near capsize in the wake of a Lake Superior freighter, a marooning on dismal Lake Winnipeg, a trigger-happy madman at Buffalo Narrows, a snarling, rabid coyote, a wild bronco ride on the unforgiving Fraser River in B.C. But somehow my five summers in the wilderness retracing the paths of the great explorer had brought about a healing of my wounded spirit.

After my trips I had received a number of letters congratulating me on my accomplishment. But it was the ones from seniors that touched me most. One in particular pointed out, "Your epic voyage has shown us that age is a state of mind. There is no barrier to doing anything ... all you have to do is get out and do it, as you have done."

Afterword

My two canoeing ventures gave me a unique opportunity as a neurotoxicologist to view at first hand the widespread changes to our natural environment accruing from mismanagement of our resources. In many cases, the pollution clearly originated in the lack of even elementary principles of environmental prudence, often arising from downright incompetence by politicians and their advisers. The extent of the devastation to the environment that was generated, particularly the genetic toxicity effects on fish-spawning beds, was a real eye-opener. Like most people, I drew much of my information on pollution and environmental disasters caused by dams or clear-cutting from sensational and incomplete reports in the media, or dry reports in science journals. However, the effect of pollution of our waterways as it specifically affects First Nations people has never received the attention it merits. This is because the media does not fully understand the intimate relationship that exists between aboriginal people and their environment and the distressing sociological changes that occur for native people when the natural environment is disrupted.

Moreover, the neurological effects arising from pollution are rarely addressed. It was not until the 1990s that government actually had a neurotoxicologist on staff. Thus, there was no one competent to assess problems such as those arising from the effects of toxins affecting the brain. At McGill University in Montreal in the 1970s, we examined the neurotoxic effects of mercury pollution produced by a major spill from a pulp mill into a river in Northern Ontario. The river was used by an aboriginal population as a source of drinking water, and its fish were a major food source for the community. The Ontario government played down the neurological effects that eating fish from a mercury-contaminated river produced on reserve residents.

At this time, a renowned Japanese neurologist visited our laboratory in Montreal. He had been studying effects of mercury pollution in Minimata Bay in Japan, which had caused crippling neurotoxicity similar to Parkinsonism among residents who had eaten fish from the river. He told our investigative team that the toxic effects of mercury contamination on residents of the aboriginal reserve in Northern Ontario were greater than he had seen in people in his own country. Although this distinguished investigator was readily available to speak to the media, nothing appeared in the press concerning his research findings in Japan and their relation to those seen in Canada.

I saw heartrending social impacts first hand and listened to painful testimony in all areas that I travelled through. People witnessed to enormous social and health problems caused by dam construction, waterway diversions, clear-cutting, and toxic chemicals. Radiation damage at Great Bear Lake resulted in disastrous social disruption to families, loss of livelihood, alcoholism and drug addictions, as well as an alarming increase in depression and youth suicide. The results overall throughout the country are close to genocide – perhaps not in the real sense of the word, but in the practical sense, it is difficult to see the difference. The belief system of the aboriginal culture is interwoven with the natural forces that govern their lives; accordingly, disruption of these forces is destined to create profound emotional upheaval. Irreversible alteration of the natural habitat by dam construction and associated water diversions, especially in northern territories, causes problems that lead to psychological carnage.

Pollution of waterways because of inadequate environmental monitoring of foreign-owned pulp and paper companies affects the ecosystem for hundreds of kilometres. Only when damage becomes catastrophic is there even modest action from government departments. In high-profile cases, this results in token punitive government action. But years of "studies" and court challenges have benefitted no one except the legal profession; the issues are quietly set aside in the musty archives of judicial limbo and environmental politics. The companies then move on to another country where environmental regulations are rarely implemented.

I observed the effects of such folly on our delicate ecosystems, many of them tottering on the brink of collapse – in the vast Mackenzie delta, or the enormous aquatic obscenities of Cedar Lake in Manitoba, Lake Williston in British Columbia, or Great Slave Lake. I observed the horrendous effects on fish populations and diverse biological species in these regions. I find it inconceivable that plans are currently underway for construction of a third dam to complement that of the other two on the Peace River. The environmental effects of large dams and diversion of rivers have been painstakingly researched by eminent investigators, and evidence from numerous studies strongly supports the conclusion that such changes play key roles in the destruction of aquatic habitat and fisheries. Seeing the face of Canada undergo such detrimental changes due to ill-conceived and poorly thought-out projects, many of which have produced social disasters, personal misfortune, and spiritual destruction among First Nations people, was profoundly depressing to witness.

Nonetheless, one thing I found uplifting in the midst of these gloomy scenarios was the remarkable example of courage of workers at the Bennett Dam on the Peace River. BC Hydro is an organization with ironclad agreements to provide power to California regardless of the permanent environmental consequences this produces. Some BC Hydro workers made a decision of conscience to resign their secure, well-paid jobs when they could no longer bear to work for an organization whose water-management policy is wreaking disaster on the wildlife habitat of British Columbia, resulting in a diminished lifestyle legacy for their children and grandchildren. Their unselfish example is inspirational. In my book, their actions qualify them as candidates for the Order of Canada.

A recent report commissioned by the World Bank and the World Conservation Union and presented by former South African president Nelson Mandela supports many of my observations on the impact of big dams. Referring particularly to the effects on indigenous peoples, the commission stresses: "Big dams have left a disastrous legacy of social and environmental damage – most of it unnecessary." Canada is particularly singled out as a "bad modern example of an industrialized country that tramples the rights of indigenous peoples. "

The report calls for "sweeping changes to the criteria by which dams are approved, instead of looking mainly at the economic benefits." It urges governments, funding agencies, and industry to pay greater attention to the risks of the project, noting that it "means nothing to build billion-dollar dams if your monuments alienate the weak."

The World Commission on Dams has set up an international protocol as a means of interpreting proposed dams' benefits and drawbacks. It urges that governments review their rules covering large dam projects and establish committees to solve problems left by those dams already built.

Considering Canada's trumpeting of our stand on human rights in the Third World, the report comes as a powerful humiliation. However, if it leads to a change in government policy towards more prudent environmental policies, especially as they apply to dam construction and the displacement of native peoples, disruption of hunting and fishing rights, and loss of sacred sites, this unwelcome publicity will have served an invaluable purpose.

Acknowledgments

It would fill almost an entire book to fully thank all the individuals who have assisted in one way or another my canoe journey across the continent. However, I would like to particularly convey my thanks to the following for their hospitality and assistance and to express a sincere mea culpa to those whose names have been inadvertently omitted.

In preparing for my trip: Alex Ross, Kingston; Jerome Orange, France.

Along the Pays d' En Haut: Peter and Janice Puddicombe, Cache Bay; Joe and Vera Meaney, Lake La Croix; Ian Mackenzie, Sault Ste Marie; Ron Clay, Winnipeg; Cameron MacKinnon, Emo; Jack Clarkson, Berens River; Glen Woodford, Berens River; the crew of CCGS *Namao* and Captain Vic Isidoro; Raymond Valiquette, Poplar River, IR; Albert Campbell, Grand Rapids; Jean and Colin McKay, Grand Rapids; George Mercredi, Grand Rapids; Blaine Landry, RCMP, Cumberland House; George Raymond, Ile La Crosse; Bill Favel, Ile La ; Karen and Dennis O'Brien, Buffalo Narrows; Craig Schnell, La Loche; Jack Fix, Fort McMurray; Maureen Duseault, Fort McMurray; Sister Martha, Fort Chipeweyan; Jack McCullough, Fort ; Ed Lafferty, Fort Resolution; Robert Ekinla, Fort Resolution; Mary Hardstick, Jean-Marie River, Peter Shaw, Fort Simpson; Sister Celeste, Fort Norman; John McGillivray, Hudson Hope; Sharon and Pat Linfitt, Hudson Hope; Pat Carson, Hudson Hope; Pat and Janet, McGee, Mackenzie; Bob Phillips, Anahim Lake; Bernie and Victor, Arctic Red River; David Malcolm, Inuvik; Magdalene Mclean, Avoch Heritage Association, Avoch, Scotland; Grigor Macintosh (a gallant Scot), Avoch; and the Hon. John Fraser, Vancouver.

In preparing this book, I would like to express my gratitude to my capable editor, Maureen Garvie, whose steady hand at the helm restrained the author from straying frequently into the treacherous shoals of trendy diversions and grammatical faux pas. Thanks also to my publisher, Laurie Lewis of Artful Codger Press for helpful and constructive comments.

And many thanks to my wife, Ishbel, whose support, encouragement and patience, towards my "retirement project" remained steadfast throughout my absence from home over five summers.

John Donaldson, August 2006

References

Bloom, Allan. *Closing of the American Mind*. New York: Simon & Schuster, 1987.

Bothwell, Robert. *Eldorado: Canada's National Uranium Company*. Toronto: University of Toronto Press, 1984.

Buchan, John. *The Thirty-Nine Steps*. Edinburgh and London: Blackwood and Sons, 1915.

De Voto, Bernard. *The Course of Empire*. Boston, 1952.

Finnigan, J. *Finnigan's Guide to the Ottawa Valley*. Kingston: Quarry Press, 1988.

Fowke, Edith. *Folklore of Canada*. Toronto: McClelland & Stewart, 1976.

Hobson, Richmond, P. *Grass beyond the Mountains*. Toronto: McClelland & Stewart.

Hutchison, Bruce. *The Fraser*. Rivers of America Series. Toronto: Clarke, Irwin, 1950.

Julien, Henri. *Canadian Illustrated News*, 1874.

Lamb, W. Kaye, ed. *The Letters and Journals of Simon Fraser, 1806-1808*. Toronto: Macmillan, 1960.

Legget, Robert. *Ottawa Waterway, Gateway to a Continent*. Toronto: University of Toronto Press, 1975.

Mackenzie, Alexander. *The Journals and Letters of Sir Alexander Mackenzie*. W. Kaye Lamb, ed. Hakluyt Society. Cambridge University Press, 1970.

Mackenzie, Alexander. *Voyages from Montreal on the River St. Lawrence, through the Continent of North America, to the Frozen and Pacific Oceans; in the Years, 1789 and 1793. With a Preliminary Account of the Rise, Progress, and Present State of the Fur Trade of that Country*. London, 1801. Reprint, Edmonton: M.G. Hurtig, 1971.

Main, John, *The Present Christ: Further Steps in Meditation*. London: Darton, Longman and Todd, 1985.

Manson, Ainsley. *A Dog Came Too*. Toronto: Douglas & McIntyre, 1992.

Mason, Bill. *Path of the Paddle: An Illustrated Guide to the Art of Canoeing*. Toronto: Key Porter, 1984.

MacLennan, Hugh. *Seven Rivers of Canada*. Toronto: Macmillan, 1961.

Morse, Eric, W. Fur *Trade Canoe Routes of Canada, Then and Now.* Toronto: University of Toronto Press, 1969.

Newman, Peter C. *Caesars of the Wilderness.* Markham, Ont.: Penguin Books, 1987.

Reid, W. Stanford. *The Scottish Tradition in Canada: A History of Canada's Peoples.* Toronto: McClelland & Stewart, 1976.

Olson, Sigurd F. *Reflections from the North Country.* Alfred A. Knopf, 1976

Robertson, Heather. *The Flying Bandit.* Toronto: Lorimer, 1981.

Ross, Alexander. *The Fur Hunters of the Far West.*, London, 1855. New edition, edited by Kenneth A. Spaulding, University of Oklahoma Press.

Smith, James K. *The Mackenzie River.* Agincourt: Gage, 1977.

Thoreau, Henry, David. *On Life in Walden.* 1854. New edition, edited by J. Cramer. New Haven University Press, 2004.

Wade, H.S. *Mackenzie of Canada, he Life and Adventures of Alexander Mackenzie.* Edinburgh and London: Blackwood & Sons, 1927.

Wallace, J.N. "The Explorer of the Finlay River in 1824." *Canadian Historical Review* vol 9, 1928.

Woodworth, John, and Halle Flygare. *In the Steps of Alexander Mackenzie.* Trail guide, John Woodworth, Kelowna, distributed by the Alexander Mackenzie Trail Association, Kelowna, B.C, 1987.

This book is set in Abode Caslon

Design and electronic composition by

LAURIE LEWIS

at Artful Codger Press

Kingston, Ontario

2006